LEARNING IN GROUPS

NEW PATTERNS OF LEARNING SERIES
EDITED BY P.J. HILLS, UNIVERSITY OF CAMBRIDGE

AN INTRODUCTION TO EDUCATIONAL COMPUTING
Nicholas John Rushby

PREPARING EDUCATIONAL MATERIALS
N.D.C. Harris

THE ORGANISATION AND MANAGEMENT OF
EDUCATIONAL TECHNOLOGY
Richard N. Tucker

ADULT LEARNING
R. Bernard Lovell

EVALUATING INSTRUCTIONAL TECHNOLOGY
Christopher Kay Knapper

ASSESSING STUDENTS, APPRAISING TEACHING
John C. Clift and Bradford W. Imrie

STUDENT LEARNING IN HIGHER EDUCATION
John D. Wilson

LEARNING AND VISUAL COMMUNICATION
David Sless

RESOURCE-BASED LEARNING FOR HIGHER AND
CONTINUING EDUCATION
John Clarke

LEARNING TO LEARN IN HIGHER EDUCATION
Jean Wright

EDUCATION AND THE NATURE OF KNOWLEDGE
R.J. Brownhill

PROFESSIONAL EDUCATION
Peter Jarvis

VIDEO PRODUCTION IN EDUCATION & TRAINING
Geoff Elliott

LIFELONG LEARNING AND HIGHER EDUCATION
Christopher K. Knapper & Arthur J. Cropley

EDUCATIONAL STAFF DEVELOPMENT
Alex Main

Learning in Groups

David Jaques

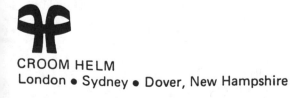

CROOM HELM
London • Sydney • Dover, New Hampshire

© 1984 David Jaques
Croom Helm Ltd, Provident House, Burrell Row,
Beckenham, Kent BR3 1AT
Croom Helm Australia Pty Ltd, Suite 4, 6th Floor,
64-76 Kippax Street, Surry Hills, NSW 2010, Australia
Reprinted with corrections 1985

British Library Cataloguing in Publication Data

Jaques, David
    Learning in groups.
    1. College teaching. 2. Group work in
    education
    I. Title
    378'.1795   LB2331
    ISBN 0-7099-0046-5

Croom Helm, 51 Washington Street, Dover,
New Hampshire 03820, USA

Library of Congress Catalog Card Number: 84-45288
Cataloging in Publication Data Applied For:

To   Penny, Damian, Sophie and Daniel,
       the rest of the Group

Printed and bound in Great Britain by
Biddles Ltd, Guildford and King's Lynn

CONTENTS

Contents

Contents

Contents

INTRODUCTION

Most academic teachers would agree that teaching
and learning in small groups has a valuable part
to play in the all-round education of the student.
Its function, in allowing students to negotiate
meanings, to express themselves in the language of
the subject, and to establish a more intimate contact with academic staff than the lecture method
permits, is generally accepted. Yet, when it comes
to it, many tutors find the leadership role difficult to perform satisfactorily and fall back with
some reluctance and disappointment on their reserve
position of authority, expert and prime talker.
New lecturers are not always given suitable
induction to group teaching: even when training in
small group techniques is given, it is not easy to
replicate the competitive tension of a seminar in a
training exercise. And if it were possible to do
so, the seminar, as a model of group interaction
would promote a rather limited view of the rich
variety of experience that small group techniques
can contribute to learning.
    My aim in this book is therefore not just to
promote understanding but to help improve skills for
tutors and students alike and to widen the range
of possible group experiences. The title 'Learning
in Groups' is meant to suggest that groups are not
merely a valuable vehicle for learning about the
skills and concepts of a subject discipline, but
are also a way of learning about groups both as a
means of enhancing academic learning and in the
development of abilities in co-operative work for
later life.
    There are several possible starting points for
the reader. Some may prefer to look at the chapter
on techniques first before referring back to aims.

Introduction

Others may need to pick up ideas on questioning techniques before gaining awareness of theoretical bases for them. What you choose to accept and use from the book will reflect your own practice and philosophy of teaching. It might therefore be a good idea if I first state my own position on learning in groups.

1. I assume that students are adults and should be encouraged to learn as adults. Knowles (1979) describes this orientation as andragogy as opposed to pedagogy. At the same time I recognise that many students in their late teens are still maturing as they cope with identity crises (Erikson 1971) and an uneasy relationship with authority. Nevertheless the assumption of an adult-adult relationship is one which brings about a more productive teaching and learning relationship.

2. Co-operation is a key word in learning groups. Competition in groups may sharpen the critical faculty of a few, but is more likely to dull the appetite for discussion among most. Co-operation doesn't just happen. We learn to co-operate through practice and this requires a clear and co-ordinated strategy for learning about working together and improving skills in co-operation. Co-operation also means each and every member of the group taking a part and sharing responsibility for its success.

3. We all learn from experiences, whether happy or bitter ones, but we often fail to extend this learning beyond the immediate fact. Thus when a group discussion grinds to a halt we may record that it has done so and that it is frustrating, but do little more. However if we were to be a little more observant about what happened, reflect on, and examine, the events and our part in them, then we would be more likely to develop rules and principles to guide us in our next, similar, experience. The "experiential" learning cycle (Fig.I.1) based on Kolb (1979), contains three assumptions:

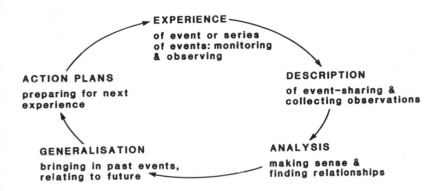

Fig.I Experiential Learning Cycle

> (i)   we learn best when we are person-
>   ally involved in the learning
>   experience.
>
> (ii)   knowledge of any kind has more sig-
>   nificance when we learn it through
>   our own initiative, insight and
>   discovery.
>
> (iii)   learning is best when we are com-
>   mitted to aims that we have been
>   involved in setting, when our
>   participation with others is valued
>   and when there is a supportive
>   framework in which to learn.

4.   Despite the pre-eminence of intellectual
     aims in learning groups it is often the
     emotional needs and undercurrents which
     are most powerful yet most frequently
     neglected. The sense of identity and
     social belonging which a student can gain
     from a well-run group should not be under-
     estimated. Nor should the inhibiting
     effect of tutor authority, a competitive
     atmosphere and the fear of students that
     they may make fools of themselves. Four
     important words seem to be missing in most
     academic courses: support, commitment,
     enjoyment and imagination. The first

three may be created in a group where a climate of open communication, involving trust, honesty and mutual respect, takes place. Imagination should blossom in this climate. It might also create it.

For most tutors the first two chapters will provide a base on which to build their understanding of groups. The field of group dynamics has no unifying theme. Rather than try to present one approach to the various problems and issues in groups, therefore, I have provided a rather eclectic view, drawing on various theoretical and research approaches which seem to shed light on problems or are a source of ideas for more rewarding and imaginative group techniques.

There follow two short chapters on learning and communication, following which the fifth chapter examines the kind of aims that are suitable to learning groups, and relates the necessary aims of groups in general to the specific ones in academic learning. The sixth chapter is a discussion of what tutors and groups might be expected to do and examines a variety of tasks and techniques. Many of these are examples of more challenging and stimulating approaches than the traditional seminar or tutorial offers.

The seventh chapter answers the question: what personal tasks and skills does the tutor have to learn in order to prepare for and handle group interaction? It particularly looks at the kinds of intervention a tutor may usefully make during the progress of discussion. In the eighth chapter the place of learning groups in the social and educational environment of the college is discussed and several case studies of real schemes are used to illustrate it. The ninth chapter provides some practical suggestions for evaluating both the leadership role and the group as a whole, and the book finishes with a set of training activities for improving participation in groups at all levels.

I have tried to write a book that is both readable and practical; one which permits flexibility yet covers the essential content. If any readers should feel like sending me comments and ideas which might help improve the book, I should be delighted to hear from them.

A final note on the problem of gender pronouns: I have tried to avoid use of 'his' and 'her' wherever possible. If there seems no other way of avoiding it I have used 'his' rather than 'her' on the grounds that I am thinking of myself in the particular situation; were I a woman I would use the female pronouns. I trust readers will understand and translate accordingly.

David Jaques,
Hatfield

This revised edition follows fast upon the first. I have not made any major revisions, merely tidied up various typographical errors and loose ends. I have also re-worked the case studies in chapter 8 and added discussion questions at the end of each chapter. The latter may be tackled by individuals but would make much more sense if discussed in groups.
Finally I would like to thank Gillian Hill for the enormous contribution she has made in making improvements for this revised edition.

David Jaques,
Hatfield

ACKNOWLEDGEMENTS

To my colleagues at the Centre for Staff Development in Higher Education (formerly University Teaching Methods Unit) for permission to reproduce various extracts from their publications and for all the ideas and experience in group teaching that I got during my five years' work with them; especially to Roy Cox and David Warren Piper.

To colleagues at Hatfield Polytechnic for their support and encouragement.

To many devoted typists who struggled both with my handwriting and with my constant re-drafting.

To other colleagues who have helped with perceptive comments on the drafts, but especially Gillian Hill.

To the Nuffield Foundation for permission to re-print large extracts from their Newsletters in Chapter 8.

To Malcolm Knowles for permission to include a section on group behaviour from his book Introduction to Group Dynamics in Chapter 2, pages 22-35.

To Jean Rudduck and the Society for Research into Higher Education for permission to reprint the various extracts on pages 84-6, and the contract on pages 244-9, from Learning Through Group Discussion.

To University Associates International for the basic format for the styles in Teaching and Learning exercise on pages 269-271 and the Group Behaviour Questionnaire on page 228.

To Hutchinsons for permission to reproduce the diagram on page 16 from The Psychology of the Learning Group by McLeish, Matheson and Park.

Finally to a host of people who have contributed ideas and material to conferences and workshops I have attended. Wherever possible I have acknowledged the source but in many cases I have been unable to trace the origins.

THEORIES ABOUT GROUP BEHAVIOUR

What is a Group?

There have been many attempts to establish clear definitions of groups and each one betrays some of its author's assumptions about what happens in groups, both in the terminology and in what he or she chooses to emphasise. Rather than trying to single out or invent a unitary definition I would prefer to list some of the characteristics most commonly described by practitioners in order to paint a more comprehensive picture of the variety of dynamic qualities within each group. A group can be said to exist as more than a collection of people when it possesses the following qualities:

1. Collective perception: members are collectively conscious of their existence as a group.
2. Needs: members join a group because they believe it will satisfy some needs or give them some rewards.
3. Shared aims: members hold common aims or ideals which to some extent bind them together. The achievement of aims is presumably one of the rewards.
4. Interdependence: members are interdependent inasmuch as they are affected by and respond to any event that affects any of the group's members.
5. Social organisation: a group can be seen as a social unit with norms, roles, statuses, power and emotional relationships.
6. Interaction: members influence and respond to each other in the process of communicating, whether they are face-to-face or otherwise deployed. The sense of 'group'

exists even when members are not collected in the same place.

7. Cohesiveness: members want to remain in the group, to contribute to its wellbeing and aims, and to join in its activities.

8. Membership: two or more people interacting for longer than a few minutes constitute a group.

None of these characteristics by itself defines a group but each indicates important aspects. However, not all of them can be expected to relate to every group and some of the qualities may be seen as part of others. <u>Interaction</u> will not take place without some need to influence, share and be responded to, all of which give rise to attempts to communicate with others. Nevertheless, if a group is consciously to regard itself as a group it must exist long enough for a rudimentary pattern of interaction to develop. Some group dynamics theorists argue that a group has to comprise at least three people before significant group behaviour can occur. For the purpose of this book however, I shall include the dyad or pair, even though it may lack some important characteristics, as a special type of group with valuable potentialities for learning.

A group may be considered as an entity, but it is illuminating to study the individual experience of members as well. Some writers, e.g. Allport (1924), argue that groups have no separate reality, only individuals are real, and that all the norms, roles, relationships, etc., exist only in the minds of individuals functioning as a collection of people. Others, Freud for instance, see the dynamics of group behaviour as a sort of collective extension of individual psychopathology. The most suitable picture for our purposes is probably one in which group phenomena are held to be real to the extent that group members respond to such phenomena <u>as if they existed</u>. In this book we shall consider the group from both individual and collective viewpoints, working on the assumption that a better understanding of group process will develop from considering both viewpoints in relation to one another.

Theory or Research?

Let us now consider what contribution theory and research make to an understanding of the complex processes which take place in a group. Opinion is divided on the most fruitful approach to studying groups. On the one hand as Shaw (1977) explains, there are those who argue that group phenomena can be validly assessed and understood only by rigorous analysis of empirical observations. On the other hand, some maintain that research evidence will almost certainly be trivial and theoretical analysis is the only means to a comprehensive understanding of the complex phenomena evident in groups. It is true that, without theory, most of the research findings would merely be a collection of random and unrelated facts but, conversely, it is impossible to construct a theory without some empirical understanding: empirical 'facts' serve to underline the broader statements of theoretical insights. Theory in its turn serves to illuminate and organise research data in a way which extend their meaning beyond the situations from which they were derived.

PSYCHODYNAMIC THEORY

Freud in his 'Group Psychology and the Analysis of the Ego' (1921) claimed that people are drawn into, and remain in groups because of emotional ties between members, and that one of the principal mechanisms in the effecting of such ties is identification - the process whereby a person wants to be like his or her parent(s). To use Freud's terms, people 'introject' a preferred person (the leader), or the qualities they like in that person, into their own being, while at the same time 'projecting' some of the bad or painful qualities of themselves onto others. When each member of a group assimilates the same qualities of the leader they can identify with each other.

Introjection and projection are two processes which are common to most relationships between people and usually take place at the unconscious level, that is the participants are not usually aware of them unless attention is drawn to them. Another Freudian concept which has relevance to groups is that of transference, a common phenomenon in which fears, loves and longings which a person has experienced in early childhood, usually in relation to parents and siblings, are re-awakened in later life when they are displaced on to another person. Although at this stage their power is unconscious it can be felt both in one-to-one and group relationships. It is not unusual for a student to reject, resent or respect a tutor to an unrealistic extent because the same feelings are triggered off by the tutor in the student (usually at an unconscious level) as by one of the student's parents. Sometimes the resentment becomes more generalised so that all people in authority and even the institution itself become the objects of hatred.

The Freudian school thus saw the basic processes in a group as outward manifestations of the inner lives of its members: the intrapersonal expressed as the interpersonal. Out of this approach has developed one of the most powerful interpretations of group interaction, that commonly known as the Tavistock Model. Bion (1961), one of its key figures, proposed that a group operates simultaneously at two levels: the <u>work group</u> and the <u>basic group</u>. The work group meets to perform a specific and overt task. However, this is frequently obstructed, diverted and on occasion assisted by certain other mental activities in the form of powerful emotional drives. The basic group behaves <u>as if</u> it shared the following tacit assumptions or motives:

(a) to obtain security and protection from one individual on whom it can <u>depend</u>. This can be the designated leader or any member who is accepted in the role. The group unconsciously assumes that some sort of magic resides in the leader. In learning groups, students frequently direct attention to the tutor's remarks, as if he were the source of all wisdom, to the exclusion of their colleagues' contributions. Even if they lose respect for a particular tutor there is a sense in which the position is endowed with authority or, at least that there is some external power which determines what should be learned whether or not the tutor is the medium. (see also pages 81,82)

(b) to preserve itself from annihilation either attacking something <u>(fight)</u>

or by avoiding the task (flight).
Commonly the group will scapegoat some
other person or group in order to avoid a
difficult problem. Flight on the other
hand takes the form of withdrawal, pass-
ivity, dwelling on the past, or jesting.
The group seems happy to distract itself
from its task by focusing on some other
harmless and irrelevant issue. 'In this
mode, the group uses its energy to defend
itself from its own internal fears and
anxieties, and consequently neither
develops nor achieves an effective
output' (de Board 1978).

(c) to engage in pairing. Two individuals
form a bond in which warmth, closeness
and affection are shown. Pairing has as
its basic assumption that the purpose of
the group is to bring two people together
who will somehow save the group from its
current predicament. Frequently this
happens when the group is bored, lost or
resentful in its discussion and is unable
to express or otherwise cope with these
feelings. In learning groups pairing may
take three possible forms. One is where
two students provide mutual respect and
support for each other to the exclusion
of other members who are thus rendered
inactive. Alternatively, the pair could
engage in intellectual battle, each
partner representing a different side of
a conflict that has been pre-occupying
the group. Again the rest of the group
are mere bystanders. Finally, the tutor
may pair with the group as a whole
and collude with them in their wish to
avoid work. Pairing is often character-
ised by a sense of unreal hope: 'Everything will be okay when we get a new
room', 'It'll come all right after
Christmas'. The need to face up to and
work through disappointments and failures
is conveniently avoided by this unreal
but seductive promise of things to come.
Pairing can also be likened to two cells
coming together in order for the group to
reproduce itself, that is to say develop
another task and direction for the group
distinct from the agreed one. Though
this coupling may not result from an

explicit sexual attraction there may
well be a quasi-sexual bonding with
its 'offspring' as the idea, the brain-
child, that will save the group from
its failings.

Dependency, Flight-fight, and Pairing are described
as the assumptions of the basic group whose primary
task is seen as survival. It is important to
recognise that the basic group which operates under
these assumptions is the same one that is engaged
in the work task; they are the same members operating under different modes. Where the overt tasks
of the work group and the covert tasks of the basic
group meet, conflict is likely to occur.

These theoretical concepts have been developed
through a wealth of experience of groups at conferences in human relations training at the Tavistock
Institute and have been applied with some degree of
success to industrial and organisational settings.
However, they are not always easy to accept and to
identify without a certain amount of training. To
some extent they may be of little relevance in a
well-run seminar group committed to its task of
intellectual development, though it is arguable
that every tutor should at least be aware of them
as a latent force lest they be drawn into a collusion on any of the basic assumptions and thus
frustrate the achievement of the work task.

The Tavistock approach has brought into
focus other issues of value in our understanding of
group dynamics. Banet & Hayden (1977) list these
concepts as authority, responsibility, boundaries,
projection, organisation and large group phenomena.

Authority: Whenever decisions have to be made about
process or the allocation of tasks, a group is
likely to experience authority problems. Whose job
is it to decide? Can the group give any one person
that sanction? Where a designated 'authority
person' exists then a group may either find itself
dependent on them, or counterdependent (attacking
authority). Freud (1921) regarded the small group
as an analogue of the family. The leader of a
group is therefore likely to have childhood feelings
transferred onto her or him; such feelings as
infantile dependency (which arouses as many bad
feelings as good) and disobedience or rebellion.
Redl (1942), quoted in McLeish (1973), provided
classroom pupils with different kinds of teacher
personalities, and discovered that within each class

there were 'conflicted individuals' who had difficulty in coping with their unconscious emotions and
images in respect of a particular teacher.   If
and when a 'conflicted individual' acts out his
repressed feelings about authority with a teacher
who happens to trigger them off, other students who
may be incapable of handling such feelings, give
tacit approval to the conflicted student as a sort
of representative of their own antipathy. In this
way a pattern of beliefs and behaviours, a classroom
'culture', is established for any group of students
with a particular teacher.

The teacher's role when authority conflicts
occur would seem to be to aid the students' growth
by refusing to join battle, and to help them understand the consequences of their action.   Many
students who object to the authority of the teacher
are not really seeking an alternative to the status
quo. They are probably fighting the tutor as a way
of avoiding the need to accept that learning is
their own responsibility and that they have to face
the consequences of the choices they make.   It is
important therefore for the teacher to create the
conditions in which the students can make conscious
choices of alternative courses of action by supportively but firmly bringing such issues out into the
open. (see contract, pages 244-49)

Responsibility: There is a feeling, in groups where
visible authority is present, that the ultimate
responsibility for each person's action and its
consequences resides in the figure of authority.
In learning groups, students rarely take responsibility for the role they play in contributing to a
successful experience.   Whether they are accustomed
to challenging authority overtly or to accepting
it with resentment and bad grace, they may never
have examined the consequences of that particular
attitude.   Somehow the responsibility for what
happens is assumed to lie firmly in the lap of the
tutor who may find himself unable to shrug it off.
Some tutors are prone to the 'mother-hen'
syndrome: they tend their 'little chicks', protecting them from the supposed deceptions practised by
others.   They may try to establish this sort of
relationship with any person or group they
encounter.   It is a pattern of behaviour they have
acquired through their own upbringing and which they
readily transfer to any willing 'brood'. Many of
us respond to a student's sense of helplessness

by offering to meet it and without questioning its nature. The problem here is that the teacher who is an incurable helper, in satisfying one of his or her basic needs, may fail to develop the student's capacity for self-growth into greater autonomy and responsibility.

Boundaries: For all of us there exists both a physical and psychological boundary in relation to others. Our own skin constitutes a physical boundary while the distinction between our private thoughts, feelings and fantasies, and the 'known' outside world constitutes another. The same can be said of the group; both in a subjective sense and a more objective and symbolic sense boundaries distinguish one group from another. The physical space occupied by a group and the time span it covers are obvious and objective boundaries. Both of these are typically under the control of the tutor. Less tangible and more subjective are the task boundary, which determines what the group should or should not do, and the input boundary which requires members to undergo certain social procedures before membership is acquired. Evidence of the strength of subjective boundaries can be readily perceived if a stranger, perhaps a new student, arrives unannounced in an established group, or if the tutor invites a colleague to sit in on a seminar.

Projection: Sometimes the negative feelings we have towards other people are too dangerous to permit of conscious expression and, as a mechanism to defend us against the anxiety that this produces, we attribute these feelings, motives or qualities to the person or persons towards whom our feelings are really directed. We thus experience the feelings as coming 'at us' rather than 'from us'. This is the mechanism known as projection. Some students may for instance see the tutor as hostile when they are in fact feeling hostility to the tutor but are unable to recognise it. They will usually hotly deny the existence of the feeling if challenged.
     Just as individuals can plant their own bad feelings on others in the group, so a group can spend a lot of time and energy in projecting its own conflicts, or inadequacies on to another group

or the institution. This is more particularly true of staff groups and student political and union meetings than of learning groups and is what happens when a group adopts the 'fight' stance described on pages 4-5.

Organisational Structure: the power relationships in the group, whether determined by outside factors (e.g. the curriculum, the tutor's position in the institutional hierarchy) or by internal concerns such as qualities or skills of individuals, can have a profound effect on the work of a group. Structural relations of this kind will probably manifest themselves in who sits where, who takes initiatives, who defers to whom, and in the pecking order of contributions. In general, structures which are not revealed and discussed, lead to feelings of mistrust. The structure of a group does not automatically exist from the beginning but develops through a process of differentiation and sorting. It can also change according to the mood of members or the special requirements of the task in hand. The recognition of this problem has led some group leaders, for instance Hill (1969), to allocate special roles and responsibilities in a group on a rotating basis. This is further described on page 151.

Large Groups: As the size of a group increases so its characteristics change. Six, in the view of Rice (1965), is a critical number for groups in all sorts of situations. With six or less the degree of intimacy offered by close proximity makes it difficult for group members to register their feelings about the group. Leadership tends to be fluid and interchangeable. As the group size increases the climate of the group changes. Individuals become less constrained by the norms of the group and become more aware of their feelings. Leadership and other roles become more established. With numbers of 12 to 25 the likelihood of full face-to-face interaction decreases and sub-groups start to emerge. When the group is over 25 in number, face-to-face interaction between everyone becomes impossible. Some people, because of the group's size, may have to sit behind others, and anyone speaking may fail to see, or be seen by, everyone in the group. When leadership occurs it takes on a more clear cut, 'external' role. Whereas

9

in the small group it is easy to think but difficult
to feel, in the large one the opposite is likely to
be the case. It becomes difficult to mobilise the
intellect, issues become polarised, splitting ('I
all right/you all wrong') takes over as a defence
against anxiety, and in order to manage the apparent
chaos people are likely to stereotype each other.
The leader or teacher, as someone who is evidently
different, is likely to be subject to these perceptions more than most and the authority/dependency
problem will almost certainly be sharper and more
acute.
Leaders become invested with all sorts of
power and expertise. But as soon as they come up
with something 'inferior' their credibility will
sag and they may be attacked for their inadequacy!
Power is the more sharply polarised and too sudden
or big a change in the power relationship is likely
to produce a flight/fight situation. If the group
challenges the leader and if in turn it is
challenged back, it might retreat or withdraw.
An example of this would be when a lecturer, after
playing a formal and omniscient role invites the
class informally to come up with some of its own
ideas.
Another experience of people in large groups
is that their identity becomes more fragile and
their sense of reality is distorted. As a result
the mechanism of projection (see page 8) is likely
to operate: unwanted parts of the self are pushed
onto others, and fantasies about other people's
motives, attitudes and intentions abound. So much
for the undercurrents. At the behavioural level,
it becomes evident that the larger the group, the
more formal and oratorical do the spoken contributions become. In the educational context we can
see that students have two kinds of relationship
open to them; one with the small discussion or
learning groups with which they already have some
identity, and one with the wider group membership,
many of whom they know from social or sporting
contacts, or even in another learning group. In
training 'workshops' (see page 137) there is a constant alternation between small groups of different
sizes and the large plenary group. In some ways
this mixture can provide for participants a sense of
a home base (their sub-group) amid the feeling of
identity loss that the large group may create.
The the tutor is able to circulate round the
sub-groups and is thus less likely to be on the
receiving end of displaced or projected bad feeling

Number of Members	Changing Characteristics	
2-6	Little structure/ organisation required; leadership fluid.	M o r e
7-12	Structure and differentiation of roles begins. Face-to-face interaction less frequent.	
12-25	Structure and role differentiation vital. Sub-groups emerge. Face-to-face interaction difficult.	T e n s i o n
25-?	Positive leadership vital to success. Sub-groups form; greater anonymity. Stereotyping, projections and flight/fight occur.	

(left margin reads: More Cohesion)

Fig.1.1   Changing Characteristics of Groups with Increase in Membership

through becoming more 'real' to participants. Yet, there will still be challenges of the authority/ dependency kind and they can be all the more powerful for having the support of a sub-group.

The complex play of relationships in a large group and the emotional swirl that is likely to go with them is thus, at least potentially, fraught with confusion, inaction and frustration. Strong leadership is both needed and gratefully accepted. As Rice points out, 'In this condition an individual who can define some positive goal can exercise powerful leadership.' How the tutor takes that role, or dodges it, is sometimes of critical importance in large groups. It is not irrelevant in small groups too.

'Habeas Emotum': Many of the above issues may seem far-fetched to academic tutors, especially those in the Physical Sciences and Engineering whose central concern is not with personal feelings and group

process but with the imparting of a body of knowledge. Yet, with these faculty areas, one hears of
constant problems to do with lack of motivation and
commitment, alienation and even 'dropout'. In a
limited number of studies where some emphasis has
been placed on 'process learning' and interaction
in small group work there does appear to be a
growth in student commitment. (See case studies on
pages 184-216). Although styles of learning and
shared values (Gaff & Wilson, 1971) may vary from
faculty to faculty the vast majority of students
prize the sense of belonging which small groups
afford students and the chance to test their understandings with their peers. Both these aims can be
put in jeopardy and the student experience in
groups can become most frustrating if emotional
under-currents are not drawn out and coped with.
This is an area where even traditional research
evidence and psychodynamic theory are in agreement.

Continually throughout this book we shall be
concerned with what Luft (1970) calls 'Habeas
emotum' - a recognition that people's emotions are
a necessary part of their existence, and that as
Rubin (1967) and Jones (1971) argue, if we educate
only the rational/intellectual person we do so at
our (and their) peril. Behaviour is determined as
much by passions, anxieties and convictions as it
is by reason, the more so when we are not aware of
the effects of our feelings. Negative feelings can
be destructive if they are ignored, submerged or
displaced into sarcasm or backbiting. Boredom,
irritation or fear can interfere with the willingness of a group to engage in the learning process.
Moreover, intellectual growth, as we shall later
discuss, is closely linked to emotional development.
It is incumbent upon tutors to recognise all this
and the part their own emotions may play in the
process. This recognition is important therefore
not merely for the effective functioning of the
group but for the more far-reaching educational aim
of developing the student as a congruent person -
one who is able to hold together the different
levels at which he or she experiences life and to
communicate responses genuinely.

Attending to students' emotional needs should
not only benefit their intellectual powers but
should also develop their capacity to tackle
the sort of relationships that are so familiar to
the industrial sector, not to speak of educational
establishments. Contemporary life places a premium
on the ability of people to get on with each other,

to be able to handle interpersonal problems rather than to avoid them, and to do so constructively and creatively. Nowhere is it more possible to practise these qualities than in small-group work when learning is not subject to purely academic limitations.

INTERACTION THEORY

Whereas Psychodynamic Theory emphasises the effect of unconscious processes in the group which exist beyond the awareness of the participant, the Interaction approach is concerned with inter-personal behaviour between members of the group. This approach has contributed a lot to our understanding of group work, particularly by providing categories for the observation and analysis of different kinds of behaviour in small groups. These categories include qualitative and quantitative considerations, and are designed to comprise all possible types of behaviour. McLeish (1973) maintains that the Interaction Analysis System should include:

1. The affective or emotional components of behaviour.
2. The cognitive or intellectual components.
3. The non-verbal or 'meta-language' components.
4. Content or message components.
5. Sociological or personal network segments of behaviour.

Although originally designed as research tools, interaction analyses have been increasingly used for training purposes to provide feedback to teachers, trainee group participants and so on. In describing apparently straightforward and overt behaviour, an interaction analysis makes it possible to provide trainees/participants with increased personal insight through objective and largely non-evaluative feedback. They may also have opportunities to practise different skills and to test them against reactions from their colleagues. Finally, in producing a comprehensive analysis of a group discussion, interaction analysis provides information on the differences between participants, the overall pattern of interaction and participation, and the development of different phases in a group's existence.

The basis of interaction analysis is that
everything which a group says or does, including
non-verbal acts, may be coded, and that includes
items like body posture, facial expressions and
tone of voice. The set of categories devised by
Bales (1970) is shown in Figure 1.2. It forms a
symmetrical pattern and describes different aspects
of group functioning. The various categories form
complementary relationships. The first three comprise the positive socio-emotional area and correspond to the last three in the negative socio-
emotional area. Categories 4, 5 and 6, in the task
area, comprise answers, while 7, 8 and 9 correspond
as 'questions'. Individual categories can be paired
off or 'nested'.6 and 7 focus on problems of communication; 5 and 8 on evaluation and 4 and 9 on
problems of control. 3 and 10 are concerned with
decision-making in the group, 2 and 11 with reducing
tension and 1 and 12 with reintegration, the
settling of emotional issues. These combined pairs
relate to phases in the evolution of groups too, as
they move outwards from communicating the task, (6
and 7) through evaluation, (5 and 8) to the making
of decisions in 3 and 10. It also demonstrates that
in the initial stages of a task, the group should be
concerned with the instrumental or task components
of the interaction, and then as it moves towards
making decisions and achieving agreement, so it
becomes more clearly involved in the emotional side
of the process.
Theoretically, this is how a group interaction
evolves. However, as McLeish argues, events rarely
follow this smooth path and whilst the sequence may
be followed in a general sense, the actual group
interaction is an unstable, everchanging process
subject to all sorts of influences. The analysis
assumes that members of the group are not radically
affected by external factors such as previous ani-
mosities or extrinsic motives in their behaviour
in the group.
Bales's position is that if one can outline
behaviours in a group as objectively as possible,
it will be easier for people to accept what
happens and change accordingly to improve group
process. Certainly it is my experience that group
members are constantly surprised at the feedback
they get from an interaction analysis in respect
of both the quality and the quantity of what they
contribute to discussion. However, it is not
always so easy to categorise behaviours in the
way indicated by Bales, more particularly in the

Theories About Group Behaviour

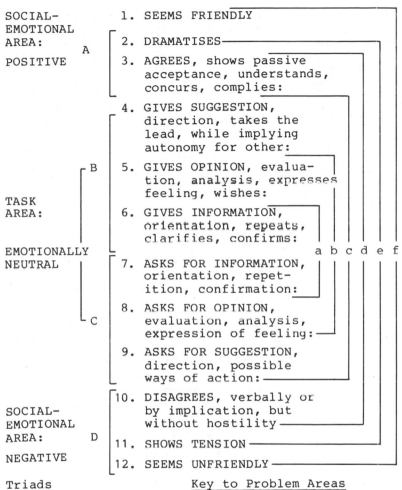

SOCIAL-
EMOTIONAL
AREA:
    A
POSITIVE

1. SEEMS FRIENDLY

2. DRAMATISES

3. AGREES, shows passive acceptance, understands, concurs, complies:

B

4. GIVES SUGGESTION, direction, takes the lead, while implying autonomy for other:

5. GIVES OPINION, evaluation, analysis, expresses feeling, wishes:

6. GIVES INFORMATION, orientation, repeats, clarifies, confirms:

TASK
AREA:

EMOTIONALLY
NEUTRAL

a b c d e f

7. ASKS FOR INFORMATION, orientation, repetition, confirmation:

8. ASKS FOR OPINION, evaluation, analysis, expression of feeling:

C

9. ASKS FOR SUGGESTION, direction, possible ways of action:

SOCIAL-
EMOTIONAL
AREA: D
NEGATIVE

10. DISAGREES, verbally or by implication, but without hostility

11. SHOWS TENSION

12. SEEMS UNFRIENDLY

Triads

A Positive reactions
B Attempted answers
C Questions
D Negative reactions

Key to Problem Areas

a Problems of communication
b Problems of evaluation
c Problems of control
d Problems of decision
e Problems of tension reduction
f Problems of reintegration

Fig.1.2

The verbal analysis of behaviour: Bales' system (1970). (All behaviour, verbal or non-verbal, is observed and classified in <u>one</u> or other of 12 categories).

socio-emotional area where people frequently keep their feelings to themselves or are trying somehow to compensate for various feelings they have towards other people or towards the whole group. The analysis makes no concession to the notion of a group culture but can be assessed as an analytical tool for visible group interaction. It nevertheless fails to reveal some of the more powerful determining forces in a group.

Six-Category Intervention Analysis

Another form of behaviour analysis is proposed by Heron (1976) and although based primarily on one-to-one interventions, can apply equally to a group setting. He calls it the Six Category Intervention Analysis and claims that the interventions deal with all 'desirable and worthwhile types of intervention: that is they exclude only negative and destructive types of intervention'. Six categories are devised in a form which contributes to self-assessment and self-monitoring for group leaders of any kind; to what extent they can be extended to ordinary group members has yet to be seen.

The six categories fall into two main groups, authoritative and facilitative. Authoritative when the leader is in a dominant or assertive role; facilitative where the role of the leader is seen to be less obtrusive and more discreet.

Under the authoritative mode the tutor can be:

1. Directing

    - Raising an issue for discussion, re-routing the discussion
    - Suggesting further work to be done

2. Informing

    - Summarising
    - Inter-relating
    - Giving knowledge and information

3. Confronting

    - Challenging by direct question
    - Disagreeing with/correcting/critically evaluating student statement
    - Giving direct feedback

Under the _facilitative_ mode the tutor can be:

4. Releasing tension

   - Arousing laughter
   - Allowing students to discharge unpleas-
     ant emotions such as embarrassment,
     irritation, confusion and sometimes even
     anger

5. Eliciting

   - Drawing out student opinions/knowledge/
     problem-solving ability
   - Facilitating student interaction
   - Enabling students to learn and develop
     by self discovery and personal insight

6. Supporting

   - Approving/reinforcing/agreeing with/
     affirming the value of student contri-
     butions

Two of these six categories are of special
importance for group work in that they form a
spectrum from student-centred learning to tutor-
centred learning.

|STUDENT-CENTRED|

1. Reflecting. Open-ended   )
   questioning (unfocused,   )
   focused, cross-referenced)   )
) Eliciting
2. Selectively reflecting.   )
   Checking for understanding.   )
   Empathic building   )

3. Closed, directive questioning   )
)
4. Summarising/interrelating/   ) Informing
   clarifying   )
)
5 Information-giving   )

|TUTOR-CENTRED|

The details of both these categories indicate

17

some of the particular skills the tutor should employ in performing the interventions. Reflecting refers to the practice of echoing back, without any special emphasis, the last few words a student says before pausing. This invariably encourages the student to expand on his thoughts in any way that has meaning to him. Alternatively, the tutor may rephrase the last few words. Reflection is a way of conveying to the student, particularly when he has paused in the development of an argument, that the tutor is paying attention and wishes the student to continue without interruption in the flow. Various open-ended questions can serve a similar purpose (see pages 162-6). Selective reflection is the skill of picking out from a contribution a few words or phrases which seem to carry an implicit emotional charge, or which appeared to cause some sort of agitation in the student. Empathic building is a way of developing a student's contribution beyond the point at which it finishes, but using the words and phrases of the student and checking that this is the way it would have developed had he or she thought of it.

Various suggestions for the use of these categories, particularly those in the facilitative mode, are suggested in Chapter 7.

Theme-Centred Interaction

As much a method as a theory, TCI is concerned with three constituent factors, each of equal importance: the 'I', the 'we' and the 'it' of group interaction. For productive discussion to occur, 'I', the individual interests must be balanced with the 'we', of group relatedness, and the 'it' of the theme or topic. The theme is treated as common property to which the individuals (which includes the 'I' of the tutor) and the group-as-a-whole relate (Bramley, 1979) and should include a gerund, as for instance 'observing accurately', in order to create a momentum and a sense of participation. These three elements are seen to be enveloped in a globe which is itself set in 'auspices' (see Figure 1.3). The globe comprises the physical, social and temporal environment in which the group takes place. It includes the shape of the room, the arrangement of the furniture and the emotional climate of the group. Auspices refers basically to the learning milieu, those external factors such as relationships to other groups, timetable constraints and prior and future concerns of the participants. Each member of the group is expected to act as his or her own chairperson in charge of an inner 'committee' which comprises four members: 'what I want to do', 'what I ought to do', 'how that might affect others' and the chairperson, who has to decide which of these should have precedence.

This basic structure is supplemented by the rule 'disturbances take precedence'; if a group member is unable to focus on the group task because of some emotional distraction - being angry, bored, upset or excited, for example - they should say so. The emotional underlay is thus revealed in a personally responsible way. TCI has strong roots in both existentialism and psycho-analysis. It provides a framework for each individual to internalise and understand his or her own place and function in a group. It is also immensely practical and can be applied to a number of group settings to which other explanatory frameworks may not be suitable. Shaffer and Galinsky (1974) is recommended for further reading.

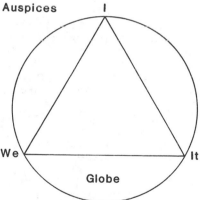

Fig 1.3   The Theme - Centred Interaction Triangle and Globe

Discussion Points

° Which of the various theoretical concepts discussed in this chapter make most sense or impact
  for you? Why might that be?
° Conduct a discussion on authority/dependency, the
  role of feelings or interaction behaviour in your
  group. Organise a fishbowl (see page 221) to get
  feedback on it.

2

RESEARCH INTO GROUP BEHAVIOUR

Over the past 50 years a wealth of information has been compiled by social psychologists working with experimental groups. Mostly their work has concentrated on the group performing practical tasks rather than processing academic material or experiencing personal growth. Typical criticism of the experimental approach is that the results are frequently trivial and even when put together do not add up to much; that they are frequently conducted with randomly selected students as subjects and are therefore unrepresentative of the population as a whole; and that they have rarely been able to touch upon the sort of complex phenomena of group interactions which appear to dominate the process in many groups. This form of research has been described by Bronfenbrenner (1977) as 'strange people doing strange things to strangers in strange situations'. However, Argyris (1968) argues that it is more or less what happens in the shop-floor situation; in both, precise instructions are given but nobody is told why. In fact, the goals are quite frequently concealed. The same might be true of the discussion group in higher education. However, there are enormous differences between the patterns of behaviour in long-established groups, such as those which exist over a period of time in an academic course or in an industrial environment, and experimental collectivities which are drawn together solely for the purpose of a particular experiment. Patterns of behaviour change as a group develops over a period of time.

Notwithstanding these criticisms, some valuable information does emerge when experimental work in areas of similar interest is compared. Yet we can never be sure of cause and effect in human behaviour: which conscious or unconscious motive does it spring from? What action will a particular motive produce? The task of providing explanations for social behaviour is highly problematical and demands careful evaluation as well as scepticism from the practitioner. On the other hand, it requires an ability to see the relationship between separate bits of evidence, and between those bits of evidence and the practical situation in which decisions have to be made.

Quite apart from the so-called laboratory experiments, we can select from a range of other studies which may loosely be described as field studies. The basic characteristic of these is that the phenomenon under investigation is studied in its natural habitat. Shaw (1977) comments 'the investigator does not create the situation or situations being studied, instead he or she examines the phenomenon as it occurs in natural on-going social events'. To this extent the evidence derived is based on local events in a special context. For the practitioner they present some problems in interpretation as there is always some uncertainty about the particular effect of the environment in which the experiment takes place - the institution, the personal qualities of the teacher and the students, the external motivating factors - such as assessment and social life - all of which can profoundly affect the outcome.

An accumulation of research evidence can, over a period of time, challenge some of our assumptions about what happens in groups and can change our understanding of problems. As practitioners, most teachers will need to test the relevance and value of research evidence in their own contexts, usually by incorporating some of the implied principles into their teaching procedures. Everyone must be his own translator.

What this all boils down to is that research evidence has to be interpreted in the light of practical experience with and in everyday groups. Knowles & Knowles (1972) provide a ready-made amalgam of research and practice in their succinct review of the common characteristics of group behaviour. The groups they refer to include families, committees and discussion groups; the properties relate to all sorts of groups and situations. All of them are relevant to the learning group and their range and variety perhaps serve to underline the limited view of group interaction we often take in our work with students. The following pages (22-mid.34) are reproduced with the kind permission of Malcolm Knowles.

Some Properties of Groups

1. <u>Background</u>: Each group has an historical background, or lack of it, which influences its behaviour. A new group coming together for the first time may have to devote much of its early energy to getting acquainted with one another and with the group's task, as well as establishing ways of working together. On the other hand, a group that has met together often may be assumed to be better acquainted with what to expect from one another, what needs to be done, and how to do it. But it might also have developed habits that interfere with its efficiency, such as arguing, dividing into factions or wasting time.

Members come into a meeting with some expectations about it. They may have a clear idea of what the meeting is about, or they may be hazy and puzzled about what is going to happen. They may be looking forward to the meeting or dreading it; they may feel deeply concerned or indifferent. In some cases the boundaries around the group's freedom of action may be narrowly defined by the conditions under which it was created, or so poorly defined that the group doesn't know what its boundaries are.

These are merely illustrations of some of the elements that make up a group's background. Some questions that help to provide an understanding of a group's background include:

How well were the members prepared to enter the group?

What are their expectations about the group and their role in it?

What is the composition of the group - what kind of people, what is their previous experience, prior friendship patterns and so on? How were they selected?

What arrangements have been made for their meeting - physical setting, resources, and the like?

2. <u>Participation Pattern</u>: At any given moment every group has a particular participation pattern. For instance, it may be all one-way, with the leader talking to the members; or it may be two-way, with the leader speaking to the members and the members responding to him; or it may be multidirectional, with all members speaking to one another and to the group as a whole. In a given group this pattern may tend to be quite consistent, or it may vary from time to time. The studies do not indicate that any one participation pattern is always best; it depends upon the requirements of a given situation. But many studies show that on the whole, the broader the participation among members of a group the deeper the interest and involvement will be. Some questions you may ask about a group to understand its participation pattern are these:

How much of the talking is done by the leader, how much by the other members?

To whom are questions or comments usually addressed - the group as a whole, the leader, or particular members?

Do the members who don't talk much seem to be interested and listening alertly (non-verbal participation), or are they bored and apathetic?

It is very easy, and often useful to a group, to chart the participation pattern during periodic segments of time, thus providing objective data about this aspect of its dynamics, like this:

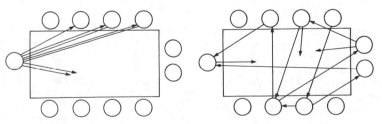

(a) Participation
Pattern from
8.00pm to 8.20pm

(b) Participation
Pattern from
9.00pm to 9.20pm

Fig.2.1 Charts of Participation Patterns in a Group

3. Communication: This property has to do with how well group members are understanding one another - how clearly they are communicating their ideas, values, and feelings. If some members are using a highly specialised vocabulary they may be talking over the heads of the rest of the group. Sometimes a group will develop a specialised vocabulary of its own, a kind of verbal shorthand, or private jokes that aren't understood by new members and outsiders.

Even non-verbal communication can often be eloquent. A person's posture, facial expression, and gestures, tell a great deal about what he is thinking and feeling. Some questions that indicate the quality of a group's communications are these:

Are members expressing their ideas clearly?

Do members frequently pick up contributions previously made and build their own ideas onto them?

Do members feel free to ask for clarification when they don't understand a statement?

Are responses to statements frequently irrelevant?

4. Cohesion: The cohesiveness of a group is determined by the strength of the bonds that bind the individual parts together into a unified whole. This property indicates the morale, the team spirit, the strength of attraction of the group for its members, and the interest of the members in what the group is doing. In the literature it is often referred to as the 'we feeling' of a group. Symptoms of low cohesion include sub rosa conversations between pairs of members outside the main flow of the group's discussion, the emergence of cliques, factions, and such sub-groupings as the 'old timers' versus the 'newcomers', the 'conservatives' versus the 'liberals', and so on. Questions about the group's cohesion include:

How well is the group working together as a unit?

What sub-groups or 'lone wolves' are there and how do they affect the group?

What evidence is there of interest or lack of interest on the part of members or groups of members in what the group is doing?

Do members refer to the group as 'my group', 'our group', 'your group', 'their group', or 'his group'?

5. Atmosphere: Although atmosphere is an intangible thing, it is usually fairly easy to sense. In the literature it is often referred to as the 'social climate' of the group, with such characterisations as 'warm, friendly, relaxed, informal, permissive, free' in contrast to 'cold, hostile, tense, formal, restrained'. Atmosphere affects how members feel about a group and the degree of spontaneity in their participation. Atmosphere can be probed by such questions as these:

Would you describe this group as warm or cool, friendly or hostile, relaxed or tense, informal or formal, permissive or controlled, free or inhibited?

Can opposing views or negative feelings be expressed without fear of punishment.

6. Standards: Every group tends to develop a code of ethics or set of standards about what is proper and acceptable behaviour. Which subjects may be discussed, which are taboo; how openly members may express their feelings; the propriety of volunteering one's services; the length and frequency of statements considered allowable; whether or not interrupting is permitted - all these and many more 'do's and don'ts' are embodied in a group's standards. It may be difficult for a new member to catch on to a group's standards if they differ from those of other groups he has experienced, since these standards are usually implicit rather than openly stated. Indeed, a group might be confused about what its standards actually are, and this may lead to embarrassment, irritation and lost momentum. Questions about standards include:

What evidence is there that the group has a code of ethics regarding such matters as self-discipline, sense of responsibility, courtesy,

tolerance of differences, freedom of expression, and the like?

Are there any marked deviations from these
standards by one or more members? With what
effect?

Do these standards seem to be well understood
by all members, or is there confusion about
them?

Which of the group's standards seem to help,
and which seem to hinder the group's progress?

7. Sociometric Pattern: In every group the participants tend very soon to begin to identify certain
individuals that they like more than other members,
and others that they like less. These subtle
relationships of friendship and antipathy - the
sociometric patterns - have an important influence
on the group's activities. There is some research
that indicates that people tend to agree with
people they like and to disagree with people they
dislike, even though both express the same ideas.
Questions which help to reveal the sociometric
pattern are these:

Which members tend to identify with and support
one another?

Which members seem repeatedly at odds?

Do some members act as 'triggers' to others,
causing them to respond immediately after the
first members' comments, either pro or con?

8. Structure and Organisation: Groups have both a
visible and an invisible organisational structure.
The visible structure, which might be highly formal
(officers, committees, appointed positions) or quite
informal, makes it possible to achieve a division of
labour among the members and get essential functions
performed. The invisible structure consists of
the behind-the-scenes arrangement of the members
according to relative prestige, influence, power,
seniority, ability, persuasiveness, and the like.
Questions to ask about structure include:

What kind of structure does the group create consciously - leadership positions, service positions, committees, teams?

What is the invisible structure - who really controls, influences, volunteers, gets things done; who defers to others, follows?

Is the structure understood and accepted by the members?

Is it appropriate to the group's purpose and tasks?

9. Procedures: All groups need to use some procedures - ways of working - to get things done. In formal business meetings we are accustomed to the use of a highly codified and explicit set of procedures. Informal groups usually use less rigid procedures. The choice of procedures has a direct effect on such other aspects of group life as atmosphere, participation pattern, and cohesion. Choosing procedures that are appropriate to the situation and to the work to be done requires a degree of flexibility and inventiveness by a group. Procedures can be examined through such questions as these:

How does the group determine its tasks or agenda?

How does it make decisions - by vote, silent assent, consensus?

How does it discover and make use of the resources of its members?

How does it co-ordinate its various members, sub-groups, and activities?

How does it evaluate its work?

10. Goals: All groups have goals, some very long-range - for example, 'to promote the welfare of children and youth'; others of shorter range - 'to plan a parent education programme for the coming year'; and others even more immediate - 'to decide on a speaker for next month's meeting'. Sometimes

goals are defined clearly, specifically, and
publicly, and other times they are vague, general
and only implicit. Members may feel really
committed to them or may merely go along with them.
Since goals are so important to the group's ultimate
accomplishment they receive a good deal of attention
in the literature. Some questions about goals
include:

How does the group arrive at its goals?

Are all members clear about them?

Are all members committed to them?

Are they realistic and attainable for this
group?

Social and Task Dimensions

It appears at first sight that there are two completely different kinds of groups. Some such as
the bridge circle, the coffee gang, and the like,
are highly informal, with few rules or procedures
and no stated goals. People belong for the
emotional satisfaction they get from belonging;
they like the people, they are their friends. They
tend to think of these as their social groups.
Membership in these groups is completely voluntary
and tends to be homogeneous. The success of the
social group is measured in terms of how enjoyable
it is.

In other groups, however - committees, boards,
staff meetings and discussion groups - there are
usually explicit goals, and more or less formal
rules and procedures. People tend to think of
these groups, which exist to accomplish some task,
as work or volunteer service groups. The membership tends to be more heterogeneous - based on the
resources required to do their work - and sometimes
brought together out of compulsion or sense of duty
more than out of free choice. The success of the
task group is measured in terms of how much work
it gets done.

As these dimensions have been studied more
deeply it has become apparent that they do not
describe different kinds of groups - few groups
are purely social or task - so much as different
dimensions of all groups. Most groups need the
social dimension to provide emotional involvement,
morale, interest, and loyalty; and the task dimen-

sion to provide stability, purpose, direction, and a sense of accomplishment. Without the dimension of work, members may become dissatisfied and feel guilty because they are not accomplishing anything; without the dimension of friendship, members may feel that the group is cold, unfriendly, and not pleasant to be with.

Group Maintenance and Group Task Functions
It is helpful, for understanding of the way in which various group functions are performed, to classify these functions as:

    (1) Group-Building and Maintenance roles — those which contribute to building relationships and cohesiveness among the membership (the social dimension).

and

    (2) Group Task roles — those which help the group to do its work (the task dimension).

The first set of functions is required for the group to maintain itself as a group; the second set, for the locomotion of the group toward its goals. For example, some group-building functions are these:

Encouraging - being friendly, warm, responsive to others, praising others and their ideas, agreeing with and accepting the contributions of others.

Mediating - harmonizing, conciliating differences in points of view, making compromises.

Gate Keeping - trying to make it possible for another member to make a contribution by saying, 'We haven't heard from Jim yet', or suggesting limited talking-time for everyone so that all will have a chance to be heard.

Standard Setting - expressing standards for the group to use in choosing its subject matter or procedures, rules of conduct, ethical values.

Following - going along with the group, somewhat passively accepting the ideas of others, serving as an audience during group discussion, being a good listener.

Relieving Tension - draining off negative feeling by jesting or throwing oil on troubled waters, diverting attention from unpleasant to pleasant matters.

And the following are some Task Functions:

Initiating - suggesting new ideas or a changed way of looking at the group problem or goal, proposing new activities.

Information Seeking - asking for relevant facts or authoritative information.

Information Giving - providing relevant facts or authoritative information or relating personal experience pertinently to the group task.

Opinion Giving - stating a pertinent belief or opinion about something the group is considering.

Clarifying - probing for meaning and understanding, restating something the group is considering.

Elaborating - building on a previous comment, enlarging on it, giving examples.

Co-ordinating - showing or clarifying the relationships among various ideas, trying to pull ideas and suggestions together.

Orienting - defining the progress of the discussion in terms of the group's goals, raising questions about the direction the discussion is taking.

Testing - checking with the group to see if it is ready to make a decision or to take some action.

Summarising - reviewing the content of past discussion.

These functions are not needed equally at all times by a group. Indeed, if a given function is performed inappropriately it may interfere with the group's operation - as when some jester relieves group tension just when the tension is about to result in some real action. But often when a group is not getting along as it should, a diagnosis of the problem will probably indicate that nobody is performing one of the functions listed above that is needed at that moment to move the group ahead. It seems to be true, also, that some people are more comfortable or proficient in performing one kind of function than another, so that they tend to play the same role in every group to which they belong. There is danger, however, in over-stereotyping an individual as a 'mediator' or 'opinion giver' or any other particular function, for people can learn to perform various functions that are needed when they become aware of them.

Often in groups one can observe behaviour that does not seem to fit any of these categories. This is likely to be <u>self-centred</u> behaviour, sometimes referred to in the literature as a 'nonfunctional role'. This is behaviour that does not contribute to the group, but only satisfies personal needs. Examples of this category are as follows:

<u>Blocking</u> - interfering with the progress of the group by going off on a tangent, citing personal experiences unrelated to the group's problem, arguing too much on a point the rest of the group has resolved, rejecting ideas without consideration, preventing a vote.

<u>Aggressing</u> - criticising or blaming others, showing hostility toward the group or some individual without relation to what has happened in the group, attacking the motives of others, deflating the ego or status of others.

<u>Seeking Recognition</u> - attempting to call attention to one's self by excessive talking, extreme ideas, boasting, boisterousness.

<u>Special Pleading</u> - introducing or supporting ideas related to one's own pet concerns or philosophies beyond reason, attempting to speak for 'the grass roots', 'the housewife', 'the common man', and so on.

<u>Withdrawing</u> - acting indifferent or passive,

31

resorting to excessive formality, doodling, whispering to others.

Dominating - trying to assert authority in manipulating the group or certain members of it by 'pulling rank', giving directions authoritatively, interrupting contributions of others.

The appearance of these behaviours in groups tends to be irritating to other members, and they tend to react to them with blame, reproach, or counter-hostility. A group that understands group dynamics is often able to deal with them constructively, however, because it sees them as symptoms of deeper causes such as valid personal needs that are not being satisfied constructively. Often, of course, it is difficult to place a given act in one or another of these categories - what seems to be 'blocking' to one observer may appear as 'testing' to another.

The Role of Leadership

In this analysis of functions necessary to the performance of groups, no distinction has been made between the functions of leaders and the functions of the members. This is because the research fails to identify any set of functions that is **universally** the peculiar responsibility of the designated leader. But the fact is that groups in our society typically have central figures with such titles as 'leader, chairman, president', and 'captain'. Ross & Hendry (1957) examine various theories that try to explain this institutional-isation of the role of leader and, after assessing them as inadequate, give this view as to the current state of thinking:

'Perhaps the best we can say at this point is that any comprehensive theory of leadership must take into account the fact that the leadership role is probably related to person-ality factors, to the attitudes and needs of "followers" at a particular time, to the structure of the group, and to the situation. Leadership is probably a function of the inter-action of such variables, and these undoubtedly provide for role differentiation which leads to the designation of a "central figure" or leader, without prohibiting other members in the group from performing leadership functions

in various ways, and at various times, in the
life of the group.'

A classic series of experiments in the laboratory of Kurt Lewin often quoted in the literature of
group dynamics bears on leadership style.   Their
purpose was to measure as precisely as possible the
effects of different types of leader behaviour on
a number of experimentally-created groups of boys.
The three types of leader behaviour tested were
'authoritarian' (policy determined by the leader),
'democratic' (all policies a matter of group
discussion and decision, encouraged and assisted
by the leader), and 'laissez-faire' (complete
freedom for group or individual decision, with a
minimum of leader participation). Their studies
produced evidence for the following generalisations:

1.   Authoritarian-led groups produced a
     greater quantity of work over a short
     period of time, but experienced more
     hostility, competition, and aggression –
     especially scapegoating, more discontent
     beneath the surface, more dependence and
     less originality.

2.   Democratically-led groups, slower in
     getting into production, were more
     strongly motivated, became increasingly
     productive with time and learning,
     experienced more friendliness and
     teamwork, praised one another more
     frequently and expressed greater satis-
     faction.

3.   Laissez-faire groups did less work and
     poorer work than either of the others,
     spent more time in horseplay, talked
     more about what they should be doing,
     experienced more aggression than the
     democratic groups but less than the
     authoritarian, and expressed a preference
     for democratic leadership.

A mounting body of research on the leadership
role since World War II supports the thesis that
some situations require authoritarian and others
laissez-faire leadership, but that, in the long run,
in normal situations, groups thrive best when the
leadership functions are democratically shared among
the members of the group.

Groups in Motion
So far we have been looking at the complicated
elements or variables that make up a group - its
properties, dimensions, and membership and leadership functions - almost as if a group stood still
in time and space. Actually, a group is never
static; it is a dynamic organism, constantly in
motion. Not only is it moving as a unit, but
the various elements within it are constantly
interacting. A change in procedure will affect
atmosphere, which will affect the participation
pattern, which will affect cohesion, which will
affect leadership, which will affect procedure,
and so on. Actually, most of the research has to
do with the dynamic interaction of these variables
in groups in motion.
There seems to be fairly general agreement
among the students of group dynamics that groups
move through more or less predictable phases of
development during their life cycle. A number of
theories about what these phases are have been
proposed, as summarised in Fig.2.2. Notice that
while each theory focuses on a different theme,
they all indicate quite similar phenomena occurring
in the early, middle and later phases of group
development.

Field Studies in Tertiary Education
Most of the research into group work in tertiary
education is naturally centred on discussion groups.
It is interesting therefore to draw comparisons
between this and the more general research evidence
described above. Beard, Bligh & Harding (1978)
claim there is general agreement that some of the
more important variables in discussion groups are:

- Seating position

- Talkativeness

- Personality of the participants

- Kind of leadership

They quote Klein (1965) who found that more voluble
members of a group tended to be popular so that a
normally silent member giving the best solution
to the problem often fails to get it accepted
without the aid of one of the more voluble participants. This is substantiated by other research done

Thelen and Dickerman (1949)	PHASE 1: Individually Centred	PHASE 2: Frustration and Conflict	PHASE 3: Attempted Consolidation of Group Harmony	PHASE 4: Individual Self-Assessment, Flexibility of Group Process, Emphasis upon Productivity in Problem Solving
Miles (1953)	PHASE 1: Unoriented, restive "talking about" irrelevant matters		PHASE 2: Abstract "talking about" Leadership and Permissiveness	PHASE 3: "Doing level" – Discussion and analysis of Here-and-Now
Bennis and Shepard (1956)	SUBPHASE 1: Dependence–Submission	SUBPHASE 2: Counterdependence	SUBPHASE 3: Resolution	SUBPHASE 4: Enchantment / SUBPHASE 5: Disenchantment / SUBPHASE 6: Conceptual Validation
	Phase 1: Dependence			Phase 2: Interdependence
Schutz (1958)	PHASE 1: Inclusion		PHASE 2: Control	PHASE 3: Affection
Bion (1961)	STAGE 1: Flight		STAGE 2: Fight	STAGE 3: Unite
Golembiewski (1962)	PHASE 1: Establishing the Hierarchy	PHASE 2: Conflict and Frustration	PHASE 3: Growth of Security and Autonomy	PHASE 4: Structuring in terms of Work Task
Bradford (1964)	STAGE 1: Ambiguity	STAGE 2: Self-Investment Participation	STAGE 3: Collaboration and Learning from Peers	STAGE 4: Motivation for Learning / STAGE 5: Experienced Behaviour and Feedback / STAGE 6: Group Growth and Development
Mills (1964)	STAGE 1: The Encounter	STAGE 2: Testing Boundaries and Modelling Behaviour	STAGE 3: Negotiating and Indigenous Normative System	STAGE 4: Production / STAGE 5: Separation
Tuckman (1965)	STAGE 1: Forming– Testing and Dependence	STAGE 2: Storming– Intragroup Conflict	STAGE 3: Norming– Development of Group Cohesion	STAGE 4: Performing– Functional Role Relatedness
Mann (1967)	PHASE 1: Initial Complaining	PHASE 2: Premature Enactment	PHASE 3: Confrontation	PHASE 4: Internalization / PHASES 5 & 6: Separation and Terminal Review
Dunphy (1968)	PHASE 1: Counterpersonal and Negativity	PHASE 2: Counterpersonal and Negativity	PHASE 3:	PHASE 4: Transitional– Negativity Membership / PHASE 5: Emotional Concerns / PHASE 6:
	Maintenance of External Normative Standard	Individual Rivalry and Aggression		Realization of Unattainable Utpian Ideals / End of Group
Tuckman and Jensen (1977)	STAGE 1: Forming	STAGE 2: Storming	STAGE 3: Norming	STAGE 4: Performing / STAGE 5: Adjourning
Napier and Gershenfeld (1981)	STAGE 1: Beginning-Hesitation and Testing	STAGE 2: Movement towards Confrontation	STAGE 3: Compromise and Harmony	STAGE 4: Reassessment–Union of Emotional and Task Components / STAGE 5: Resolution and Recycling

Fig. 2.2   Phases of Group Development
          – Various Theories

by Tuckman and Lorge (1962) who found that contributions of members of low status were normally ignored
in arriving at a group solution to a problem.
Compare this with Deutsch (1949) who studied
the effect of giving different information on the
assessment of a group to members of different
groups. He noted that where groups were to be
assessed collectively, in co-operation, they showed
'more co-ordination of effort, diversity in amount
of contribution, subdivision of activity, attentive-
ness to fellow members, mutual comprehension and
communication, greater orientation, orderliness and
productivity per unit time as well as more favourable evaluation of the group and its products
compared with groups who were informed that each
individual would be assessed independently. Davey
(1969) in an experiment with 800 groups of different
sizes concluded that with up to approximately seven
group members the permissive style of leadership
seemed most productive, but above that a con-
trolling style seemed to work better. This leads
to consideration of the value of tutorless groups.
Marris (1965) found that when staff were absent
from groups students felt less inhibited and
frequently discussed their work with each other.
They felt that seeking help from staff was viewed
as a confession off incompetence. Of course sub-
groups within a larger group are a form of tutorless
group and Beard (1972) points to the success of
discussion in pairs (buzz groups) before students
raise questions more formally with the teacher.
   The presence of a tutor does not of course
imply his or her active participation in discussion.
Abercrombie (1979), for instance, developed a
technique of group work in which the tutor played
the part of an onlooker who asked the occasional
question or made a comment, rather in the way that
a group psycho-therapist might do. In this case,
the task was specific; it was to help students
to consider evidence carefully and to make valid
judgements on their observations. The objects of
scrutiny were radiographs or an account of an
experiment. Some students were clearly unsettled
by this procedure and others rejected it out of
hand, though nearly all were amazed at the degree
to which unconscious assumptions had appeared to
influence their judgement. Upon testing at the end
of the course, it was apparent that participants in
this class were able better to distinguish between
facts and inferences, made fewer false inferences,
explicitly considered alternative hypotheses more

frequently and were less often fixed in their view of the problem by dint of previous experience, than were a control group. This experience had apparently helped them become more objective in making assessments of scientific material.

It thus appears that groups are demonstrably valuable for many of the more sophisticated aims of higher education to do with critical thinking, making diagnoses or decisions, solving problems, and changing or maintaining attitudes to the subject under study. Indeed Bligh (1972), surveying the research evidence on different forms of teaching, concluded that discussion methods are more effective than didactic methods (e.g. the lecture) for stimulating thought, for personal and social adjustment, and for changes of attitude, and were no worse than the lecture for effectively transmitting information.

There is a vast amount of research evidence on group work and it is in a constant state of expansion and revision. The fact remains that it is work done by other people in other places for other purposes and this provides a ready excuse for teachers to reject it or at least ignore it. The notion of the teacher as researcher therefore has a lot to commend it.

Teacher as Researcher

The concept of a teacher as one who is putting into practice ideas developed by others is not an appealing one, nor is it realistic, as Pring (1978) argues. Each teaching situation is governed by a unique set of variables which no general researcher could conceivably take into account: the personality of the teacher, the special characteristics of the students, the effects of the learning milieu in that institution, the structure of the particular curriculum being taught, to name but a few. If teachers are to research their own teaching the question arises: how can the objectivity and rigour demanded by research be obtained? As Pring says:

'being objective is opening to public scrutiny the basis upon which one's judgements are made so that counter evidence and contrary arguments might, if they exist, be levelled against what one says. I may be correct in declaring at the end of the lesson that things went well, but my judgement is subjective insofar as there is no evidence against which another might test the truth of what I say'.

In order to conduct classroom research one would need to formulate hypotheses and choose an appropriate test procedure. Such hypotheses would be unlikely to embrace all the variables, yet as long as they are regarded as provisional and are stated clearly, they can be very instructive. Among test procedures one might use, are:

- An interaction analysis (for example, the one on Page 15)
- Recording either with audio or video tape
- Recording one's own comments in a diary
- Drawing out the students' perceptions.

None of these would on its own stand up as reliable research evidence, but taken together they could be employed as a 'triangulation' technique in which each account of what happened is tested against the others. This proposal of the teacher as an activator in research, rather than as a recipient, is an exciting one in that it implies a greater sense of direction and self-autonomy for the teacher. It is firmly supported by Rowan and Reason (1981) who propose an interactive style of research in which the mutual influences of researcher and 'researched' are acknowledged.

Discussion Points

° Take the sets of questions on pages 22-28 and answer them for, or in, your group.
° Consider the chart on page 35. Discuss various groups including your present one in terms of the various developmental phases.

3

RESEARCH INTO LEARNING

Any scepticism towards research into group dynamics applies equally to learning theory and educational research, particularly when the latter is concerned with student learning. Yet where this research is accepted as a source of helpful explanatory concepts, then its real value increases in leaps and bounds. The effect of research is thus indirect.

> 'Research evidence gradually changes teachers' assumptions, and the way they interpret their role. It "sensitises" teachers to aspects of the teaching-learning process which had previously lacked significance. It points up anomalies in the existing situation and may provide hints at alternative solutions. But it cannot indicate the single best way of tackling either lecturing or studying.'
> Entwistle (1977).

Let us now turn to an examination of recent research into the ways students learn.

Student Performance

The personal characteristics of 1531 students from seven English universities were tested in the late 60s and early 70s by Entwistle and others at Lancaster through a battery of psychological tests administered in the first year and again in the final year. A cluster analysis of the characteristics revealed that students achieve success in different ways, with a variety of combinations of aptitudes, attitudes and personality traits. The analysis suggested that there were two contrasting types of student with above average degree results. They were:

  (A) highly-motivated; emotionally stable, tending to tough-minded conservatism; well-organised in study methods; not particularly active in social or sporting life, or in aesthetic interests.

  (B) highly neurotic and bounded by the syllabus (the characteristic of some students who work hard on set work but rarely take the risk of going beyond it); had low self-esteem, no active social life or aesthetic interests.

Though these are but two examples drawn from several possible clusters they appear to display different kinds of motivation - A, looking towards success, and B, fearing failure. These patterns were subsequently confirmed in interviews.

  While we may be sceptical about the validity of a 'type-sorting' analysis it does remind us that students differ considerably in their ways of achieving success. The implication for group work is that many quite reticent students may be just as successful academically as those who consistently 'play the system', and even more successful than those whose creative flair we most value in discussion. We should perhaps ask ourselves to what extent our styles and methods of teaching and our assessment system encourage and sustain either of the above qualities and whether that is what we want. There are also ethical issues involved. Are we, by promoting and encouraging the more extrovert and radically-minded student in discussion groups implanting a value which could mislead? Do we allow the tough, goal-orientated students to benefit at the expense of their more inspired, value-conscious and open-minded colleagues? Clearly these are not precise questions as the above research was describing ideal-types, and not real, individual people, but it does at least go part way to explaining the resentment which many students feel - that somehow, though they have 'made all the running' at seminars, it is their quieter, less open-minded colleagues who collect the best marks.

Learning Styles
Rather different aspects of the students' approach to learning have been revealed through a series of studies by Marton and Saljo (1976) and their colleagues at Gothenburg. They have indentified

two distinctive approaches among students in the way they read texts.

(a) <u>Surface-level processing</u> - in which students take a <u>passive</u> approach and are concerned with:

- covering the content
- how much they have learned
- finding the 'right' answers
- assimilating unaltered pieces of knowledge
- learning verbatim

(b) <u>Deep-level processing</u> - in which students take an <u>active</u> approach. They are concerned with:

- the central point
- what lies behind the argument
- the whole picture
- what it boils down to
- what it is connected with
- the logic of the argument
- points that are not clear
- questioning the conclusions

The surface-level processes divert their attention therefore to the <u>sign</u>, and the deep-level process to what is <u>signified</u>. In general those adopting 'deep' approaches are more successful in exams. Surface processors tend to pass only when they manage to overcome the tedium which that form of learning often induces.

Deep processors are more versatile: they find it easier to tackle 'surface' questions than surface processors do 'deep' questions. Strong motivation increases the likelihood that deep-level processing will occur, while anxiety induces a hurried fact-grabbing strategy. This will doubtless be familiar to the experienced tutor, who will have noticed the increasing desperation among students to memorise 'facts' and know 'what is what' as exams approach.

In a parallel investigation, Pask (1976) in London distinguished between two clear strategies among students for drawing up a classification system. <u>Holists</u> adopted a broad perspective and looked for a variety of interrelationships, whereas <u>serialists</u> were typified by their attention to detail and a pattern of learning by increments.

Holists ask a different order of questions too, 'about broad relations and (they) form hypotheses about generalisations' as opposed to serialists whose questions are 'about much narrower relations and (whose) hypotheses are specific'. Lest it be thought that holists are successful in all respects it should be added that they are likely to over-generalise and to make remote and often mistaken connections. Serialists on the other hand, are often victims of their own caution and their inability to make connections often makes integration of knowledge a difficult task for them. Pask's continuing research into learning strategies has indicated, not surprisingly, a further category - the versatile learner who is able to adopt the holist or serialist strategy according to the task in hand. He also demonstrated that holists are not good at learning serialist material; nor are serialists with holist material, but students whose learning style matched the material learned it quickly and accurately.

Intellectual Development

It would be sad if we reviewed student learning solely in terms of processing information and finding ways of 'working the system'. In tertiary education students are free, possibly for the first time, to learn in their preferred way, and to develop their own sense of what is worth learning.

In an interview study of students at the Liberal Arts College of Harvard, Perry (1970) found a coherent progression in the manner in which students approached learning, experienced values and construed the world during their college experience. He identified a sequence of nine positions through which students appear to have progressed as they moved through college. Basically the sequence comprised a development from a dualistic, authority-accepting position, through a relativistic 'anything goes' phase to a final stage of open-minded commitment.

Position 1:   There are right and wrong answers to everything: 'authority' knows these and has to teach them; knowledge is the accretion of discrete correct facts.

Position 2:   Uncertainty and diversity of opinion are perceived, but seen as either unnecessary confusion amoung poorly-qualified teachers or a subterfuge by them to encourage better learning.

Position 3: <u>Diversity and uncertainty are accepted as legitimate</u> but only on the grounds that 'authority' hasn't found the right answer yet (but surely will).

Position 4: <u>Diversity and uncertainty are part of an academic ritual</u> - they are what authority expects of the students.

Position 5: <u>All knowledge and values are perceived as relativistic and contextual</u>; dualism (position 1) is a subordinate special case of this.

Positions 6 to 9 are less clearly distinguishable and cover the gradual movement from <u>feeling the need for a tentative commitment, trying it out, exploring its implications</u> to finally <u>experiencing commitment</u> as a continually unfolding activity through which the personal lifestyle of the student is expressed. One would hope that most students will 'join the boat' at a stage beyond Position 1 and progress at least to Position 5 by the end of a full-time course at tertiary level. However, it is rare that a student reaches the stage of maturity implied by Position 9. Even the acceptance of relativism as a perception of the world represents revolutionary change in thinking and values for many students and as such is a challenge to some of their fundamental beliefs. As such it is akin to the restructuring of scientific theory which takes place from time to time in the history of mankind (Kuhn, 1973). Such a profound transformation is thus one of great significance in the intellectual development of the student, yet paradoxically it is one which is often the most quietly realised.

Perry also describes forms of 'deflection', or reversion in the process, which offer a way out at critical points. These are <u>temporising</u>, where a student bides his time in one position; <u>escape</u>, a sense of withdrawn disenchantment; and <u>retreat</u>, an entrenchment in the dualist, absolutist framework of Positions 1 and 2.

Perry's study raises questions about structure and sequence in course design, above the presentation of knowledge and the ways in which students are grouped for teaching, about the techniques and skills that tutors bring to discussion, and about

ways of assessing students. To what extent is it
possible, particularly in group discussion, to
assist students to growth points in their development, while allowing for the emotional dispositions
to which intellectual forms are often wedded? Is
Perry's scheme applicable only to the so-called
liberal arts, or is it equally relevant to the
learning of science and technology? Whatever the
answers may be, and they will doubtless vary
according to circumstances, there is little doubt
that the studies of Marton, Pask and Perry stimulate
thought on the nature of student learning even if
they present a somewhat simplified picture.

Implications of Learning Research
As yet we can only speculate on what the research
of Marton, Pask, Perry and others implies for
teachers at any level of education. Although it is
likely that we can equate surface processors with
serialists and with those in Perry's dualistic stage
(and even with Hudson's (1966) convergers) and the
deep processing with holists, relativistic reasoning
and divergers there are no clear indications of what
the teacher should do about it: the research was
all investigatory rather than applied. However, we
could venture a few working hypotheses based on
them:

1.   that many courses, especially those with
     high student contact-hours and heavy
     pressure of exams, are likely to inhibit
     deep, holistic, relativist thinking.
2.   that deep, holistic, relativistic students
     are more likely to prefer the openness
     of small discussion groups to the more
     formal, distant relationships of highly
     structured lecture courses.
3.   that the teaching style of tutors will
     reflect their own way of thinking about
     knowledge and will vary accordingly.
4.   that a mixture of formal lectures, small
     group work, individual study and project
     work may be best for the majority of
     students and that a course sequence which
     uses these methods increasingly in this
     order will prove acceptable on several
     counts.

5. that the most academically successful students will be able to recognise differences in teaching styles and learning tasks and adopt strategies of learning appropriate to them.

There may be implications of a need, as Entwistle suggests:

'to think more clearly about the formation of large and small group methods in relation to the particular intellectual skills, or cognitive style, they are expected to foster and whether the assignments and examination questions given to students provide sufficient encouragement for deep-level processing.'

Surface processing may be the only strategy possessed by many students when they arrive at college. Whether this is a kind of personality trait or is something more superficially acquired as a means to success in school, and therefore easily shed, are further questions over which to ruminate. Certainly, if we can accept what Perry says about the often traumatic nature of change it will follow that tutors require sensitivity and skill in accommodating the variety of student styles within a climate of intellectual growth (not to speak of the tutor's own styles and predilections). Students too readily slip into disillusionment and consequent failure because the range of demands is too great. But are they always the right demands, and is their response to the demands appropriate? What we as tutors must do is to help students understand what choices there are in approaches to learning and to give them opportunity and support in making their choices. Small groups provide what is probably the most suitable environment for this to occur.

Discussion Points

o Describe (in writing) what, in general terms, you or your group learns. How?
o In what ways can a group leader encourage deep processing, holistic thinking and intellectual development. Where are _you_ in all this?

4

CONCEPTS IN COMMUNICATION

No amount of understanding of group behaviour is sufficient for successful participation in groups unless each person in the group has the capacity to communicate effectively. It is through communication that people achieve an understanding of one another and are thus able to influence, and be influenced by, others. Only if there is a predisposition to accept and accommodate others will honest communication take place and this implies a degree of trust and openness between participants. Without these, mutual understanding and influences are liable to distortion: co-operation is unlikely.

The Process of Communication

Communication is often thought of as little more than the process of passing and receiving information. Concern for improving communication usually centres on the skills of writing, speaking, reading and, less frequently, listening. Typically, the emphasis will be on qualities like clarity, conciseness, precision and logical sequence. Yet many, and possibly most, errors in communication occur because of psychological rather than logical factors. The feelings, attitudes, behaviours and relationships of those involved in communication are all likely to determine whether it is effective or not.

The process of communication is far from being the rational or mechanical exercise (pictured below) that many people think:

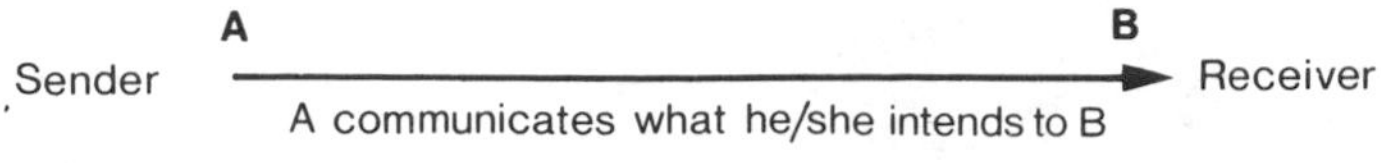

A   **B**

Sender ————————————————————▶ Receiver

A communicates what he/she intends to B

Fig.4.1   Model of Communication 1

It is more than person A saying something to person B and the latter hearing it, interpreting it and acting on it correctly. Communication is not just about words. As Kolb, Rubin & McIntyre (1979) put it:

> 'Person A brings to the interaction with person B much more than just the content of the message he wishes to convey. He brings himself as a person. Person A has an image of himself as a person and, to varying degrees of specificity and intensity (it may be a first impression), he also has a set of attitudes and feelings towards person B. The message to person B, therefore, in addition to certain content, may well contain some cues as to who A feels he is as a person (e.g. confident and secure versus tentative and wary), how A feels about B as a person (e.g. warm and receptive versus cold and uncaring) and how A expects B to react to his (A's) communication.'

If the issue were as simple as that, we might have a reasonably easy task in communicating. The trouble is we are not always aware of what it is we are actually putting across. We convey things we do not intend. The message thus gets distorted so that the above picture now becomes:

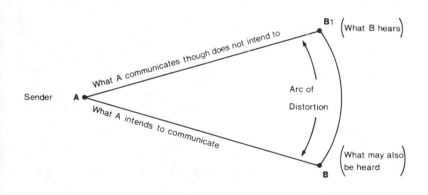

Fig.4.2   Model of Communication 2

In addition, we often have more than one intention when we communicate something: sometimes the
secondary intention becomes the stronger one, and
where this is at a less-than-conscious level the
message may well be distorted beyond recognition.

A teacher, for example, who looks 'po-faced'
when a particular student speaks, whilst saying
'Yes, that's really very interesting' is communicating a 'message beyond the words'. So, too, is
the lecturer who though meticulously correct in his
exposition shows no enthusiasm for the subject or
his students, and the tutor who always sits as far
away as possible from one particular member of the
tutorial group. These distorting messages are conveyed by the tone of voice, facial expression, body
posture, gesture or physical location. Though,
as Hobbes said, people often 'use words to disguise
their thoughts' it is the underlying feelings and
thoughts which frequently come through most powerfully through non-verbal cues.

Those on the receiving end of a communication
may also be party to the distortion. They have to
listen and interpret appropriately and this is not
at all easy when they are simultaneously receiving
contradictory messages.

Yet the 'receiver' may be equally at fault in
distorting otherwise ideal communication. A common
problem in interpersonal communication is failure
by the receiving party to attend fully to what is
being said and thus miss the important points of a
message. Sometimes this is because the receiver is
preoccupied, or has a particular way of thinking
about something (a mental set) which predetermines
the interpretation. Stanford and Roark (1974) give
an illustration of this (though it may be as much a
sign of the times - early 70s - as it is of a mis-
apprehension). A counsellor had been giving a
class on homosexuality when she was approached
by a student. The conversation went like this:

Student:	Do you have a book on careers?
Counsellor:	No, I don't have any books on the subject.
Student:	Well I just wanted to take a look at what I could do when I get out of high school.
Counsellor:	What did you say you wanted a book about?
Student:	Careers.
Counsellor:	What?

    Student: Careers.
    Counsellor: Oh, careers, I thought you said
                   queers.

Hearing only part of a message may also serve the receiver's purposes too, especially when there are contradictory signals being expressed and he has a legitimate choice.

The receiver's part in the hearing and interpreting of messages may be represented by a diagram complementary to the one above:

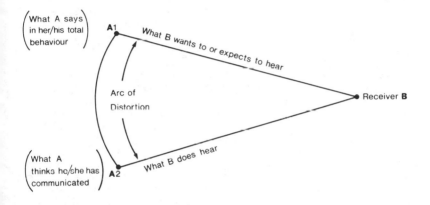

Fig.4.3 Model of Communication 3

Figs.4.1-3 are based on Nylen, Mitchell & Stout (1967)

At times, we may consciously wish to convey more than one intention at a time. For instance when we <u>express</u> our thoughts in an interview we are often trying to <u>impress</u> the interviewers. When we express ourselves we are revealing ourselves to others as we are; when we impress we are trying to present ourselves in a favourable light. A lot of classroom behaviour is to do with impressing: students trying to demonstrate their knowledge, their interest, their regard for the teacher; tutors trying to maintain an aura of objective expertise and control. There is nothing wrong with trying to impress provided it is appropriate and one is aware of it. It becomes a problem, particularly for us as teachers when, in trying to create impressions with students, we are 'detected' and lose credibility and the students' trust. Students are very astute at finding chinks in our armour. On the other hand, we may find that some behaviours are difficult to perform and may consequently respond to some requests in a confusing way. Suppose a student is asked to present ideas in a seminar, based on reading he had volunteered to undertake, but has failed to do. He is unable to say he is sorry and to express embarrassment and guilt; instead he laughs it off with 'What me? Didn't I say I couldn't do it?' or responds angrily with 'There's just too much reading to do!'

It is an unfortunate fact of life that we all lack certain behaviours in our repertoire or feel inhibited about displaying them when the climate is aggressive and defensive: for instance, the ability to say 'sorry' or to be angry, or to give or respond naturally to compliments. Almost certainly the above student would have betrayed his embarrassment, guilt or anger through his non-verbal behaviour and this would almost certainly be picked up by the others in the group as a conflicting and therefore confusing communication.

We are also likely to distort what we hear because of our <u>personal</u> needs. The need to be liked or to have everything neatly categorised, for instance, may blur our perception of what we are being told. Rather than attending to the complete message we may block a lot of otherwise important information. Our need to be liked might cause us to be over-sensitive to negative components in a communication: our need for order and neatness or <u>control</u> might predispose us to miss some excellent ideas from students who find it difficult to express themselves clearly. What we intend to do with the information when we have it can also cause us to filter and select. Students picking up clues on what to include in an essay or, more significantly, an exam, are more than likely to listen and respond only to that academic knowledge which suits these particular purposes.

An added factor which may contribute to distorted reception is <u>threat</u>, whether it manifests itself in a direct personal challenge from a group or an individual or in a more general and ill-defined way. The distortion or denial that occurs as a result of threat derives from either the need to protect our

self-esteem or from the anxiety which has its roots
in early childhood experiences. Fear or criticism,
reproof, rejection or ridicule inevitably set up
defensive barriers, yet because they are at a
conscious level they are at least open to scrutiny
and change should we so wish. Not so amenable to
change are the distortions resulting from childhood
conflicts, repressed because of the danger they
originally posed, and reawakened at an unconscious
level by particular people or events in adulthood.
Both of these threats may be revived by a specific
thing somebody does or says to us or by an environment which has a high degree of evaluation,
control and competitiveness.

The Content of Communication
The words with which we choose to make our communication are important too, not just for the
precision and clarity they offer but because they
give colour and light to what we say. Students
starting with a group are often at pains to learn
how to handle the accepted vocabulary of the subject, and can easily gravitate towards the use of
cliches and labels. 'Oh that's a case of X' can
cut out the possibility of open discussion when X
is a concept which has been invented mainly to box
in uncertainty about a phenomenon. More commonly
one might hear 'That's a Mathematics problem' or
whatever the subject in question is, as a way of
foreclosing discussion on a topic.
    Style and meaning are of relevance too in how
people communicate. Statements which begin 'it is'
or 'there are' are intentionally more distancing
than those starting with personal pronouns, especially 'I think' or 'I like'. A psychological
distance is also established by the use of theoretical rather than personal understandings. Stanford
& Roark (1974) divide the problem into five categories of meaning: Theoretical, Abstract, Objective,
Personal Cognitive and Personal Experiencing.

    'Theoretical explanations are the fabric by
    which we write bits of experience into
    comprehensive explanations. Psychologically
    they are impersonal and distant. Theories,
    abstractions and objective referents can be
    verified by opinions of others and are thus
    open to consensual agreement. But personal

meanings are open to our scrutiny only; we are the sole judge.'

Discussion, and even lectures, which focus entirely on 'what is' or 'what other people have said' may help students in jumping academic hurdles but have little personal impact on them.

We often speak as if:

'subject matter has the only "real" meaning and the students' personal meanings are irrelevant or secondary at best. The effect over a long period of time, especially for students with different experiential backgrounds from the teachers is to drive them away into a world where their meanings are nearer those of their environment and accepted as having worth.' (Stanford & Roark, ibid).

The effect on students is probably to encourage in their minds and culture a split between that which is acceptable for academic discussion and their personal experience in the college as a community - a division, that is, between educational knowledge and everyday knowledge. The tendency of many students to seek solace and rewards in the social and political life of their college to the exclusion of academic work may well relate to this 'academisation' of knowledge.

Improving Communication

As we have already seen, the lack of trust and the existence of threat in any interaction can have a distorting effect on communication. The establishment of honest and meaningful communication can be achieved through two precepts, simple to say but not so easy to practise:

1. develop a sense of mutual trust and openness.
2. correct distortions in communication through constructive feedback.

The first demands a willingness to be open to oneself (recognising and accepting one's own feelings), to others (being able to disclose these feelings discreetly) and to the world around us. The Johari Window (Luft, 1970) is a helpful device for analysing and working on this problem.

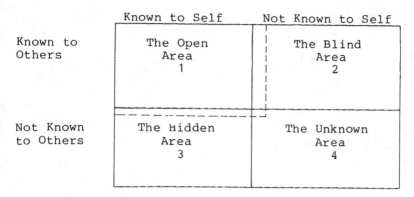

Fig.4.4   The Johari Window

The window (Fig.4.4) is used for increasing personal and interpersonal awareness. It comprises four quadrants:

Quadrant 1;   the free and open area refers to behaviour known to self and to others.

Quadrant 2;   the blind area, refers to things about us that others can see but of which we are unaware.

Quadrant 3;   the avoided or hidden area indicates things we prefer to keep to ourselves (hidden agendas or personal feelings).

Quadrant 4;   the area of unknown activity represents the sort of things that are accessible neither to us nor to others, but which may eventually be revealed. Such behaviours and motives could have affected our relationships, without our knowing it, all along.

Luft suggests that a change in any one quadrant will affect all the other quadrants.

By disclosing some of our own feelings or private experiences we expand quadrant 1 into quadrant 3. This makes it more possible for other people to let us know something about ourselves

that we were unaware of, e.g. 'You always smile
when you are angry' which in turn expands quadrant
1 into quadrant 2. This leads to the more open
form of communication indicated by the broken line.
Exercises using the Johari Window may be found
in Pfeiffer & Jones (1974) and Kolb, Rubin &
McIntyre (1979).

Feedback

Feedback must always be handled with sensitivity
and judgement. It is more effective if:

1. It is descriptive rather than evaluative.
   Describing one's own reaction leaves the
   other individual free to use it as he sees
   fit. Avoiding evaluative language reduces
   the need for the other individual to
   react defensively.

2. It is specific rather than general. To
   be told that one is 'confusing' will probably not be as useful as to be told 'when
   you ask us a question you seem to rephrase
   it so many times that we get confused.'

3. It takes into account the needs of both
   the receiver and the giver of feedback.
   Feedback can be destructive when it serves
   only our needs and fails to consider the
   needs of the person on the receiving end.

4. It is directed toward behaviour that the
   receiver can control. Frustration is
   increased when a person is reminded of
   some shortcoming over which he or she has
   no control.

5. It is solicited, rather than imposed.
   Feedback is most useful when the receiver
   has asked for it and accepts it without
   argument.

6. It is well timed. In general, feedback is
   most useful at the earliest opportunity
   after the given behaviour (depending, of
   course, on the person's readiness to hear
   it, on support available from others,
   etc.).

7. It is checked to ensure clear communica-

tion. One way of doing this is to have the receiver try to rephrase the feedback he has received to see if it corresponds with what the sender had in mind.

8. When feedback is given in a group, both giver and receiver take the opportunity to check with others in the group on the accuracy of the feedback. Is this one person's impression or an impression shared by others?

(Adapted from Kolb, Rubin & McIntyre, 1979).

Feedback is probably the best way of getting evidence on the effectiveness of our communication. It enables us to learn about how others see us and about how we affect them. It is thus a vital ingredient in the process of evaluation which we shall examine in more detail in Chapter 9.

TRANSACTIONAL ANALYSIS (TA)

A simple but powerful model for analysing the processes of human interaction is that devised by Eric Berne (1968) and later amplified by Thomas Harris (1973). Taking Freud's concepts as a starting point Berne proposes that each person comprises three basic 'selves' - the Parent, the Adult and the Child - each of which is capable of affecting the tone of communication.

These 'ego-states', as they are called, exist within each of us as a result of our early life experience. They are not, like Freud's superego, ego and id, elements of our inner world operating on each other at an unconscious level. Rather they are conscious experiences of everyday life imprinted in the person as a result of internal and external events encountered during the first few years of life. Transactional analysis addresses itself to the interaction between people, rather than to their inner psyche and is therefore more readily available for a study of relationships in teaching and learning.

The Parent in us acts according to how we perceived our mother, father or parental figure behaving. The parent is often concerned with prescribing the limits to behaviour, issuing moral edicts, teaching 'how to', protecting, nurturing and fostering; and these functions are typically accompanied by the tones of voice and the non-verbal expressions which partnered them when we experienced them in their original form. For obvious reasons teaching frequently puts us in the position of behaving parentally or at least of being tempted to do so. Institutions provide a broadly parental function (and in view of this it is not surprising that young people often take it out on the physical fabric of schools and colleges). That is not to say that the functions of the Parent are intrinsically either good or bad. The important thing is that we be sufficiently aware of the Parent in ourselves so that we can use it or not according to our interpretation of what is happening in any transaction.

The Adult is that part of us which is concerned with the gathering and processing of information and with rational action in the 'real' world. It derives from the time in our childhood when we began to manipulate objects external to ourselves and to realise we could achieve something worthwhile through our own original thought. The Adult in us is ruled by reason rather than emotion; it is not however synonymous with 'mature'. The sort of functions specific to the adult are therefore the acquiring and sorting of data (even about one's Parent, Adult and Child states) the choosing of alternatives and the planning of decision-making processes. The Adult may thus manifest itself in a variety of ways and is the side of us most concerned with analysing the very transactions it is part of.

The Child in us is the residue of emotional responses experienced and recorded in early childhood. These responses are essentially internal reactions to external events. The re-creation of similar events in later life is likely to trigger the corresponding reactions. There are many different 'children' within us and they experience the same feelings now as they did when we were little. Where the feeling derives from parental impositions or restrictions it is likely to be that of frustration, anger, fear, rebelliousness or conformity. Where it comes from the glorious excitement of first discoveries it is likely to connect with curiosity, creative delight, desire to explore, spontaneity and trust. Other biographical traces may also include competitiveness (from sibling rivalry) and dependency.

Each of us comprises all three ego states. None of the states is better or more important than the others. 'Appropriate' behaviour is determined by the situation, the Adult's analysis of it, and the Adult's ability to control the Parent and Child according to perceived circumstances.

Needless to say, the psychopathology of individual human beings is never as simple as this model proposes, but TA is nevertheless a convenient and, at times, telling way of analysing what goes right and wrong in human communication. It can be important for the tutor to acquire the ability to pick up the verbal and non-verbal cues signifying the existence of a particular ego state. In the world of teaching one might come across cues of the kind shown here.

Verbal Cues	Non-Verbal Cues
	(Not directly related to verbal cues)

Parent -(P)

Verbal	Non-Verbal
'If I were you...'	Pursed lips
'There's no question...'	Wagging fingers
'That's ridiculous...'	Horrified look
'Well done...'	Pat on back or head
'This is the way to do it...'	

Child -(C)

Verbal	Non-Verbal
'I'd like...'	Delight
'I don't care...'	Rolling eyes
'I can't stand...'	Shrugging shoulders
'Wow!'	Laughter
'Oh no!'	Teasing
	Raising hand for permission to speak

Adult -(A)

Verbal	Non-Verbal
'My view is...'	Open alertness
'In what way?'	Giving attention
'Can you say more?'	
'I think...'	
'Why, what, where, etc.'	

Fig.4.5 Verbal and Non-Verbal Cues in Transactions

Transactions: In diagrams of transactions, the ego states are commonly represented by their initial letter and communication is indicated by arrows in the appropriate direction.

A transaction is complementary where the ego state of the responding person is that to which the communication was directed. It is crossed where this correspondence is not achieved and ulterior where one correspondence is intended but another conveyed. (The broken line indicates the last-named transaction.)

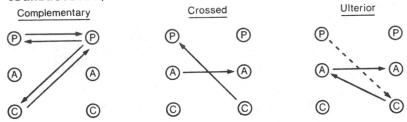

Fig.4.6   Complementary, Crossed and Ulterior Transactions

Crossed and ulterior transactions clearly lead to unsatisfied, frustrated or angry feelings.
Here is an example of these three kinds of transaction.

A student comes to see his tutor:

> Student: 'I don't know, I feel like giving up the course - it's all just one big muddle.'

This could be intended as a (C) --> (P) communication. For there to be a complementary transaction, i.e. (P) --> (C):

the tutor might respond:

> 'I'm sorry to hear that. Here take a seat while I make a cup of coffee' (Nurturing Parent).

or,

> 'Now come on, pull yourself together, nothing's that bad' (Admonishing Parent).

Alternatively the tutor might say:

> 'I see, well it seems to me you've got the following alternatives.' or 'OK, well what do you see as your choices?'

which would be (A) --> (A) responses. This would constitute a crossed transaction, one in which the sought correspondence is denied. It is therefore likely to be inappropriate as an initial move.

If, on the other hand, the tutor responded:

> 'Oh, I thought you were going to go and see the counsellor.'

it might well sound like an Adult response with overtones of critical Parent or even irresponsible Child. Either of these would constitute an ulterior transaction typically leading to a tangle of ill-feeling.

To quote another example from teaching; a student might say:

> 'I'm fed up, none of the articles is in the library like you said they would be.' (C) --> (C), or (C) -->(P)

The tutor could reply either:

> 'If you were a bit quicker off the mark there would be no problem.' (P) --> (C)

or

> 'Never mind, I've got a few copies here you can have.' (A) --> (C)

or

> 'That's not my fault.' (C) --> (C)

It is typical and proper that teaching should function a great deal at the Parent level. Education does after all involve the setting of standards, advising, guiding, fostering and so forth, but there is always the danger that teachers will direct such transactions indiscriminately to the 'Child' rather than making open choices appropriate to a given situation. A generalised Parent-like posture can

easily produce in students a corresponding Child-
like response which in turn confirms the original
Parental status.

Transactional Analysis does not end with the
subject of ego-states. It includes in its orbit
several other useful ideas for teaching and
learning. For example, Harris has expanded Berne's
original scheme of transactions to include the
following 'life positions'.

I'm not OK	-	You're OK
I'm not OK	-	You're not OK
I'm OK	-	You're not OK
I'm OK	-	You're OK

and these are likely to determine the quality of
the Parent-Adult-Child transactions. Many instances
of these in education will doubtless spring to the
mind of the reader. Needless to say it is the last
transaction, 'I'm OK, you're OK', which is the most
healthy and creative, though least often encountered.

Another useful TA concept is that of <u>strokes</u>.
Strokes are the recognition of someone else's existence. Everyone needs them. There are <u>positive</u>
strokes such as 'Hello John, how nice to see you,
come in' or, the sort of knowing wink which evokes a
sense of 'I'm OK, you're OK'. Equally there are
<u>negative</u> strokes like 'I'm not interested in what
you want' or the avoidance of eye contact which
creates a feeling of 'I'm OK. You're not OK';
<u>conditional</u> strokes such as 'I'd be happier if you
could come and see me some other time of day' and
<u>unconditional</u> ones: 'It's terrific working with you'
or 'you look very smart today'. Transactional
Analysis considers strokes to be necessary for one's
emotional well-being. The ability to give as well
as to receive unconditional and positive strokes is
an important social skill.

One of the strongest and boldest claims that
TA brings to the world of human relationships is
the belief that people, through self-awareness,
are able to change themselves and develop their
potential to change others. By recognising what can
cause hurt, misunderstanding and frustration in
relationships they are better able to break out of
unproductive communication and bring more creativity, enjoyment and freedom into their social
environment. This is a large claim and one which
needs careful examination through both practice
and research. It certainly provides a valuable

explanatory framework for human interaction, one
to which it is easy to relate and to develop in
everyday communication.

Discussion Points

° What barriers to communication do you notice in
(a) your everyday life, (b) your work generally
and (c) groups which you belong to or lead? How
do they arise and how might you tackle them?
° What kind of transaction seems to govern your
relationships in the various groups you belong
to? How does this work out (a) for you and (b)
for the group?

5

AIMS AND OBJECTIVES OF LEARNING GROUPS

Groups in the wider context form and are formed for many purposes: pooling resources, making decisions, mutual support, sharing ideas, creating something, to name but a few. Though the learning group may share some of these purposes to varying degrees, it has two additonal distinguishing features. First, the group members are (generally) drawing on know-ledge from outside the group in order to process it within, and subsequently use it outside. Second, and this is a particular feature of the traditional seminar, the group includes someone (the tutor) who is responsible for both selecting the external knowledge and supervising its processing in the group and checking its use beyond the end of the group through some form of assessment.

There are three questions arising from these thoughts which we might bear in mind in this chapter:

1. To what extent do learning groups have to involve a procession of knowledge from outside to inside and outside again?
2. Does it have to be the tutor who controls the input, processing and output of knowledge?
3. What can the learning group in its academic world incorporate from the aims and purposes of other kinds of group?

Before we look at these questions let us con-sider what aims, and educational aims in particular, are all about.

Educational aims seem to appear more often in course documents than in discussion between tutors and students. As a public statement of values, they reflect what teachers, and those who influence them, claim to prize in what they principally do. Some of these values may relate to personal qualities like social skills, or intellectual discipline, and may reach across many fields of study; others are more specific to a subject area and represent what is regarded as important as subject matter for the syllabus.

Several writers have described the use of aims and objectives as instruments of course design (see Taba 1962, Wheeler 1967, Rowntree 1978 and Stenhouse 1975, for instance), and this is not the place to get involved in the weighty arguments of curriculum theory. However, as group discussion is an important part of tertiary education, it is appropriate to examine questions about the place of aims in small group teaching. Such questions as 'What are aims and objectives?', 'Where do they come from?', 'Why bother to specify them, especially in group teaching?', 'What are typical aims for groups?' and 'How can we make sense of them in terms of classroom practice?'.

The Nature of Aims

Teaching and learning are purposeful human activities. That is to say, they may be described in terms of what we as teachers or learners believe we are doing or what we intend to achieve by it. Of course, as we carry out our day-to-day work we are not always conscious of our intentions or of what our actions achieve. Sometimes we employ, out of habit, a strategy whose origins and true functions are lost in the mists of time; or we imitate what we have seen others do without questioning its value or purpose. In some cases it seems that a teaching procedure exists purely because teachers and students expect it to be there - it has become a time-honoured ritual - and any attempt to change it will be doomed to failure. The traditional seminar, for instance, comprising groups of 10-20 students discussing critical summaries presented by one of them may fall into that category. It is used because it is used. Nevertheless, aims are implicit (albeit obscurely) in all teaching procedures and there is no doubt that many students value seminars as a learning technique. (See NUS, 1969.)

Aims, where expressed, serve to focus attention on the direction of teaching and act as a reference point in our choice of what we teach. In the words of Dewey (1944), the aim as a 'foreseen end':

(a) involves careful observation of the given conditions to see what means are available for reaching that end and to discover hindrances in the way,

(b) suggests the proper order or sequence in the use of means,

(c) makes choice of alternatives possible.

If we do not make such aims explicit, and therefore negotiable, then participants in a group discussion may be following their own hidden agendas and lacking in any common frame of reference. The function of aims therefore may be not only to help establish a direction in learning but also to clarify the opportunities offered by a situation. It may also lead to a better sense of collaboration among the group in achieving the aims.

Intrinsic and Extrinsic Aims

Some of the aims of group discussion may be viewed as outcomes; they are about what the group may be expected to achieve as a result of the discussion. In this sense they are extrinsic to the process and might possibly be realised by other teaching methods. Such an aim might be 'to attain a deeper understanding of educational theory'.

However, other aims (and these are frequently the most highly valued) are _intrinsic_ to the processes: the end is also the _means_. For instance if the concern in science education is 'to develop an enquiring attitude towards environmental phenomena' then this, unlike the acquisition of theories, principles, concepts, etc., may be achieved only through practising the processes of enquiry and through repeated emphasis on the requisite attitude of mind. A student might make an optimistic attempt at acquiring such skills and attitudes through guided reading, programmed learning and so forth, but this would be learning only in the conventional sense: 'learning about' rather than 'learning to be', and it is likely that students would not become committed to these processes without the rigour and incentive of group interaction.

Many of the accepted aims of higher education are of an 'intrinsic' nature:

Aims and Objectives of Learning Groups

- developing imaginative and creative thinking
- developing a critical and informed mind
- developing an awareness of others' interests and needs
- developing a sense of academic rigour
- developing a social conscience
- developing a willingness to share ideas
- developing an ability, and sense of enjoyment, in lifelong learning.

All of these aims have two things in common:

1. they appear to be of more personal interest to both student and tutor than is the acquisition of knowledge and may thus have a greater long-term value.

2. they are processes which are experienced mostly if not totally within well-organised discussion groups.

The aims of group techniques are therefore among the most central aims of tertiary education. Nevertheless, there is no clear way of knowing when a student has achieved the aims, nor of measuring their attainment. Perhaps the best that can be said for them in terms of 'behavioural' principles is that the students have been given maximum exposure to the experiences implied by them.

Aims and Objectives

Objectives are commonly distinguished from aims through their emphasis on what is called 'terminal' behaviour. Where aims in essence indicate broad directions for teaching, are closely related to values and learning processes, and are impossible to pin down in a measurable form, objectives are generally taken to be descriptions of what a student should be able to do by the end of a learning occasion. Though objectives give no indication of how they are to be attained, the achievement of objectives should in principle be measurable. An example of the distinction between aims and objectives comes from the Open University Course Unit T100/26. One particular aim is 'to discuss methods of objective measurement and subjective assessment of external noise' and two of the objectives arising from this are that students should be able to 'list some physical measurements that may be made on any noise, that distinguish between noises, and that are related to subjective reaction', and to, 'carry out measurements of background levels using the sound indicator'.

Objectives may therefore be similar if not identical to assessment questions. They are also part of what some educationalists would call a rational and systematic approach to the curriculum. Teaching, so the argument for specifying objectives runs, is a rational activity, and one of the conditions of rational activity is the conscious pursuit of a goal or objective. To satisfy the needs of a well-designed course, one must specify an objective, choose the means of achieving it and then measure this achievement so as to evaluate the effectiveness of the strategy.

Objectives are therefore a translation of aims into specific behaviours. Aims must necessarily precede objectives even if only in an implicit sense, and serve to guide them. 'Aims provide the ethical standards against which objectives are judged' (Rowntree 1978). Objectives also give us some clues about tasks for so-called 'structured' groups (see pages 91-94 and Wilson, 1980).

The Place of Aims and Objectives in Group Teaching

While it is perfectly logical to set objectives, human activity does not in reality follow such a rational pattern. People tend to act on inspiration, on intuitive shifts and changes, and to respond spontaneously to the immediate situation. Nowhere are these unpredictable factors more evident than in discussion groups.

The pursuit of a specific objective in a group discussion could also destroy the possibility of achieving many other equally valuable aims such as those to do with creative thinking, autonomy or democratic learning. In other words, for the educational experience in a group to be valuable, the student must enjoy the freedom to question, to disagree, and to make interpretations and this may take the individual and the group in a direction other than that which was intended by the tutor or the course planner - or the examiner. In the experience of many tutors, what continually happens is that, to quote Pring (1973), 'one's conception of the enquiry or activity is altered in the very pursuit of it... the ends in view are constantly changing as one gets nearer them'. Group discussion is more of a conversation than a one-way programme.

What is more, there are few rational connections between means and ends, except where, as previously indicated, the two are coincident. Even if it were possible to select a method to achieve a particular objective, other concomitants such as the group mood, tutor/student relationships or contextual issues like the proximity of examinations could frustrate the intentions of the tutor. This is part of the problem of selecting educational objectives as if they existed prior to and independent of the students and, more importantly, of the group upon whose very existence and energy their achievement is dependent.

On the other hand, the specifying of aims can provide an intentional framework in which intuitive and spontaneous changes can be made. It enables tutors and students both separately and together to discuss the desirability of a set of aims (and their hidden values). Aims and the means of achieving them can thus be negotiated in the interests of all concerned, and a versatile tutor can propose alternative approaches. All this should contribute to a sense of shared responsibility for learning, particularly because it focuses attention on what the student learns rather than what the tutor knows but also because it releases the students from an over-reliance on the tutor's agenda. In these ways, the expressing, sharing and negotiating of aims in group teaching help to achieve a further aim - that of creating a sense of self-direction in learning.

Nowhere is this more important than in science and technology where mastery of content is often stressed as an end in itself, and little is done to help the student relate to his personal goals and frames of reference.

If and when choice is exercised in the curr-iculum it is usually by the tutor. The students are deemed unqualified to select what is to be learned - or how. It may well be, as Entwistle (1981) suggests, that students tend to specialise in subjects where the teachers suit their own personality and patterns of abilities. Yet, as we have seen on Pages 42 to 45, there is a contra-diction in students being presented with an implacable intellectual authority in subject areas (e.g. science and technology) where our understand-ing of the world and the techniques for harnessing its forces are in a constant state of evolution and even revolution (see Kuhn 1973); where change is the only stable factor.

The acceptability of (the vaguer) aims rather than (more specific) the objectives is based firmly on the assumption that the nature of group discussion is discursive and open-ended. However, in science subjects, there are also aims connected with 'mastering the substance of a curriculum', helping students to achieve a firm grasp of principles through discussing them and learning to communicate in the 'language' of the subject. Certain specific content objectives (like those listed on page 66) will be highly relevant to a science course, and these may not be negotiable because of inflexible requirements of the assessment system. Abercrombie (1979) describes Blunt & Blizzards' (1973) approach to this problem in an Anatomy course where, at each tutorial, student groups were given a set of exercises related to a general objective and its accompanying specific objectives; assessment was closely related to these objectives and indicated the depth of study involved.

Here the idea of setting objectives is applied in an original way, using the group process as a source of motivation. Yet there is a danger that students learning in this way may be exposed to an excessively serialist style of teaching (see page 41). Perhaps the most suitable way of avoiding this tendency to serialism is to use the Associative Discussion method (pages 124 to 127) in which students are expected to regard their evidence and arguments critically.

Of course it is debatable whether this approach is a case of using group process to achieve individual content aims, or of using subject matter as material for learning more sophisticated aims; aims such as 'awareness of others' interests and needs' and a 'a willingness to share ideas' or 'the application of interpersonal skills'. In one sense, the task is the means to the end of group process aims; in another, the group process helps the completion of the task.

There are two further circumstances in which the specification of objectives may be particularly valuable for group work. One is where the students undertake a personal or peer responsibility for the conduct of their own work. In some cases this can lead to their assessing their own work. Syndicates and peer tutoring cells (see Chapter 6) may be given a direction by the tutor's specifying objectives for this sort of work. The other is in projects or other self-directed work where students may be encouraged to develop their own individual

objectives in groups and thereafter pursue them
with group support. (See page 204, Student
Planning in the Dip.H.E.) In both these cases, the
specification of objectives may be seen as a way of
investing the authority of the absent tutor in a
set of guidelines and standards. Knowles (1975)
describes a personal learning contract in which
students decide their own learning needs, strategies
for achieving them, evidence of their accomplishment, and criteria and means of evaluating them.
The development of the contract is facilitated by
the tutor who encourages the students to use
various combinations of teamwork in pursuit of
their goals.

Sources of Educational Aims

In general, educational aims are based upon people's
conception of what it is to be educated and on the
notion of some sort of professional person – 'the
engineer', 'the historian', 'the sociologist',
etc. Such aims may be described as instrumental or
vocational. However there are others which are
essentially part of the educational process itself –
the so-called 'intrinsic' aims. The various sources
of aims for group work in higher education are
depicted in Figure 5.1:

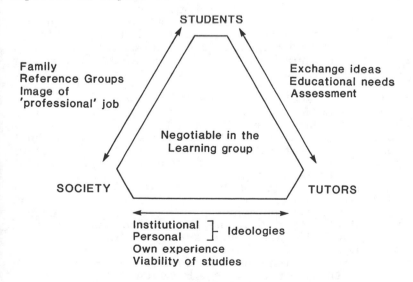

Fig.5.1   Sources of Aims for Group Work

Three basic sources can be identified:

Society: which includes the personal background of both tutor and students as well as the wider community.

Students: who draw upon their own background and on their perception of the outside world.

Tutors: whose aims derive from similar sources to those of the students but who are strongly influenced by the climate of learning in the educational setting.

Although a simplified model, this diagram is capable of more complex reading. Not only can the aims be seen to originate from students, tutors and society but there are several which occur either through the movement from one source to another or from the direct interaction of one with another, or indeed from a belief held by one about the other. For instance, the value of working in small groups derives from a notion that man is a social animal: most people start their life in small groups, in the family unit, and there is therefore something natural about discussion in groups. Such aims are transported by students from society into the educational setting. Conversely, the development of teamwork skills derives from the movement of students from the educational setting into society.

Let us look now at the base of the triangle. Some of the new universities in the UK have been designed both administratively and educationally to give pre-eminence, or at least greater emphasis, to small group work. In some cases, this policy has arisen from a desire expressed in policy documents HMSO (1963) and HMSO (1964) for a change from the old educational order. In other cases it seems that academics have felt the need for students to learn in a democratic environment where critical issues can be faced more openly.

Along the right hand side there are aims which are purely to do with educational needs; those for instance concerned with gaining feedback on student progress, the tutor and student each seeing how the other views the world, and so on. In addition, there are aims and ideas which, although initiated by the tutor, may be modified through interaction with students in group work. An example of this could be the tutor's wishing to develop the students' skills in analysing a piece

70

of ecological evidence where the students are more concerned with the ethical considerations of it. Aims like these lie in the open centre of the diagram. It would be comfortable to think that all these aims are naturally subject to a continuing, if not always conscious, revision, as the parties involved identify and reflect on all the contributing sources and the values they imply. However, aims and their inherent values are not often made explicit. The intellectual rarefaction for which academic life is popularly caricatured may set in, with a consequent risk that the institution will increasingly succumb to the 'ivory tower' syndrome. This could be the result of tutors equating their proper subject expertise with 'knowing what is best for the students' or failing to negotiate their beliefs and values with the flux of ideas deriving from the outside world as it is mediated by the students.

Tutors are often reluctant to make the aims of their teaching explicit, whether because their hidden power is thereby diminished or simply because they feel threatened by change. Small group discussion involves a critical interchange of ideas, opinions, values, judgements and so forth, and one of the essential elements in any form of education which purports to be adaptable and sensitive to the changes in a rapidly changing world is that the values and judgements implied by educational aims should also be open to discussion.

Another source of aims and objectives for the group tutor is educational theory. Bloom, in what has become a classic educational text (1956, 1964), classified objectives into 2 basic divisions: knowledge and intellectual skills; and the development of attitudes. Clearly when it comes to the process of learning it is impossible to discriminate between these categories of behaviour. Skill is required to learn a piece of knowledge, to apply it or to write about it and our attitude to both knowledge and its application in a particular environment is important in determining how well we perform these operations or indeed whether we do them at all.

In the UTMU (1978) book 'Improving Teaching in Higher Education', Bloom's classification has been written as a set of associated verbs:

Knowledge: write; state; recall; recognise; select; reproduce; measure

Aims and Objectives of Learning Groups

Comprehension: identify; illustrate, represent; formulate; explain; contrast

Application: predict; select; assess; find; show; use; construct; compute

Analysis: select; compare; separate; differentiate; contrast; break down

Synthesis: summarise; argue; relate; precise; organise; generalise; conclude

Evaluation: judge; evaluate; support; attack; avoid; select; recognise; criticise

While we may sometimes feel that the specification of desired behaviour can be an intolerable constraint on the 'democratic' processes of group discussion, a list such as this could provide tutors with a useful focus on two counts:

1. each could form an operative verb in the instructions for a group task (see page 82).

2. a tutor could develop a repertoire of questions based on these verbs to have 'up his sleeve' and draw out as spontaneously as possible during the progress of a discussion. For instance the verb 'summarise' might suggest an intervention from the tutor like, 'Would anyone like to put all that together now?' (see page 155 et seq for further proposals on tutor interventions).

What are Groups For?

'No-one says anything. You've prepared a lot of work and then find it's taken over by the tutor. Some just talk for 2 hours solid. You learn to switch off after a while.'

Some tutors regard group work as little more than an extension to the lecture. The so-called seminar takes the form of a monologue in which the tutor expounds the ideas which he has been unable to complete or treat in such detail in a lecture. Others, mainly in science and engineering, regard the tutorial discussion as an opportunity to clear up misunderstandings from a lecture; in other words, it is little more than a compensation for the inadequacies of the lecture method. Still other tutors, more especially in the arts and social sciences, see the seminar as an opportunity for intellectual analysis and the making of critical judgements about the subject, and yet have little concern for the social and emotional aspects of group discussion. Groups run in this manner tend to be highly intellectual and competitive and they frequently descend into an exercise in point scoring. (See the student view of seminars on pages 96 to 101).

Whatever the overt intentions of group work, there is little doubt that they serve purposes other than those stated. Small group dicussion provides the opportunity for students not merely to engage in intellectual discourse but also to create a social 'family' to which they can belong and become identified with. It also allows students to learn ways of communicating their thoughts, and occasionally feelings, and of gauging their understanding of subject matter firstly by expressing it and secondly by comparing it with the understanding of their peers. Clearly, the atmosphere in the group will determine whether this can be conducted in an open and co-operative manner as opposed to a closed and competitive one.

How do learning groups compare with the generally accepted basic functions of groups? In terms of group dynamics, the two major areas of aims are those concerned with task and with main-tenance. In the academic context, 'task' aims will usually be the so-called intellectual ones, e.g. the exercise of critical judgement, the ability to analyse statements and cases and to question underlying assumptions and values. They will also include those of a pastoral or remedial nature, such as recognising when students are in difficul-ties, checking for misunderstandings in reading or lectures, etc. Group maintenance on the other hand will include aims like creating a sense of belonging in an otherwise anonymous institution, generating a sense of trust and openness, handling conflict in a constructive way and so forth. Maintenance aims may be said to facilitate or underpin task aims. However, 'maintenance', as in its more normal usage, implies repeated attention and adjustment to the running of the group if the task is going to be achieved. Readers may also recall, from the section on group behaviour (pages 9 to 11), that maintenance aims become increasingly more relevant as the size of the group increases. It is quite common for instance for small groups of three and four to work on a task without concern about who is doing what or any formal leadership role being needed; where a class is divided into small sub-groups (see pages 90 to 95) the maintenance problem is very much subsumed to the task. However, in a larger group, the opposite is frequently the case. If the task aims are to be achieved, either members of the group must be extremely aware of the dynamic processes within it and be skilled in handling these, or the tutor himself must take on a firm leadership role. It will be seen, therefore, that in a large group, certainly one in excess of seven members, the problems of agreeing on how to set about the task and how the distribution of responsibilities within the group should be made will take a predominant role (at least in the early stages) before the group can set about its academic task. Of course it is always possible, especially in the social sciences, for the task and the maintenance aims to be combined. For instance, the explicit task of the group could be to examine the processes of social differentiation or of leadership within the group (though this can become a very difficult and confusing activity to students who are not fully aware of the processes in which they are involved).

Typical Aims and Purposes for Groups

It may be important to distinguish between the aims which are achievable by a learning group as a group and those which are principally achieved through the application of the sort of special techniques described in the next chapter. As we have already seen, some group aims of the former kind, the more personal, social and emotional ones, go largely unrecognised. Whether tutors are aware of them or not, however, they will be advanced to some extent in any competently-led group. The range of maintenance or socio-emotional aims is well summarised in UTMU (1978).

> 'Some staff may feel that the emotional welfare of their students really hasn't got much to do with their small group teaching, the essential purpose of which they say is to make sure that students have really understood what they have been trying to get across in lectures. Careful questioning they argue, can bring out the major misunderstandings and difficulties and many of these can be dealt with by the teacher in a way in which he can be sure that the students have really understood. Under the extreme pressures

often felt by both students and staff to cover
the ground effectively, such a view of the main
purpose of group work is very understandable.
But if this purpose is pursued vigorously and
efficiently, it may also mean that other
purposes will not merely be ignored but will be
actively discouraged. Strategies which may
produce effective learning within the highly
structured formal education system can leave
students with little ability, or even desire,
to cope with learning and relearning when they
leave the formal supportive structures of
higher education behind them. Nevertheless,
work there will be in structures of a different
kind and many professionals now find themselves
working in teams.

It could be said therefore that an important
function of group work in higher education is
to enable students to know enough about themselves and about others to enable them to work
independently and yet co-operatively within a
team. Such teams may or may not have formal
leaders, but the style of leadership is likely
to be very different from that of the more
traditional seminar leader who controls the
activity of the class in such a way that
students learn to feel little responsibility
for what happens in the group beyond doing
required background reading.

The group experience can, in fact, be extremely
important in achieving freedom from dependency
if the students learn to play a variety of
roles in the group and begin to develop a
sense of responsibility for its success or
failure. In the process of learning these
roles they will need to develop more acute
self-understanding, to become aware of their
own inhibitions, defences and assumptions, and
be able to recognise the difficulties which
other students have and begin to help them to
overcome them. In learning to become more
sensitive to different points of view and ways
of thinking and to work co-operatively with
others using the varied skills of the group,
they may begin to develop a surer sense of
social identity, and a feeling of belonging
and commitment. This can encourage not only
enthusiasm in the subject but a willingness to
reveal abilities which are so often effectively
hidden, even from themselves. Students' oral
skills moreover, are unlikely to develop

very highly simply in response to probing questions.
There needs to be a genuine sense of opportunity for self-expression and this may be very difficult in a context where the main object is to increase understanding and correct misconceptions and faulty reasoning.'

There is plenty of evidence both from research and experience that groups of all kinds operate at both a task and a socio-emotional level. If we look at groups in an academic context we can see that they can be viewed as functioning within both intrinsic and extrinsic dimensions.(see page 64). Figure 5.2 demonstrates the inter-relationships between these four aspects in a matrix format.
The tendency in tertiary education is to give least attention to the intrinsic dimension. Teaching tends to be solution-orientated rather than problem-orientated and seems to take external requirements as its starting point rather than the needs and interests of the students. Moreover, a lack of attention to the socio-emotional dimension means that many of the task aims cannot be achieved. Without a climate of trust and co-operation, students will not feel like taking the risk of making mistakes and learning from them. To achieve this, the tutor would have to balance his concern for academic standards with a capacity to understand and deal with the workings of group process as well as an attitude of generosity and praise for new solutions to old problems.
The students might correspondingly applaud his resourcefulness in introducing them to new experiences in group learning.
If, finally, we return to the questions posed at the start of the chapter, it will be evident that learning groups are amenable to a much wider range of aims than is commonly supposed and that many of these bear a similarity to the aims and outcomes of groups in the wider world. Insofar as learning groups comprise a meeting of human beings with some shared goals, it seems probable that processes like pooling resources, making decisions, gaining mutual support, sharing ideas, creating something and so on would always exist, at least subliminally. Yet if they could be made more explicit perhaps by incorporating them into more practical, real-world tasks not only to create more stimulation and variety of opportunity in learning for students but also to develop their awareness of group and teamwork

Aims and Objectives of Learning Groups

	TASK	SOCIO-EMOTIONAL
I **N** **T** **R** **I** **N** **S** **I** **C**	Expressing selves in subject Judging ideas in relation to others Examining assumptions Listening attentively Tolerating ambiguity Learning about groups	Greater sensitivity to others Judging self in relation to others Encouraging self-confidence Personal development Tolerating ambiguity Awareness of others' strengths and weaknesses
E **X** **T** **R** **I** **N** **S** **I** **C**	Follow-up to lecture Understanding text Improving staff/ student relations Gauging student progress Giving guidance	Giving support Stimulating to further work Evaluating student feelings about course Giving students identifiable groups to belong to

Fig.5.2 Types of Aims and Purposes in Group
        Teaching

matters for their future careers.

These practical aims have nevertheless to be converted into acceptable and realistic activities in the classroom. This is the central concern of the next chapter.

Discussion Points

° What kinds of discrepancies appear to exist between the express aims of groups you belong to, or lead, and what actually happens? How do they arise?

° Draw up a chart like Fig.5.2 for the aims of your own group(s). To what extent do they vary within the group or between groups? What values and assumptions lie behind the aims?

TASKS AND TECHNIQUES

If aims and objectives are to represent a bit more
than good intentions, they must, as we have already
discussed, be related to corresponding <u>tasks</u> and
<u>techniques</u> and each of these demands of the tutor
particular skills and the playing of a special role.
Tasks specify the activities in which the students
individually or collectively are engaged, whether it
is to do with a process like 'observe the behaviour
of a white rat' or an end-product like 'list ten
issues that strike you as important and rank them'.
<u>Techniques</u> are the ensemble of tasks, rules and
procedures which comprise a coherent educational
experience. In order to establish and maintain a
task or technique, a tutor needs both imagination
and skill in prescribing the structure, monitoring
what is happening, gently enforcing rules or adjust-
ing them to advantage, and avoiding the risk of
being drawn into the sort of relationship with
the group which could subvert the purpose of the
exercise. Here is an example of the way aims,
tasks, techniques and roles might fit together:

Aim: To develop students' awareness of different strategies for solving problems.

A suitable set of group tasks might be:

(a) to try and solve a given problem
(b) to monitor the strategies involved
(c) to share the findings and compare them
with research evidence
(d) to draw up a classification of the
findings

A technique or procedure which could match this
might be to organise sub-groups with observers in

a 'fishbowl'* layout. The tutor's job would be to prepare any materials, explain and check agreement on the tasks, monitor their development and control time boundaries.

Setting Tasks

As explained on page 67, students are often unsure about what to do in groups and might well take up the pursuit of separate individual goals while ostensibly engaged in collaborative discussion. In seminars the very vagueness of the task often means that students fail to get their teeth into anything substantial and end up with a feeling of dissatisfaction. They are unsure about whether they have achieved anything or even what it was they were supposed to achieve. The task might, after several meetings, become clear to them but even then, it may well be diffuse and perceived differently by each student. What is more, the rules or conventions of behaviour may not be explicit and may possibly be unrelated to the task. There seems to be tacit confusion about all sorts of things and this creates uncertainty and stress. Stenhouse (1972) suggests that students evolve a secondary task of their own, which is to study the tutor's behaviour in order to understand the situation in which they find themselves. If this muddled situation is to be avoided, it is important for the tutor to make the task, and his role in relation to it, explicit. Sometimes, especially with a large class working in sub-groups or where students have to do work outside the classroom, it is essential that the task be carefully worded and written out. On other occasions it may be better to negotiate a task with the group, especially where this is the first time it has been tried.

Sources of Tasks

By placing the emphasis on task, the tutor can partly side-step the ever-present problem of authority and dependency in the group. The tutor may think up, or encourage the students to invent, a task which establishes common ground between them, organise any structuring of sub-groups, set time limits, confine his authority to a position which is set by agreed rules and procedures, monitor what is happening and make consequent adjustments.

*see page 221

Such a sequence can have a cyclical form in which the act of monitoring informs the tutor when a switch of task may be necessary and that he may be required quickly to dream one up which is relevant to the immediate concerns of the group. Sometimes, ideas occur spontaneously with remarkable results. Abercrombie (1979) reports the experience of Felicity Baker (1974) who converted the uninspiring experience of a group studying French prose into a 'small new awakening' by giving responsibility to the students for the assessment of each other's work as a group task.

Whenever a group appears to be getting bored, a change of task can have remarkable results. The boredom may be due to a lack of 'grounding' in the discussion, that is, it is not rooted in the personal experience of the students. The sort of real-life process encountered in case study, role play, or marking each other's essays - can re-activate the dormant energy of the group. On the other hand, boredom can arise from the group being trapped in an authority/dependency tangle (see pages 4 & 6), and a tutor may be wise to spend time getting the group to look at its assumptions about the teaching/learning relationship.

Group discussion is frequently unrelated to personal experience or real-life processes. This problem is discussed by Parker & Rubin (1966) who argue strongly for the introduction of real-world experiences (as opposed to academic artefacts) in the classroom. One model they suggest for this purpose comprises four stages:

1. Creating and acquiring knowledge: students observe phenomena, read expository material, collect evidence and listen to presentations.

2. Interpreting knowledge: students derive meaning from what they have learned; they relate new knowledge to old. The necessary skills include analysing, reorganising and experimenting with information and relating it together.

3. Attaching significance and communicating knowledge: students infer generalisations, relate information to new situations and learn to reorganise the information in new ways. These activities precede communication.

4.   Applying knowledge: students use information to recognise, clarify and solve
problems.

Several of these processes could be converted
into group tasks and elaborated as the discussion
progresses.   Parker & Rubin's approach reminds us
that we can learn a lot about ways of educating by
considering 'natural' activities in the outside
world.   Many of the tasks and techniques listed on
the following pages are derived in this way.
It is worth mentioning here that, whilst any
task or technique may embody a unique complex of
aims and objectives, any one aim could be achieved
by a number of tasks or techniques.   Tutors who can
build a repertoire of tasks and techniques should
thus find themselves more versatile in the pursuit
of all sorts of aims.

Types of Task
The possibilities and permutations of tasks are end-
less.   All we can do here is to look at some broad
categories and suggest some specific examples.

Tasks for groups as a whole, or sub-groups

Argue with tutor/students - disputation
Discuss presentation
Discuss misunderstandings
Draw up list of similarities and differences
List items from experience
List items from observation in group
List items from reading
Mark own or each other's essays
Set criteria for essay marking
Generate ideas
Make categories
Clarify problem/solve it/evaluate it
Enact
Discuss critically
Diagnose
Argue relative merits
Share anxieties
Share essay plans
Share study methods
Watch video
Read and evaluate text
Report back on previous session (see page 221)

Tasks and Techniques

Tasks for individuals followed by discussion in groups

    Mark off checklist
    Rank or rate and compare values
    Make decisions/proposals about case
    Construct model, etc.
    Observe group process
    Make choices
    Analyse text
    Allocate individual tasks - project work
    Suggest thesis and argue it
    Solve problem

Tasks for peer tutoring (see page 108)

    Teach
    Question to check learning
    Prepare questions
    Prepare tasks
    Counsel

    Resourceful tutors will doubtless dream up a host of other tasks as they consider the ways in which knowledge in their subject is created, interpreted, communicated and applied.

Structuring Tasks

As we have already seen, large groups (ten or over) find some difficulty in working cohesively on a task and will tend to split into sub-groups unless held together by strong leadership. When it is important to mobilise a sense of commitment and immediate purpose among a largish group of students therefore it may be sensible to capitalise on the group's desire to divide into smaller units by 'doing what comes naturally'. We might for example invite the students to first work individually on a listing task for five minutes, share their ideas in pairs for ten minutes and finally, in groups of four to six, write up categories on a large sheet of paper for 25 minutes of open discussion between groups. We could explain our role as that of wandering round to check that everyone understands and accepts the task and is doing it in an appropriate way, and to help students in formulating categories. The nature of the students' encounter with each other would thus vary over a period of time and with each change would come a different kind of learning experience. The skills required of the tutor in setting up these 'task-orientated' groups differ somewhat from those required in tutor-led groups. They are more to do with a considered negotiation of a mutual contract than a sensitive response to the unfolding group process. These skills are discussed in more detail in Chapter 7.

Group tasks alone do not lead to integrated learning. They have to be co-ordinated into a schema which not only pinpoints roles and relationships within the group, but also puts them in a valid and coherent learning sequence. Though the following task from Nisbet (1966), and quoted in Rudduck (1978), is elaborate, it is a nice example of such integration. The amount of detail thought necessary may be an indication of the number of pitfalls inherent in the traditional seminar which must consciously be avoided if new structures are to take shape. The course is in Theory of Education.

'Each student chooses a field of study and has two-and-a-bit meetings in which to complete the task. At the introduction meeting, the tutor explains the procedure. Within each field the student responsible must first produce six statements worth making. What this involves has to be clearly understood: a "statement worth making" (worth making that is in the context of this seminar) is one which is clear, succinct and important: which is controversial enough to require careful decision before it is accepted or rejected, and which represents the personal belief, based on study, experience and reflection, of its author. To put it negatively, statements not worth making are high-sounding platitudes, trivialities, vague abstractions whose acceptance or rejection would make no observable difference in practice, disingenuous 'OK' phrases, inadequately grounded opinions, or assertions that no-one is likely to dispute. Each statement must consist of only a single sentence but the author will in due course be given every opportunity of providing supplementary details and explaining why he chose to formulate each statement in its present form. No attempt must be made to "cover" the whole field. The six chosen are to be regarded as a selection from the hundreds he could presumably produce in the given area of study if called upon to do so. When a student has made up his list he is expected to provide enough copies (with recommended references to relevant literature appended) to go round the group'.

The second meeting begins with the distribution of the copies of Student A's statements and a short talk by him to introduce them. The remainder of the meeting is devoted to free and informal discussion. 'Spontaneity and freedom are the characteristics of this meeting.'

At the third meeting the statements are quickly reintroduced and in an atmosphere of <u>discipline</u> and <u>urgency</u> (in contrast to the previous meeting), Student A tries:

'to obtain unanimous agreement for each statement in turn. Whenever this is not immediately forthcoming he and the other group members, including the tutor, suggest amendments which might (a) satisfy the critics and yet (b) retain the support of those who approve the statement as it is and (c) still leave "a statement worth making". If, after a long discussion a compromise proves impossible, the dissident member(s) will be left to compose a "minority view" on the statement in question. Each member of the group including the tutor, knows that when the list is promulgated in its final form his name will appear as one of the supporters. At the end of the meeting (Student A) takes home the group minute book to write up the official account of the two meetings for which he has been responsible.'

(These minutes are checked with the group at the beginning of the next meeting.)

What seems particularly interesting here is that the task is similar to that of the traditional seminar in which a student presents views on prior reading, yet it places a very explicit and more comprehensive set of demands on the students. Above all, <u>decisions</u> have to be made and this almost invariably draws out values and beliefs into open conflict - they cannot be avoided by mere verbal felicity. The alternating of free and disciplined styles of discussion is a structure worth looking at also. Too often a group vacillates between the two styles, so that the benefits of neither are convincingly achieved.

In these seminars then, the broad ground rules for discussion are clear and explicit. (We shall return to this matter later on page 153). The role of the tutor is also made clear:

> 'The method makes it easy for the tutor to sustain his rightful role as <u>primus inter pares</u> - "primus", in that he is chairman, and is responsible for the conduct of the meetings, occasionally supplying factual information, tactfully bringing in the less vocal members, keeping an eye on the clock, and exercising self-restraint by remaining silent where necessary, even when he would like to say a lot; "inter pares" because he participates in the discussion on the basis of equality, criticising and being criticised, asking and answering, revealing his own personal values as well exploring those of the students.'

These tasks, rules and roles are of vocational benefit to the students, the writers claim. For post-graduate students (average age 27), the practice of shaping a consensus view and reconciling opposing positions has direct relevance to their professional work on committees and the like. They are also of great value to the tutor who cannot fail to be stimulated by the flux of new and unexpected ideas and confrontations. (See also Wilson, 1980).

The above tasks emphasise processes of discussion and decision-making. Another fruitful task field is evaluation and assessment. Students may be asked to do one of the evaluation exercises described on pages 226-31 or to assess what they have learned (in perhaps a general sense) and what they have contributed to, and got from, the course. This latter task can be given a keener edge by asking students to rate themselves on a numerical scale according to agreed criteria on work or performance. These criteria can be worked out by the class as part of the exercise. Following this, the students might rate each other and compare their self ratings with the mean of the peer ratings. If these are then put alongside the assessment of the tutor, a fascinating discussion can ensue as a result of which students begin to internalise some of the criteria and standards of academic learning. This task is yet another which could equip students for more autonomous learning and self-appraisal in their subsequent careers. It also introduces the idea of triangulated assessment (self-peer-tutor) in which a degree of objectivity is obtained by having three separate judgements on the value of the student's achievement.

Clarifying tasks and roles can be enormously helpful to group project students too. Projects (in this context) consist of several successive and overlapping tasks. Choosing a problem or topic, choosing partners, researching solutions, analysing results, writing a report, doing a presentation and so on, all occur with varying degrees of overlap and weight. Pervading all of these is the task of group maintenance - how to get the best out of a collection of students with disparate experience, skills, knowledge and personal qualities. One task for the tutor in this regard is therefore to alert students to leadership issues and decision-making processes as the project progresses. Kuiper (1977) suggests an 'internal' contract for project groups which comprises aims and values on which members can agree and an 'external' one which describes the practical purpose to which the project is to be put. The external contract usually involves a third party in the university institution. We shall return to the subject of projects later in this chapter.

Game Tasks

Making rules, roles and procedures clear is important enough in group teaching but sometimes it is useful to introduce some imaginary scenario into the task, as in a role-play or simulation. In an engineering laboratory several years ago, I introduced three new experimental tasks:

(A) 'Dear Sirs,
I am designing a series of submerged pipelines to cross rivers in different parts of the UK (details given). I am in urgent need of a reliable check on the forces I might expect them to withstand and would be most grateful if you could test various models in a wind tunnel in order to give me some working data. Please send me your report within three weeks from this date. Yours, etc.'

(B) 'The 1st year students are currently interested in the differences between static and dynamic forces. Could you please conduct the following experiment to check on the nature and magnitude of these differences and, having undertaken suitable rewording, write out a set of explanatory notes for the 1st year students.'

(C) 'The valley of Erehwon (map and relevant data enclosed) is being considered as the site of a huge new dam and reservoir. You are to divide into three professional groups: engineers, technicians and journalists. The engineers must conduct a feasibility study on -

(a) dam structure
(b) water supply and
(c) hydro-electric power

The technicians must determine measuring techniques for (a list of purposes given) and the journalists must compile a public relations brochure on the study. Your written reports should be submitted two days before the meeting of the study commission where they will be formally introduced and discussed.'

In these three cases, and especially the last one, the rules and procedures, though not very explicit, are no longer embedded in the teacher-student relationship but are invested in understanding of everyday life <u>outside the educational system</u>, to do with the consultant/client relationship, students in a teaching role and feasibility studies respectively. Policies of this sort are admirably suited to group-teaching in subject areas which have low intrinsic interest and need some imaginative boost to get them going. Games and simulations are indeed most valuable in this regard. Many examples of their use in Language Teaching are given in 'Take Five' (Carrier, 1981). However, we must not conclude that this approach lends itself only to 'remedial' purposes, where a subject is basically boring. Games and simulations appear to be of enormous benefit in developing professional, communication, and problem-solving skills, in integrating learning at different levels and across disciplines and in achieving unexpected insights into other people's views. We shall return to this topic later (page 116) but the interested reader might like to note the existence of the Society for

the Advancement of Games and Simulations in Education and Training which publishes a quarterly journal containing many helpful ideas on games.
Chapter 8 provides further examples of various group tasks in the context of the curriculum.

A VARIETY OF TECHNIQUES

Thus far we have looked at aims and tasks and the educational and psychological principles that support them. When these are integrated into an established pattern of rules, roles and procedures, we have an ensemble of means - a technique. In this section we shall look at some of these techniques and the principal aims they are designed to serve. Subsequent chapters describe the skills required of the tutor in preparing and operating these techniques, and how they may be organised into the curriculum.

Neat classifications of social processes are generally a futile venture and make for lazy reading. The following descriptions of group techniques are therefore organised within a fairly loose framework. Any reader interested in re-classifying them according to different criteria might find it a helpful way of getting new insights into their further use. The way the various techniques are used will vary enormously from group to group. Some, like synectics, a creative problem-solving technique, are fairly specific in their format; others like the seminar are infinitely variable. Some are incorporated with others. Whichever category system one uses there are always too many exceptions.

The techniques are grouped in three categories:

(1) those concerned with mainly cognitive objectives (knowledge, comprehension, application, problem-solving, analysis, evaluation)

(2) those involving creative objectives (seeing new relationships, connecting the emotional and the intellectual, producing imaginative solutions)

(3) those developing individual or group awareness, personal growth, communication skills, participation and the breaking down of interpersonal barriers.

Within each of these broad categories, there is a progression from <u>tutor control</u> to <u>student freedom</u>, though even these terms are quite clearly problematical. One of the most creative and liberating techniques, 'brainstorming' has a set of fairly strict rules for discussion in the group.

The open intention of this chapter is to encourage tutors to break out of the traditional mould of seminars and tutorials and to recognise the range of variations and alternative techniques or methods they can use; techniques which are less frustrating, more enjoyable, which challenge and stimulate the minds of students and which give credit to that under-used faculty of mind - the imagination. Many of these less-than-familiar techniques may be included within the bounds of what is, for timetabling purposes, called a 'seminar'. Others may need to be pursued in their own right.

The first two techniques are of particular relevance for larger groups where the communication of knowledge is clearly directed through the tutor. Others, like 'syndicates', indicate the tutor's role in relation to several groups, but say nothing about what happens within each of the syndicates. In other words some are to do with the inner processes while others define external features. The nature of the experience in each group will in any case be determined to a large extent by the points at which control is applied and the manner of its application.

Controlled Discussion

This technique is commonly used with a class, rather than a group, as a means of checking for knowledge and understanding of presented material. Discussion is controlled by the tutor; either students ask questions or make comments, or the tutor fires questions at students in the manner of a Socratic dialogue.

Advantages: convenient to organise at the end of a lecture, gives quick feedback, large and 'economical' number of students.

Disadvantages: social situation inhibiting, reticent students not heard, little peer discussion.

Step-by-Step Discussion

Though similar to controlled discussion in its communication pattern, this technique is based on a prepared sequence of subject matter. The tutor draws out and guides the students' knowledge in discussion and, by using open-ended questioning skills (see page 165), allows students some freedom to explore the realms of their own knowledge. The input for step-by-step discussion may be a sheet of notes, or a text shared by tutor and students alike, or even a video/audio tape where a 'stop-start' procedure can be employed (see page 242). This technique brings together several of the qualities of the lecture and the seminar.

Advantages: makes economical use of large groups; 'authority' can be invested in shared text or tape – students not dependent on tutor for content; combines information-giving, processing and feedback aims.

Disadvantages: as for controlled discussion but to a lesser extent; sequence and structure of discussion pre-ordained – may not correspond with students' needs.

The next four techniques are ways of achieving the same basic aims as for the previous two, but within a much more 'democratic' climate.

Buzz Groups

Frequently where the group is large there is a need for a break in the more formal proceedings in order:

(1) to provide a stimulating change in the locus of attention.

(2) for the tutor to gain some idea of what the students know.

(3) for the students to check their own understanding.

If, therefore, during the course of a lecture or other one-directional communication, students are asked to turn to their neighbours to discuss any difficulties in understanding, to answer a prepared question, or to speculate on what they think will happen next in the proceedings for just a few minutes, a sense of participation and some lively feedback are quickly achieved. Buzz groups enable students to express difficulties they would have been unwilling to reveal to the whole class without the initial push of being obliged to say something to their neighbours. Taken by itself, the buzz group technique has little meaning. Yet in the context of a lecture or other large group event it can re-kindle all sorts of dying embers. Its incorporation into a pattern of teaching events is described on pages 178 to 180.

Advantages: can be used in any teaching situation for as short or long as desirable; helps students and teacher check on misunderstandings; creates a stimulating break.

Disadvantages: can destroy intellectual and emotional cohesion if timed badly.

Snowball Groups (Pyramiding)

Buzz groups can easily be extended into a progressive doubling in which pairs join up to form fours, then fours to eights and these finally report back to a plenary session. This developing pattern of group interaction is known as a 'snowball'. This technique is amazingly effective in ensuring comprehensive participation especially when it starts with individuals writing their ideas in the first stage before sharing them. Lest students become bored with repeated discussion of the same points, a sequence of increasingly sophisticated tasks is often desirable. See Fig.6.1.

Advantages: good for encouraging the evolution of well-integrated ideas: allows students to think for themselves before discussing; creates full and lively participation in plenary discussion.

Disadvantages: breaks up cohesive feeling in some groups; takes time to unfold.

Tasks and Techniques

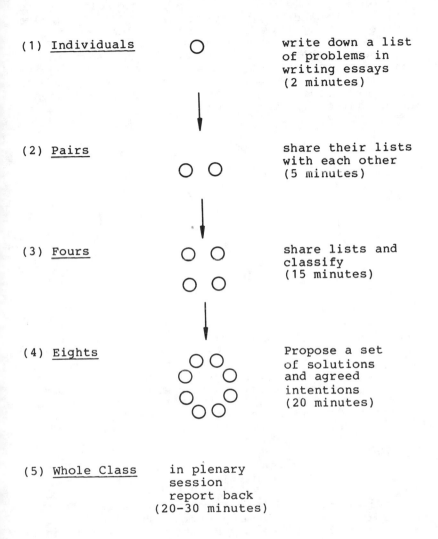

(1) <u>Individuals</u>   ○   write down a list
                                      of problems in
                                      writing essays
                                      (2 minutes)

(2) <u>Pairs</u>   ○ ○   share their lists
                                      with each other
                                      (5 minutes)

(3) <u>Fours</u>   ○ ○   share lists and
                        ○ ○   classify
                                      (15 minutes)

(4) <u>Eights</u>   ○○   Propose a set
                       ○ ○   of solutions
                       ○ ○   and agreed
                        ○○   intentions
                                      (20 minutes)

(5) <u>Whole Class</u>   in plenary
                          session
                          report back
                          (20-30 minutes)

Fig.6.1 Snowball or Pyramid Groups

<u>Cross-Over Groups</u>
One continual problem with the division of a class
into sub-groups is how to avoid a tiresome plenary

session when each group reports publicly to the others. In the crossover technique, students are divided into groups such that the number in each group is approximately equal to the square root of the total number participating. There are then two (and possibly more) ways of proceeding, each requiring group members to meet at least one from each of the other groups. If we take a group of 9 students and organise them as follows:

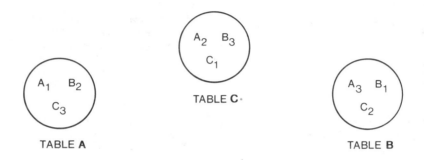

Fig.6.2 Cross-Over Groups

and hand each a card marked A1 B2 etc as in Fig 6.2, the two distinct procedures are:

i.   after a given time, all suffix '2' people move to their 'home' tables (i.e. A2 goes to table A, B2 to Table B and C2 to Table C) and then, after a similar period of time, suffix '3' people move to their 'home' tables.

ii. at a given time all As join each other, all Bs and Cs similarly.

Alternatively, a colour coding rather than a numerical one can be employed. The task of each student as he or she moves into a new group can be to report what has been said in the previous group before discussion in the new group proceeds. This technique is helpful in mixing a new group of students and, according to Bligh (1976), is of particular value on part-time courses where the circulation of ideas is never very rapid.

Advantages: excellent for mixing people and information; simple to organise,

> students enjoy it, avoids plenary discussion.

Disadvantages: can lead to confusion about learning outcomes; can break up absorbing discussion.

Horseshoe Groups

This describes a way of organising a class so that it can alternate with ease between the lecture and discussion group formats. Rather than the students facing the front in serried ranks, they are arranged round tables in a horseshoe formation with the open end facing the front:

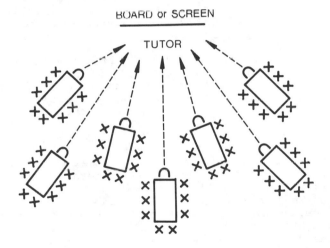

| X | Students |
| ∩ | Empty chairs for tutor(s) |

Fig.6.3 Horseshoe Groups

A tutor can thus talk formally from the blackboard for a time before switching to give the groups a task such as a problem or an interpretation; the task should of course be one demanding collaboration among the students. The horseshoe formation can be of great benefit in science and engineering exercise classes if students are given problems at the start and then the tutor circulates round the groups, listening and asking or answering questions. Should any general problem emerge an explanation can be offered by the tutor to the whole class, or indeed by any student.

Whether the groups are given identical, similar, or entirely separate problems there is always the opportunity to open up discussion of a sticky point or to ask groups to explain their solutions or decisions to each other. If a sense of inter-group competition can be infused into the situation, the level of interest and work can be heightened as well as cohesion in each group.

This format may also be used for syndicate meetings (see page 105).

Advantages: students can clear up misunderstandings, share uncertainties and teach each other, tutor has flexibility of talking or listening, students help each other.

Disadvantages: some students do little or nothing, tutor cannot easily identify students in difficulty (unless 'remedial' exercise set up) many 'problem' tasks not suited to group work.

Seminars

Though a formal title for a timetabled group session, the word 'seminar' is generally taken to mean a group discussion with fairly intellectual aims, led formally or informally by the tutor and focused on issues arising from the subject matter rather than on student difficulties (c.f. tutorials). The number of students is usually in excess of 8 and less than 20; traditionally, one of them will be asked to present a critical analysis or other work to introduce the discussion. Seminars, or the tutors' leadership of them, have been the butt of much criticism in recent years. An Education student, Treadaway (1975), described eight types of seminar which served to illustrate some of the common problems.

1.   The monologue or 'sitting at-the-feet of the master' type.

2.   The highly structured or 'I know what you want to say' type.

3.   The duologue or 'wrestling match' type

(one bright or forceful student wants to impress the tutor and a duologue ensues on areas which no-one else knows about).

4. The anecdotal or 'did I ever tell you?' type.

5. The essay-reading or Oxbridge type.

6. The article-summary or 'We've all read this anyway' type (if a student summarises without making critical comment then his colleagues may not bother to read it; the tutor may not have read the article for years and the discussion can thus become sterile).

7. The examination cramming type (the tutor seems concerned mainly with the students passing the exam, sometimes more so than the students).

8. The 'I don't believe in structured discussion' type.

Treadaway continues his analysis of seminar problems seen through the students' eyes:

'The first necessity is that the leader of the seminar should be clear what his purpose is and should ask himself whether a seminar is actually the best way to achieve this. If his purpose is merely to impart information, to put forward a particular point of view or to cram for an examination he may, and I think probably should, decide that a seminar is not the best method for doing this. The fault of many seminars, therefore, lies in trying to use the method for purposes for which it is not suited.

The next problem is size. There is no rule, of course, but my experience both as tutor and student suggests it is difficult to have a discussion in which everyone takes part fully, if the group is larger than ten. In an hour or so, even the actual time is against you - six minutes per person is not very much to develop a serious argument. But, more important, observation in this Institute and elsewhere has shown me that a significant proportion of people find it difficult to speak easily and confidently to a larger group. This may be due to personal inhibition, unfamiliarity with the Institute, the country or the language or a combination of these. It is very noticeable, for instance, how overseas students may be silent for a whole seminar but may be leading the discussion in a small informal group afterwards. The size of groups is of course, an administrative problem and staff/student ratios often make large groups inevitable. But, if the group is large, the answer is not, I suggest, to attempt discussion in spite of the size but to spend as much time as possible in smaller sub-groups. I have found that it is in these groups, especially when given a particular problem or project, that most learning takes place. At the same time, if the tutor feels he has particular information or ideas to put across, there is nothing wrong with spending part of the time in the larger group while the tutor gives a lecture or holds a question-and-answer session, provided he plans it as such and realises that this is different from a discussion seminar.

The second basic organisational factor is the physical one. You cannot expect a discussion if people are facing each other's backs, if they are miles apart across a huge room or table or crowded into a tutor's small room all facing his desk, or even if the room itself is dirty or cold. All these problems cannot always be solved, of course, but at least tutors should be aware of the importance of the physical arrangement and should not be surprised if discussion fails to develop when they neglect it.

The next decision is who should lead the seminar, and how. There are no rules about this, of course, and equally successful seminars can be led by tutors or students. Most tutors seem to feel, probably rightly, that it should be led by a student, as the student himself gains a great deal from having to lead it. On the other hand, few students have much experience at leading seminars and it is essential that they should be given guidance on this. This is rarely done and the result is sometimes a waste of time for the rest of the group. Whoever leads, however, the most important thing to remember is that a seminar

is supposed to be a discussion. This means
that the introduction should be fairly short
and should deliberately raise points which will
be the basis for discussion, rather than merely
summarise an article or other material. The
actual material for discussion should have been
distributed and/or read in advance and without
this a good seminar is unlikely. Sometimes, of
course, the object of the seminar is to discuss
a particular article. More often, however, an
article or book is meant to be the starting
point for discussion of a wider topic. If so,
this should be stressed to the leader and he
should be encouraged to use the article as a
starting point to bring in his own viewpoint
and experience. Often the seminar becomes a
discussion of one article when it was supposed
to cover a whole topic. It is up to the tutor
to decide this, however, and to make clear to
the leader what is needed. In some cases, he
may have the delicate task of stopping students
who go on too long or summarise rather than
discuss. Many tutors, quite naturally not
willing to offend, fail to do this when
necessary; but is it worth destroying a whole
seminar by being unwilling to risk offence to
one student? Advice to all beforehand should
in any case make the choice unnecessary.
The most crucial factor in a seminar is, of
course, the role of the tutor. This is very
difficult. He has to provide sufficient
guidance and structure to give the seminar a
meaningful shape without dominating it and
forcing it into a shape he has predetermined.
Ultimately, there are no rules and a seminar
can only be guided intuitively as it progresses. The problem is that students get the
impression that some tutors are not sensitive
enough to the difficulties. A good seminar
leader has to ask himself constantly whether he
is leading too strongly or talking too much;
whether everyone has made a contribution or a
few students are dominating and others need to
be encouraged by careful questioning; whether
some time in smaller groups might be useful; or
even whether he should withdraw altogether for
a while and let the group continue on its own.
An unstructured seminar is usually as unsuc-
cessful as a tutor-dominated one. To strike
the balance successfully is a difficult skill.
I would suggest it really needs some definite

training. I know this would have helped me considerably when I started to lead discussions amongst trainee teachers. Perhaps we too easily assume that teachers need training while tutors who teach teachers do not?

There may be occasions in a seminar, of course, when tutors can help best by their absence. Whether they like it or not, tutors are seen as authority figures and some people will be reluctant to speak, and perhaps show lack of understanding, when they are present. Sometimes a whole group can be inhibited in this way, with everyone silently thinking they are the only one who does not understand. I have often found, therefore, that the best way to get a discussion going is to leave the group, or even the room, for a while. Often a group who seemed to have no ideas of their own when I was present were almost at the point of fighting each other when I came back ten minutes later, and had by then gained the self-confidence to continue the discussion with my participation. There are some occasions, therefore, when a seminar, divided for at least part of the time into a number of small groups with a peripatetic tutor, works much better than a single group with the tutor present all the time.

It would be very valuable if official encouragement could be given right from the beginning of each course towards forming small informal groups for projects or discussion. It is often more useful, for instance, for a seminar to be prepared and led by a group who meet together and discuss the topic beforehand. Similarly, it is useful for groups to meet together after the seminars to follow up, practically or theoretically, some of the ideas raised by the seminar or some of their difficulties. This will usually only happen with some encouragement by the tutor.

My ideal seminar, then, would be one prepared by a small group of people who had met in advance, discussed the topic and distributed any necessary material to the whole group. They would present the topic to a group who had already read something about it and would emphasise points for discussion rather than just summarise. Depending on the size of the group there would then be discussion by the whole group or by sub-groups with the tutor

moving from group to group guiding rather than leading the discussion. There would probably be a short summary at the end by the tutor or the group leaders and encouragement for those particularly interested in the topic, or with any difficulties, to get together for further discussion later.
Finally, my definition of a seminar as learning through discussion should not preclude the use of other teaching methods, where appropriate (within the boundaries of the seminar).'
Treadaway (1975).

Treadaway's analysis of the 'seminar experience' highlights problems both about group teaching in general and about the traditional seminar. We should remember that the word seminar is as often used to describe a timetabled discussion period of any kind as it is the sort of intellectual battleground described by Treadaway. The three unconscionable problems of the latter seem to be:

(a) the weight of academic authority and expertise invested in the tutor

(b) the inability of tutors (and students) to recognise and try out alternative approaches - they both prefer to continue a respected tradition

(c) a pervading anxiety about assessment with a consequent feeling among students that they should speak only when they have something 'safe' to say.

The seminar at a research or postgraduate level, as Bligh (1976) remarks, can be very useful particularly when new ideas and proposals for research are being discussed. In such a case, it is a discussion among equals. Bligh is singularly critical of the seminar as a method of teaching. He describes it as 'simply inappropriate'. Its success is dependent on too many chancy factors: the 'lead' student may not do a competent job either in preparing or presenting: the essay is often not a good way to introduce a topic for discussion; there may be collusion among the students not to criticise a colleague in front of a tutor; the balance of dynamics in the group with a student leader and a tutor may be a precarious one.
In a survey conducted by the British National

Union of Students in 1969, students regarded the seminar as being particularly valuable for the following purposes:

'To encourage learning and to facilitate the interchange of ideas'

'To provide a stimulus for creative thinking'

'To improve students' self-expression'

but less so:

'To provide an occasion to study in depth'

on the other hand they were critical of seminars in the following respects:

'Tended to be dominated by one or two students'

'Students tend to wait always for a lead from the staff members'

and

'Students avoid doing sufficient preparatory work'.

The students were also of the opinion that the maximum working membership of the seminar was six to ten. (NUS, 1969)

These more statistical views reflect the same sort of problems, and the consequent ambivalence among students, that Treadaway describes. Potentially, seminars provide an intellectual stimulus that is difficult to match. In practice, the dynamics of the group and the tutor's handling of it make this technique an unsatisfactory experience for many students. The exceptional tutor may succeed in elevating the seminar to a memorable level of intellectual ferment. Mere mortals might be better advised to try alternative means of achieving the same educational objectives and, in the process, achieve some which they had not previously considered.

Advantages: procedures accepted by general convention, intellectual atmosphere stimulating when well run.

Disadvantages: task rarely clarified; leadership

roles confused; little regard for
social and emotional dimension.

Tutorials

Where the seminar is usually devoted to a critical
and searching discussion of subject matter, the
tutorial, at least as distinguished by the Hale
Report (HMSO, 1964), is concerned with the development of the student's powers of thought.   The
tutor's task is to 'use the subject to what he
considers the best advantage to promote that development'. This distinction is one of emphasis rather
than of strict demarcation.   The tutorial is aimed
towards teaching the subject as well as the student
and the seminar increases the students' intellectual
powers as well as teaching them the subject.
Numbers, however, do seem to be important.   In
a one-to-one tutorial the tutor may focus attention
entirely on work prepared by the student; when the
number of students increases, less and less time
can be devoted to each individual concern and
correspondingly more has to be applied to the
subject matter as a way of spreading the focus.
The tutorial is thus transformed into a seminar: the
Hale Committee chose four as the critical number for
this to happen.

Readers may well recall that four to six
students appears to be the critical number in other
situations, particularly in leaderless groups.
Below that sort of number, no leader is considered
necessary for certain defined tasks.   With more
members, unless a leader is designated, a group may
break into disarray as leadership conflicts are
fought out.   What function then does a tutor serve
in a group whose size does not necessarily justify
a leader?   If the answer is none, then it follows
that the tutor's presence in any tutorial is likely
to be a dominant one.   This is not to suggest that
there is anything inherently wrong with such a
dynamic - it may be very necessary for certain
purposes - but if as tutors we wish to avoid over-
direction of student learning, with its consequent
dependency problems, we may want to consider other
techniques which allow the students more autonomy.
This is never more true than in the one-to-one
tutorial where, in the words of the Hale Committee,
'the inequality of intellectual power and attainment between tutor and pupil is often too great for
any real discussion'.   One-to-one tutorials are
also extravagant in the use of tutors' time - but

that is self-evident.

Tutorials appear to serve three main functions: to provide a regular meeting ground for the checking of student progress, a means of locating misunder- standings in lectures and an opportunity to give special scrutiny to a piece of the student's work. In two, if not three, of these respects the tutorial conforms to an authority-based pattern of learning. However, the pastoral role of the tutor should not be under-valued; in this capacity some tutors manage to combine all the above functions quite happily. They hold a regular meeting with three or four 'tutees' where they look at a piece of written work (not necessarily for submission to them), check what difficulties the students may be experiencing in particular areas, and relate this to any reports they have of students' progress. If they are able to use the group potential skilfully, for instance by getting students to assess each other's written work, they may increasingly divest some of the responsibility for these concerns to the students to the point where the tutorial group becomes a sort of 'learning cell' with the tutor as a resource. In this setting, learning can develop into a more mutually supportive exercise than is typically the case in tutorials.

In science and engineering the word 'tutorial' is often used to describe an exercise class of up to 30 in which students work individually on set problems while the tutor circulates. In a way the exercise class is a form of rotating one-to-one tutorial with all the virtues and drawbacks that entails. The tutor does have a chance to check how students are getting on but many students will be wary of admitting mistakes or lack of effort to the tutor, and can quickly acquire stratagems for avoiding him or her during the all-too-short one hour period that is conventionally allocated to the class. The alert tutor may well choose to divide the class into sub-groups with tasks demanding collaboration between the students alternating with individual work (see Horseshoe Groups on page 95). Readers may find some interesting references on problem-solving in Polya (1957), Wicklegren (1974), Frazer (1977), Woods et al (1977).

Advantages of
Tutorials: focuses attention on individual
                 student work and ways of thinking;
                 helps tutor keep an eye on student
                 progress; provides continuity in

tutor/student relationship.

Disadvantages: can be expensive of tutor time (especially with one-to-one); tutor in dominant role.

Syndicates

A dilemma which commonly faces tutors in seminars is how to exercise control over the content while at the same time giving students room to express their own ideas in their own terms; to a great extent this is resolved in syndicate learning. The technique is described in two articles by Collier (1966 and 1969). The students in small tutorless groups (five to six members in each) are given joint assignments which require reading, discussion and written work. The tutor's first task is to prepare the assignments; these may cover the same ground as a lecture course and comprise a developing sequence of questions and references. Here by way of illustration is part of one of the assignments Collier describes as it is presented to the students:

'Organisation Structure: Principles of Interpretation

1. What are the characteristics of the 'organic' and 'mechanistic' forms of organisation described by Burns & Stalker? In what circumstances does each have advantages? What features of the organisation of Plant Y under Messrs Stewart and Cooley's methods of administration do not come within Burns & Stalker's analysis? See Burns & Stalker: The Management of Innovation, Chapters 5 & 6.

   Revans: Standard for Morale, Chapters 1, 8, 9 & 10
   Guest: Organisational Change, Chapters 2-5
   Thelen: Dynamics of Groups Work, Chapter 4

Some assignments may be considered sufficiently important to be worked on by all the syndicates while others may be covered by some of the syndicates on behalf of the class as a whole. The students distribute the reading, discussing and writing tasks among themselves within the groups, and meet during what would otherwise be a lecture period, to work on the tasks while the tutor circulates among them. Plenary discussions are held at various points during the course. The collection of student views emerges in either a written or an oral report; dissenting opinions where they arise are included. The tutor summarises the reports in a formal lecture suggesting any changes and improvements in the work produced and extending ideas beyond the students' material where appropriate. A final plenary session follows.

The students are thus given both the security of specific content and a clear task, and the freedom to exercise their own skills and judgement in analysing and synthesising information. Collier claims that syndicate learning cuts across any of the fundamental assumptions about teaching and learning which the educational system may have established in the students:

(a)   the students are placed in a situation where, in the first instance, they form views derived from their reading and experience and from discussion with their peers, rather than from the teacher;

(b)   the students form bonds within their syndicates which give them some support in the face of the teacher's authority;

(c)   the relations are no longer controlled by the naked confrontation of the teacher with a number of separate individuals and can thus become more easily personal and informal.

In this way, whereas the teacher's authority in respect of discipline and procedures within the group is either neglected or rejected, his authority as subject expert is, if not intact, then clearly a separate issue to be treated on its own merits. This may of course raise problems for some students who find it difficult to function in groups without the guiding hand of a tutor, but it is equally possible that it is liberating to those students who have problems in expressing themselves freely in the presence of a tutor. Syndicate learning also appears to combine the two ingredients of high motivation - competition between groups leading to cohesion and purpose within them. There is nevertheless a tight prescription of task and the boundaries of knowledge are firmly controlled.

Advantages: combines control of content with freedom in discussion; authority is clearly delegated; groups take pride in achievement, work harder; disparate knowledge is integrated.

Disadvantages: some students (possibly) not able to cope with tutorless groups; discrepancy between kind of learning and assessment methods; overall control of what is learned tends to be un-negotiable.

Case Studies

A standard technique of teaching in Management and Business studies, the case study, is, in a sense a kind of simulation in which the experience is secondhand and probably condensed. The important merit of the case study is that it allows a problem to be studied in a complex form, including elements of real-life events which it might be impossible to reproduce in the classroom. Typically the students are provided with case notes in advance and are expected to prepare their own solution to the problem or problems presented. Case studies open up opportunities for role play (q.v.) where it becomes necessary to shed light on particular encounters rather than general issues. In some ways, case studies have the edge on simulations in that students are not tempted to trivialise; there is, however, little of the sense of risk-free competition and personal involvement which appears to be an inherent part of games and simulations.

The main virtue of case studies is the way in which they can efficiently integrate a wide diversity of subject matter. They are mainly used in Applied Social Sciences but there is no reason why they should not be used to advantage in science and engineering, for instance in respect of socially related issues and design failures. The Open University 'Open' Files of written material on their Technology Foundation and Man-made Futures Courses are excellent examples of this approach. Bignell (1976) is another useful source of 'failure' case studies.

Case studies can also be used as examination questions in order to test a student's power of synthesis (Easton, 1982).

Advantages: integrative - encourages a 'broad view'; develops a sense of objectivity; demands tolerance of several points of view.

Disadvantages: requires some maturity and prior experience of students; makes heavy demands on the tutor in holding the discussion together; is time-consuming.

Peer Tutoring

It is clear that a lot of teaching is done in courses by the students themselves - perhaps more than many teachers would wish to recognise. In laboratory groups for example it is quite common to see students explaining points to each other and helping one another over basic misconceptions and more advanced problems. Not quite so apparent is the mutual help and support which exists outside the curriculum in the refectory, the halls of residence or in the library.

Peer Tutoring is a way of harnessing these valuable processes within the bounds of the curriculum. According to Goldschmid & Goldschmid (1976), peer tutoring can be supported on the following grounds:

socio-psychological - it offers close personal contact in an otherwise remote environment; pedagogical - students are active as learners, teaching enhances learning for the 'tutor', and there is increased co-operation, motivation and self-esteem; economic - a saving on staff time and energy; political - it helps students effectively adjust to the curriculum as a 'system'.

Examples of different models of peer tutoring are:

(a)   senior students acting as regular seminar leaders;
(b)   'proctors' who help test and guide more junior students through a programme of individualised instruction;
(c)   self-directed student groups;
(d)   the learning cell, in which students in pairs alternately ask and answer questions on commonly read material.

(e) parrainage* where older students counsel incoming freshmen firstly over practical matters to do with settling in, and later over study problems.

Because they have long been trained in the passive 'reception of information' and in 'success through competition' students may need to be inducted to the academic and social skills necessary for peer tutoring. Moreover not all students will be suited to the role of peer tutor and in some of the above schemes care may have to be exercised in both role choice and training. In others, everyone will perforce be involved in the operation. For further reading on Peer Tutoring see Cornwall (1979) and Boud (1981).

Advantages: student is actively involved - learns by teaching; integration of students into course facilitated; inexpensive.

Disadvantages: students require training - needs regular monitoring; not all students good at it; may demand constant staff supervision for success.

Projects

Put simply, a project is a learning task in which the students have choice of topic and direction and whose outcome is therefore unpredictable. It demands initiative, creativity and organising skills of the students: they are required to produce a report, plan or design which comprises the solution to a problem. In pursuit of this goal the students have a considerable amount of time to develop their own learning strategies according to where the project takes them and generally rely on a supportive relationship with a tutor/supervisor.

Projects are thus more of an educational strategy than a technique, as they involve a comprehensively different philosophy of learning. Students are responsible (to a greater or lesser extent) for the direction and range of the work they undertake, which may carry them beyond the tutor's own area of subject expertise either in breadth or depth. Consequently projects are likely to create all

*the nearest translation from the original French is 'sponsorship'

manner of anxieties in both tutor and students as
to direction, progress and personal competence.
Various studies of project work (SRHE, 1974 and
Jaques, 1980 and 1981) show a fairly consistent
pattern of events. Sinclair Goodlad (1978) summarises these in UTMU: Improving Teaching in Higher
Education:

> 'First, students should be actively involved
> in the choice of the subject; this increases
> their involvement with the task. Secondly, the
> student should be encouraged to discover for
> himself the implications of the constraints of
> conceptual fruitfulness in the discipline,
> availability of resources (library informa-
> tion) or institutional arrangement. It is a
> delicate task for the tutor to strike a balance
> between over-direction of a student's work
> (which can destroy the distinctive benefits of
> project methods) and under-direction (which can
> lead the student into muddle and frustration).
> Thirdly, some teachers have found that a
> student's enthusiasm is closely related to the
> production of documents - high at the beginning
> (when an outline and bibliography are being
> prepared) and at the end (when the final pres-
> entation is being fabricated), but low to
> the point of despair during the period of
> gestation. It has been found wise to arrange
> an input of teaching (presentation of ideas at
> a seminar, brainstorming session, simulations,
> discussion of rough draft, etc.) in the middle
> of the lifespan of a project and just at the
> beginning.'

Group projects present students with two additional problems. One is that the choice of partners
is often confused with the choice of topic and tutor
and this may be too much for students to unravel -
a bit like choosing who to marry and where to work
at the same time! It is not unusual to find a group
project resolving itself into a collection of individual, if related, tasks.

One procedure for tackling this problem is
operated at the City University in Electrical
Engineering (Edwards, 1980) where groups are
organised as follows:

> 1. Topics of interest to the class are
>   listed

2. The topics are whittled down, through discussion, to a small number

3. Each student ranks the topics in order of personal preference

4. The course tutor then allocates topics to students according to these preferences: the groups are thus constituted

5. Tutors' names are not revealed or allocated till the groups are established

In another rather different scheme at Worcester Polytechnic Institute, Massachusetts, the tutors advertise the projects they are prepared to supervise, or a starting point from which they will negotiate, and in some cases attach persuasive posters to their doors!

On the other hand it might be preferable to allow the project to emerge as an expression of the combined interests of preselected groups. The tutor in this case might, having formed the groups, give them a file of papers covering a range of issues (e.g. Open University files)* and then assist them in the formulation of a problem to be solved, perhaps using another OU resource, the PIG Problem Identification Game (OU, 1975). Of course this pre-supposes there is no 'hassle' about who teams up with whom. Either the grouping must be done arbitrarily according to some principle (e.g. random selection or heterogeneous mix) or the students must take part in a team-building exercise such as 'Card Exchange' described on page 275.

The second problem about group projects arises both logically and psychologically out of the first. Notwithstanding the use of a clarifying procedure for selecting topics and projects, it may in many circumstances be too much to ask a group of students to handle both the uncertainties of project work and the problems of working in a team concurrently. Aware of this problem, tutors at Delft in Holland offer their project students in Town Planning a prior training course in group dynamics and team-work. However, prior training has to be followed

*Several 'Files' or 'Case Studies' have been produced by the Open University, on problematical issues, as 'supplementary' material to their course units.

up with procedures for monitoring the unfolding progress of the group if it is to be of enduring benefit. If learning about teamwork is one of the critical aims of the project then students might learn much through monitoring the group process, not merely about the personal and collective problems of teamwork, but of their priorities as individual learners. Various checklists and exercises (see pages 226 et seq) should be of help in this respect. So might the keeping of a group diary or logbook which could form the basis of a commentary on the work of the project to be submitted, but which is not assessed, with the project report. If, on the other hand, the students are being asked to learn about teamwork issues the hard way', one may wish to give them some help with their programming of the work - it is all a matter of time and priorities. A more elaborate form of the diary idea is the portfolio: 'a permanent record of a personal journey' and 'a basis for continuing reflection' (Boud et al 1985). The portfolio can include ideas, pictures, cuttings and reflective comments on these. It works best when treated as confidential.

The following planning guide is used at Mount Royal College at Calgary in Canada.

'On Page ..., you find a graph containing a breakdown of the approximate percentage of time taken by each major project phase. Although the percentages will vary, depending on the amount of research necessary and the type of medium chosen, the graph will give you a general idea of how much time to spend on each phase. Use this graph to complete the "Flow Chart" on the next page. (Fig 6.4)

Before you begin Phase I of this guide, determine specific dates for the completion of tasks noted in the flow chart. Do this in consultation with your instructor. The use of the flow chart in the planning process will virtually assure you of completing your project on schedule. A Word of Caution: You may not have time to do certain projects which involve complex productions. If you are not sure, check with your instructor.'

There follow the Phase Group and Flow Chart shown overleaf.

Tasks and Techniques

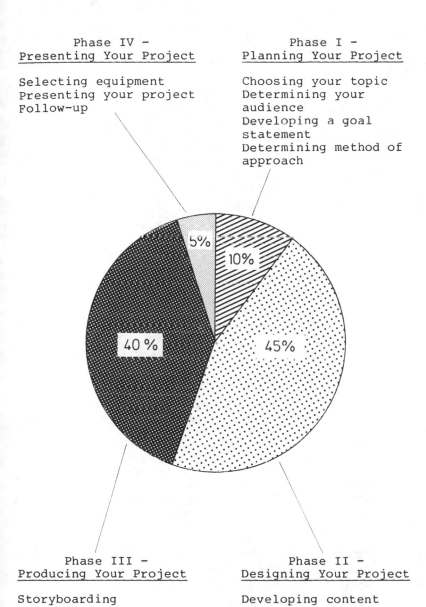

Phase IV -
Presenting Your Project

Selecting equipment
Presenting your project
Follow-up

Phase I -
Planning Your Project

Choosing your topic
Determining your
audience
Developing a goal
statement
Determining method of
approach

Phase III -
Producing Your Project

Storyboarding
Scripting
Producing audio
and visual components

Phase II -
Designing Your Project

Developing content
Research
Organising content
Selecting media
Developing evaluation

Fig. 6.4 Phase Group for Project Work

113

FLOW CHART

Dead-line	Project Phase		Instructor's Initials
	Phase I –	Planning your Project	
	Step 1 –	Choosing your topic	
	Step 2 –	Identifying your target audience	
	Step 3 –	Developing a goal statement	
	Step 4 –	Determining your method of approach	
	Phase II –	Designing Your Content	
	Step 5 –	Developing your content material	
		Stage A – Determining relevant questions	
		Stage B – Selecting appropriate resources	
		Stage C – Researching your project	
(Research Completed)		Stage D – Writing a content outline	
	Step 6 –	Selecting the most appropriate medium	
	Step 7 –	Evaluating your project	
	Phase III –	Producing Your Project	
	Step 8 –	Preparing your storyboard	
	Step 9 –	Writing your script	
	Step 10 –	Preparing audio materials	
	Step 11 –	Preparing visual materials	
(Production Completed)			
	Phase IV –	Presenting Your Project	
	Step 12 –	Selecting your equipment	
	Step 13 –	Presenting your project	
(Presentation Date)			
	Step 14 –	Following up the presentation	

Fig. 6.5 Flow Chart for Planning Project Work

Projects offer students a unique chance to develop skills and capacities that might never be apparent in other kinds of learning. They give students feedback on their ability to handle freedom in relation to the constraints of the outside world, to cope with real problems, and, if all goes well, to build up a continuing interest in them beyond the completion of their studies. The learning potential of projects is therefore enormous. Group projects add the further benefits of pooling resources, division of labour and the enjoyment of interpersonal learning. However, assessment, yet again, presents a problem. It is very difficult to compare one student with another when the report is the result of a group effort. Students differ in their skills, their rates and levels of working, and their styles of learning. Who is to say the student who held them together and constantly inspired the group yet contributed nothing to the report should receive no academic reward? There is at least one method in use for dealing with this problem (see pages 207, 208). It makes sense nevertheless for a group project to be assessed according to criteria that demand a co-operative effort and that these criteria should be clearly negotiated with the group near the start of the project or, at the very least, before irrevocable decisions are made.

A clear step forward in clarifying goals, relationships and responsibilities in project work is the use of a learning contract. Knowles (1975 and 1979) describes contracts for self-directed learning which are evolved through a set of class discussions. The contract comprises Learning Goals, Strategies and Sources, Evidence of Accomplishment and Criteria and Means of Measuring Accomplishment. Heron (1981) proposes a scheme for self-monitoring and assessment which, though less clearly prescribed, is clearly worth considering in projects where one of the critical aims is for students to learn about themselves as learners.

The kind of learning that can be achieved in project work, given commitment, energy and imagination from all concerned, is potentially vast in both variety and depth. Our understanding of the processes and their scope nevertheless has a long way to go.

Advantages: freedom to study at depth and in breadth; chance to tackle real problems, provide solutions that can be tested in 'real world';

learning active; comprehensive challenge to students.

Disadvantages: things can go radically wrong; challenge and freedom too much for some students - some tutors not able to function in non-directive role or outside area of subject expertise; assessment a problem.

Games and Simulations

There is a growing interest at all stages of education in techniques which allow students to act out the problems and issues under discussion and to make decisions about them based on a more personal understanding of their nature and implications. If we were to take a cynical view this interest might be viewed as a response to the sense of alienation among students towards the learning of knowledge as if it existed independently of them and for purposes (examinations) extrinsic to the knowledge itself. From a more positive standpoint the interest in games could result from a recognition that enactment of issues can serve to integrate even pedestrian knowledge into the framework of values, beliefs and even the personal behaviour of students. The medium for this 'gestalt' is the imagination, that faculty of mind so often written off because of its association with fun and the supposedly childish connotations that holds. The assumptions which underpin this argument were exposed over half a century ago by Dewey (1916):

'- the difference between play and what is regarded as serious employment should not be a difference between the presence and absence of imagination, but a difference in the materials with which the imagination is occupied. The result (of overlooking this) is an unwholesome exaggeration of the fantastic and 'unreal' phases of childish play and a deadly reduction of serious occupation to a routine efficiency prized simply for its external tangible results.'

In the UK this split between work and play was further reinforced by the Victorian ethic which regarded work as a virtue and play as an indulgence to be enjoyed once 'penance' had been done. Though it may be strange to think of this ethic prevailing in tertiary education of the 1980's we have only to think of the silence and respect demanded in lectures or the seriousness of discussion in seminars to be reminded of its enduring nature.

Part, or even all, of the problem appears to be tied up in the high esteem for the rational, with equivalent disregard for the emotional, experience of learning. 'Emotive learning', as Dewey calls it, provides 'unity or integrity of experience'. It allows 'art, science and politics (to) reinforce one another in an enriched temper of mind instead of constituting ends pursued at one another's response'.

Before we discuss the games and simulations as techniques, a few definitions are called for. The word _game_ is usually taken to describe a group exercise in which players co-operate or compete towards a given end within a regime of explicit rules. Players behave as themselves (even if they do display exceptional behaviour at times!). Cricket, chess and charades are obvious examples of popular games; educational games include 'The Colour Game' (six people with hidden agendas have to agree on a colour), 'Back to Back' (where a drawing is described so that a back-to-back partner can draw a copy) and 'Starpower' (players trade tokens to acquire power). Games are generally given no real-life context and people act as themselves. A game becomes a _simulation_ when a scenario is provided - it thus constitutes a simplified representation of life. The scenario might be a public meeting, a classroom, or a radio station. If play is not prescribed by rules then it is usually shaped by _roles_, and the roles may be fixed:

'You are the city architect who has been fighting a losing battle over the provision of pedestrian precincts.'

or free, where people act themselves in a given situation. Sometimes roles are written as aims:

'Your aim is to become chairman.'

What is described as _role play_, is often therefore an exercise in which interpersonal encounters can be explored with some degree of freedom. Whereas in games the interplay occurs within a pattern of clear and often artificial rules, in role play what happens is governed by the implicit rules of everyday life in a defined situation.

117

All of these definitions are a matter of degree and balance - combinations abound. It is possible for instance to have a simulation in which communication between groups is governed by rules, where the activity in the groups is determined by roles and where each group has a singular objective to fulfil in competition with the others. Most simulations are covered by the following diagrammatic model.

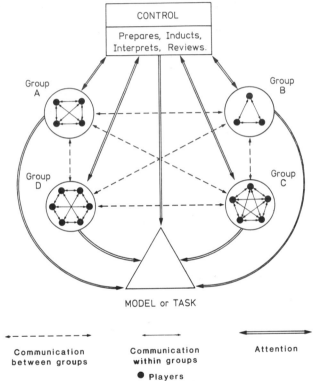

Fig. 6.6 Diagrammatic Model of Games and Simulations

This model may be contracted or expanded to suit. As depicted here it comprises a number of groups A, B, C and D, each with a goal and possibly a shared role (e.g. a pressure group). The inter-group communication may replicate what happens in real life (e.g. if there is a hierarchical relation-ship there might be more communication channels available 'downwards' than 'upwards'). The rel-ations between each group may be ordained by roles. Each group's attention is focused on a model which may be a concrete object (e.g. a 'Lego' town), or map, or an imagined problem scenario. The task of the tutor in a simulation/game is usually that of referee (though this may be delegated) who plays a benign 'God', and who supervises the setting up, smooth running and de-briefing of the exercise. All of these operations require qualities often ascribed to a deity - prediction, an element of mystery, apparent control of events, the creation of ad hoc roles and rules, and not always answering requests.

De-briefing, the review of a game or simulation is the most important part of the task education-ally. This reflective discussion helps students to generalise from their particular experience and to think beyond the immediate experience. The following pattern for de-briefing is one which seems to put the students' learning into perspective.

(a) How are you feeling right now?* (Often this needs to be asked in order to tap some of the emotional charge of the exercise.)

(b) What was going on in the simulation? Who achieved what? What different perceptions were there of what happened?

(c) What did players learn about themselves, each other, social groups, social systems, limitations of science and so forth?

(d) What did the simulation tell them about the 'real world'?

(e) How did it parallel the 'real world'?

(f) How could the simulation be improved?

(g) How is everyone feeling now*?

(h) What might you do differently as a result of your experience in the simulations?

The de-briefing discussion, though typically conducted as a plenary, can often be enlivened by dividing the class into sub-groups, especially ones

*These are particularly important questions to put when, by accident or design, a lot of intense feelings have been aroused.

whose membership cuts across the grouping in the simulation. Following the de-briefing the often loose and variable learning can be better tied up and consolidated with students in syndicates or task-orientated groups with tasks like:

(a) discuss and report back on generalised insights

(b) make links with learning from more traditional sources: lectures, reading, for instance.

or, if it can be video-recorded:

(c) a video-playback to look at why's and wherefore's of interaction in the simulation (a step-by-step discussion (q.v.) works well here).

Games and simulations are considered to be particularly valuable in promoting social and professional skills: communicating, role-taking, problem solving, leading, decision-making, and so on, not to speak of their less academic but more affecting function in opening the eyes of participants to what it feels like to be in someone else's position. Games and simulations are also claimed, with good justification, to increase the level of motivation and interest in the subject matter, develop a greater sense of self-awareness and personal power, and create a freer and more democratic climate. As for cognitive learning, apart from the impact of all the above in energising the learning process, they can facilitate the understanding of relationships between separate areas of subject matter, particularly those where personal action is demanded. Nevertheless without the consolidating effect of de-briefing and further tasks a lot of this learning may remain only half realised.

The number of possible permutations of the game and simulations format is vast; as varied, one might suppose, as life itself. Ready-made and tested exercises with full instructions for the tutor/organiser are available from a variety of sources. Reference to these may be found in books such as Davison and Gordon (1977), Krupar (1973), Taylor & Walford (1972) and Pfeiffer & Jones (1972, 73, 74, 75, 76, 78, 79, 80, 81, 82, 83 & 85). The Society for the Advancement of Games and Simulations in Education and Training (SAGSET) includes many examples in its journal, 'Simulations/Games for Learning' and produces resource lists for different subject areas. Should readers want to design their own exercise, some helpful advice may be found in Stadsklev (1974) Davison & Gordon, and Chesler & Fox (1966). Such an exercise could come under any of the following categories, or combinations of them:

> Public Meeting
> Assessor's Panel
> Communication Network
> Competitive or Co-operative Interaction in Group
> Committee Role play
> Critical Interactions Role play
> Board Game
> In-tray Exercise
> Card Game (usually with Rummy rules)

Guided fantasy is another and more economical way of simulating, provided the participants find it acceptable.

Finally, as an indication of the scope of games and simulations, here are descriptions of three exercises covering different formats and subject areas.

Star River Project: Eight interest groups, including industry, the local authority and residents are involved in a series of joint meetings to prepare and negotiate their cases on the planning development of a river estuary. They must also process a lot of scientific and technical information (political, economic, social, historical, biological and chemical) in order to present their case at a final public meeting. A newspaper covers events and keeps all informed on policy trends.

This simulation aims to develop an understanding of the conflicting issues that arise in planning a community's environment. It requires upwards of 20 participants and lasts anything from three to eight hours.

Moco: Four players in competing pairs choose various elements of an engineering structure which are represented by plastic magnetic pieces designed to stick on a metal board. Each pair then tries to complete as high a scoring structure as possible using some or all of the elements according to specified conditions. The first pair to finish scores an extra point, but must submit their structure to inspection by their opponents. Participants are thus compelled to apply their understanding of the 'nature' of structures to the problem in question without involving themselves in the detailed and more remote analytical calculations. The duration of MOCO depends on how many rounds are played.

For a description of the game see Cowan & Morton (1973).

Role-Reversal: This involves an improvised role play. Participants are invited to recount an incident or continuing problem to do with their social or personal life. The problem might, for instance, be that every time a student goes to see his tutor he gets the feeling he is not welcome and ends up tongue-tied and frustrated. In the role play the student would first be asked to describe the encounter, and then be invited to play the role of the tutor in question; another student is asked to be the one with the problem. The roles are thus switched and this enables the 'student' to experience the nature of the problem from the tutor's point of view. The original student, it is hoped, will gain insight into not only what his own behaviour may provoke in the tutor, but also into the frame of mind of the tutor and how he, the student, might tackle the problem more constructively. Variations on this strategy may be the introduction of the 'alter-ego's' who either advise or take the place of the role players at agreed junctures, or the re-enacting of critical moments, perhaps using video playback in order to explore alternative tactics. The tutor/student relationship is but one example of this role play. It can be used for any number of encounters where things are perceived to go wrong. Any role play may be conducted either by the central players only, with the rest of the class watching, or simultaneously by several small groups. Role play is a particularly helpful technique when, in discussing a social or professional issue, it becomes apparent that interpersonal behaviour is a significant and casual factor. Role-reversal requires at least half an hour to set up and run. It would be impossible to put a time on the process of de-briefing.

Role play used in this manner can sometimes be a bit threatening to participants. In a sense they are on stage and the rest of the group or class is watching them. Gibbs (1984) describes a peer learning method in which participants, working in <u>tutorless sub-groups</u>, take full responsibility for their own role play and de-briefing. For the scenario described above for example the roles of tutor, student and observer(s) would be designated and rotated in groups of three for as many cycles as needed. The observer(s) would be responsible for the time boundaries and the de-briefing.

It is sometimes said that games and simulations are manipulative in that they constrain people to behave according to the designer's model of reality with all its attendant values. This is an indisputable danger, but can readily be countered through a proper de-briefing in which such issues are brought out.

Games and simulations can, as may already be apparent, be used within a scheduled group meeting or at a specially convened, extended, session. As such they can be of great value as a stimulus for further discussion or in illuminating particular issues. Alternatively they may be used to bind together the disintegrated elements of a course either in the form of a grand finale or by constructing the whole course as a 'partial' simulation in which students participate only at certain scheduled times and otherwise work on tasks demanded by or related to the simulation. For the imaginative teacher there is no end to the possible variations in the style and scope of games, role plays and simulations.

Advantages of
Games and
Simulations: experience is first hand and concentrated; motivation intrinsic to activity, learning well retained; high level of interest; removes teacher-student polarisation; learning occurs at divers levels.

Disadvantages: time-consuming, demands a lot of preparation; some students don't or won't participate; colleagues regard games as trivial; materials often expensive, learning unpredictable and difficult to evaluate; dangers of hurtful stress in some, especially where not carefully handled by tutor.

As a footnote, readers may like to learn that three publications, Lewis & Mee 1981, Jaques in Cryer (1982) and Van Ments (1983) give clear counsel to tutors in the handling of role play and similar 'experiential' exercises.

Free or Associative Discussion

The benefits of giving people freedom in a controlled environment to talk about whatever comes to mind have long been understood in psychoanalysis and group therapy. The therapist is trained to listen and generally to refrain from comment while the patient 'freely associates', thus revealing underlying patterns of thought and feeling. Free discussion operates on a similar principle. The tutor says very little but encourages spontaneity of speech among the students. What the tutor does say is by way of directing students' attention to anomalies and inconsistencies in what they have said, pointing out patterns and relevances in what might otherwise seem a vague and rambling discussion, and helping them 'to see themselves as capable of change' (Abercrombie, 1979).

Although free discussion may comprise a great number of apparently random exchanges, its permissiveness allows the student to become increasingly aware of some of the habitual attitudes and assumptions which to a large extent determine his ways of thinking about the subject. McLeish (1974) states that:

'Students discover, in the course of discussion, that they have highly specific, even idiosyncratic reactions to problems, to situations, to individuals; that they always slow down their ability to solve problems. An understanding of the nature of knowledge, and self insight, is given them in a manner no other teaching method can provide. It is first hand, personal experience of the shifting character of experience, the ambiguity of evidence, the tenuous nature of our most profound convictions.'

In these senses free discussion is a means to intellectual growth - the sort of personal development that Perry describes as students move from the dualistic to the relativistic phases, and even onward to commitment (see page 42-3). The tutor's job is not to correct mistakes (other participants quickly pick up this task) but, with a good sense of timing, to inject comment on the nature of the argument; otherwise to listen attentively. By clearly specifying the aims and by intermittently restating them in the context of what is being said, the tutor sets a direction. By occasionally expressing feelings - 'I don't know what I've done to shut you all up' - the tutor encourages a recognition of the important part that emotions play in our thinking; by referring to his or her own habits when students are talking about theirs, and encouraging 'oscillation of attention between different contexts', e.g. from the present group to the whole class or profession, the tutor promotes the transfer of learning and a reflexive understanding of problems. The tutor's role is therefore to clarify the field of discourse and set its boundaries as well as to draw associations within the general aim. For this reason Abercrombie expresses preference of the word 'associative' rather than 'free' to describe the group discussion.

In her earlier book 'The Anatomy of Judgement' - a classic text which merits study by all teachers and students - Abercrombie (1969) describes tasks set to groups of medical students. The tasks were designed to elucidate 'for the participants some of the factors that had affected their judgement on scientific matters'. Each of the tasks was of course undertaken in the climate of free/associative discussion.

Task 1.   Students were shown two similar but different radiographs and asked to 'list the differences you can see between the two hands'.

Task 2.   Students were given a short extract from a book in which the words 'normal' and 'average' occurred. They were asked to 'Write what you think the author means by these terms and give all definitions of 'normal' you can think of'.

Task 3.   Write a short essay on classification and discuss in the group.

Task 4.   Students first read a scientific

paper reporting an experiment and its conclusions. They were then asked to answer the following:

1. Quote a statement which summarises what the author claims she has discovered.

2. Compare this with observation actually made.

3. How could you set out to test the hypothesis that...
(Author's hypothesis stated).

The students were thus being asked to reveal how they interpreted, ordered, commented and judged scientific information, and to improve in and through the process. Several students claimed this caused them to think seriously and to continue doing so well beyond the group session. In some cases it appeared that the time effect was delayed by months. One student claimed that it was two years after he had finished the course before he understood it. It was remarked that the course helped students express themselves clearly, to understand what others were saying and to listen. The last, as Abercrombie remarks, is a much neglected skill.

A variation of the free/associative group model was used by Smythe & Besly on a basic Biology course in Sydney. The tutor was originally placed <u>outside</u> the group and the students were told she was <u>present</u> only as a resource and would not enter discussion unless the whole group agreed it was necessary. Later a five-minute limit for 'non-intervention' by the tutor was introduced. Tasks ranged from the arrangement of specimens, diagrams or cards to intriguing questions: 'Was Jack's Beanstalk possible?'. Two of the themes that come through strongly in all the literature on these groups are the somewhat painful silences that accompany the transition of the students from dependency to responsibility, and the need for some sort of training for tutors in what is a very unnatural role for most. The authority/dependency conflict is one which is deeply rooted in the culture of teaching and learning. It takes a lot of courage, care and personal insight to handle it successfully.

Advantages: promotes intellectual growth, greater student responsibility for learning, encourages flexibility, has long-term value.

Disadvantages: apparently rambling kind of discussion, time needed for adjustment to process, learning difficult to assess by traditional means as often very internal.

Brainstorming

This is the best known and most frequently employed procedure to stimulate creative thinking. It was devised by Osborn as long ago as 1938 in reaction to much of the cramped thinking he saw being applied to the solution of problems at business meetings. In fact, it is only one part of a creative problem-solving procedure: that designed to generate ideas. The full procedure, includes the following stages:

fact finding
idea finding
solution finding

Fact finding involves the definition and preparation of problems; definition in the picking out and refining of the problem; preparation in the gathering and analysing of relevant data. Idea finding deals with the production and development of ideas through brainstorming. Solution finding relates to the evaluation of tentative solutions and the choosing and implementation of the agreed one.

The two main principles of brainstorming are the Deferment of Judgement: evaluation and criticism inhibit the freedom of creative thinking, and Quantity breeds Quality: based on the premise that we have to work through conventional ideas before we can get to original ones.

During brainstorming sessions four rules operate:

Criticism is ruled out - any attempt at evaluation must quickly be ruled out of order; this also includes discussion as it usually raises doubts and qualifications.
'Free-wheeling' is welcomed - the wilder the idea the better. 'It is easier to tame down

127

than to think up (ideas).'
<u>Quantity is wanted</u> - the more ideas suggested,
the greater the likelihood of an original one
coming up.
<u>Combination and improvement are sought</u> - parti-
cipants are encouraged to build on and improve
each others' ideas and combine them to form new
ideas.

The participants in a brainstorming session
should ideally have knowledge of the problem areas
though not be too close to the problem, and be of
such a mix as to provide a variety of experience and
personal style.   Osborn regards the ideal size of
group as 'about a dozen' and this is the experience
of most practitioners.   The leader must be both
alert and pushing yet be able to maintain a friendly
and informal atmosphere.   A typical session might
proceed as follows:

1.   The leader makes sure that the problem has
       been properly defined and background
       information prepared.

2.   Having arranged everyone so that open
       communication can take place, the leader
       runs a warm-up session (especially for
       novitiates).   For this purpose the leader
       may place an object, e.g. a plastic
       beaker, brick, paper clip into the middle
       of the floor and invite a quick generation
       of ideas on possible uses of the object.
       In order to free members from the usual
       inhibitions he or she might throw in some
       less conventional ideas: very often those
       of a lavatorial, aggressive or sexual
       nature have an astounding effect!

3.   The leader reminds everyone of the rules
       and principles and prepares to write up on
       a board or large sheet a title for each
       of the contributions; constantly pushes
       for more, proposing own ideas where
       necessary, stimulates further lines of
       thought by asking how the 'thing' could
       be changed in terms of colour, shape,
       motion, etc.

In a brainstorming session on the problem of
'How to Remove Oil Slicks from the Surface of the

Sea' the dialogue might go as follows:

- Burn it
  (write 'burn it')
- Let it get washed ashore and scrape it up off the beaches
  (write up 'scrape beaches')
- Sink it with sand
  (write 'sink with sand')
- Blow it out to sea
  (write 'blow out to sea')
- That won't get rid of it
  (reprimand for evaluating)
- Soak it up with seagulls
  (write 'soak with seagulls')
- Harness it to seagulls
  (write 'harness to seagulls')
- Train gulls to dive down and suck it up into straws and drop these into a waiting tanker
  (what shall we write down for that? - sucking gulls!)

and so on.

5. The ideas may be evaluated by the same group, a completely different one, or a mixture of the two. As a first step it is often fruitful to ask 'What is the wildest idea on the list?' and try to translate this into a practical proposal. Other ideas are then given a more practical bent and subsequently classified in terms of cost, simplicity, feasibility, acceptibility, etc.

6. Finally, discussion focuses on the implementation of the chosen solution(s).

Brainstorming has been well tried and successfully proved in the production of creative solutions to real-life problems. In an education system which generally pays much lip service to creativity but does little to actively promote it, the very simplicity and quickness of this technique makes it well worth a try, especially in design, project work or other areas where open-ended problems are of consequence.

Advantages: Simple, easy to learn; good fun; can easily be generalised to include many aspects of life.

Disadvantages: Can be facile and unproductive; some
people unable to function in it.

Synectics

A more structured and thorough scheme for creative
problem solving was developed by Gordon (1961 and
1971) and Prince (1970). Synectics is built around
many of the psychological states known to be helpful
in overcoming blocks to creative thinking. It uses
analogies and metaphors, encourages a wide range of
ideas, and pays particular attention to the role
of the leader in this. The 'psychological states'
are:

(a) <u>involvement and detachment</u> – an oscillation between close personal resonance with
the problem and detachment from it

(b) <u>deferment</u> - avoiding the danger of the
quick and superficial solution

(c) <u>speculation</u> - the freedom to let ideas
flow easily

(d) <u>hedonistic response</u> – a recognition that
the feeling aroused, as a solution is
approached, is an indication of where
the discussion should go

These psychological states are induced through a
series of 'operational mechanisms' which serve to
'make the familiar strange': people are distanced
from the problem in order to free them from their
prior concepts of it - or 'making the strange
familiar' in order to bring them closer to it. The
operational mechanisms are:

(i) <u>Personal Analogy</u>: each person is invited to
imagine themselves to be the object under consideration, to merge themself with its physical existence.
In the case of a concrete object such as a spring,
or an oil slick (the problem is being considered)
the individual would attempt to feel the tension,
the glutinousness, or whatever. With personal and
social problems role play may do the same thing.
     In personal analogy group members are asked
first to describe the facts about their identified-
with-object, its everyday experience and how it
feels about its existence.

(ii)   Direct Analogy: now the group thinks of instances where comparable modes of operation, function or movement exist.   The oft-cited case is that of Brunel getting his idea for the design of caissons from seeing shipworms tunnelling into wood.

(iii) Symbolic Analogy: here the emphasis is on finding a visual or metaphorical image which helps to free the mind from the constraints of literal thinking.   One group used the Indian rope trick as a symbolic analogy for the design of a jacking device to fit into a box four inches square.

(iv)   Fantasy Analogy: the value of fantasy is in the way it can act as a releasing mechanism for the unconscious motives and wishes we all have.   Fantasy analogy is based on Freud's notion that creative work is the result of 'wish fulfilment'.   It is an effective way of making the familiar strange.   The group is asked to abolish their rational understanding of the object or problem and indulge in daydreaming.   For instance members might be asked, in tackling the problem of inventing a vapour-proof closure for space-suits, 'How in your wildest fantasies do you want the closure to operate?' Alternatively the group may be led into a story fantasy based on how the initiator of the concern senses the problem.   The 'hedonistic' responses (see page 130) are picked out to see what they reveal. In a synectics session on how to design a training workshop for administrators a fantasy story led into the notion of poodle dogs floating down from the sky by parachute.   This was quickly 'forced' into the somewhat more practical proposal that random individual tasks be 'showered' upon participants at the beginning of each day.

Unusual techniques abound in Synectics. Because creative thinking is essentially a free-flowing and undisciplined process, structure has been built in to help clarify and emphasise what is happening.   The interested reader should refer to Stein (1975) for a review of all the procedures of Synectics as well as the original work of Gordon and Prince.

Apart from its use for stimulating creative thinking, Synectics has potential for more general learning purposes.   For instance in metaphorical thinking for 'unsticking' discussion (cf Pirsig, 1974) students are encouraged to suggest what something is like e.g. the influence of Socrates on the Athenians — maybe a river cutting into a bank of clay — and to play with that for a while.   This approach seems to have been particularly successful with under-achieving students. It has even been used with success in the teaching of philosophy.

The role (described by Prince) of the Synectics leader in facilitating the creative process is illuminating to a host of group dynamic problems. Prince is concerned, as is Osborn, about the effect of prematurely evaluating ideas in a problem-solving group and in avoiding comment on their negative aspects. He offers the following advice to the leader:

1. 'Never go into competition with your team' - everyone else's ideas have precedence over the leader's.

2. 'Be a 200% listener to your team members' - in order to understand someone's view the leader might paraphrase or build on it.

3. 'Do not permit anyone to be put on the defensive' - there is value in what everyone offers and the leader's job is to find it; those seeking negative aspects should be asked what it is they like or would prefer.

4. 'Keep the energy level high' - the leader should be alert, interested, involved and demonstrate this with his body movements; he should use humour, challenge and surprise.

5. 'Use every member of your team' - verbose members should be thanked rather quickly after a contribution, their eyes avoided when inviting a response and if all else fails, talked to frankly; quiet members should be brought in.

6. 'Do not manipulate your team' - whatever ideas of his own the leader may want to have adopted he should work towards the group over solutions being reached; his job is to keep them informed on their stage in the synectics process.

7. 'Keep your eye on the client' - the person presenting the problem should be constantly referred to.

8.   'Keep in mind that you are not permanent'
      - the leader is the servant of the group,
      and must keep lines of communication open
      and emphasise imagination and flexibility;
      assuming that traditional leaders accrue
      power and that everyone wants the role,
      the leadership should be rotated.

Synectics is both a problem-solving technique
and a means of training people to be more creative.
In utilising so many of the conscious, preconscious
and even unconscious psychological mechanisms of
human ability it appears to stimulate hard work,
spontaneity and a happy connection between the
rational and the emotional. For these reasons some
of its procedures carry lessons for us in the more
straight-laced context of tertiary education.

Advantages: Taps subconscious mental processes,
              stimulates creative thinking, people
              work hard and intensively; provides
              clear procedures.

Disadvantages: Demands considerable skill and time;
               is unusual - not usually germane to
               academic learning.

Why Have Variety?

As explained at the beginning of the section this
list of techniques is by no means exhaustive and
there are undoubtedly many others which could lay
claim to inclusion. Nevertheless they do embody a
multitude of principles and procedures for groupwork, many of which might be combined or used in
sequence by the versatile tutor. Their inclusion
within the repertoire of a tutor is no guarantee
of success - external issues and personal factors
may be paramount. Yet the value of acquiring a
repertoire of tasks and techniques seems undeniable
for the following reasons, if not more:

1.   Students' learning styles vary, and
      implicit in each of the activities
      described is a different approach to
      learning.   (Ramsden in Marton et al, 1984)

2.   Each student needs variety of stimulus
      and experience.

3.   As students develop intellectually and

133

emotionally a change in their relationship to knowledge and its 'agent', the teacher, is necessary.

4.   It is possible to cast the teaching and learning net over a wider range of aims than would otherwise be feasible.

5.   Students who have experienced a variety of approaches to learning and to human interaction should achieve increased choice and awareness in ways of working in later life.

6.   It is impossible to predict the way any teaching/learning interaction will go: a tutor therefore needs to be adaptable and resourceful to maintain interest and momentum.

7.   In making choices and exercising a wider range of skills the tutor becomes more alert.

8.   Evaluative feedback is easier: a student can make critical remarks about a procedure without seeming to criticise the tutor.

But perhaps more important than becoming skilled in a variety of tasks and techniques is our resourcefulness in any specific situation. How do we handle the knotty problems? Can we recognise the part we are playing in any interpersonal relationship? Are we able to find time, space and a clear head to make decisions about what to do and when to do it? We shall, I hope, make some progress towards answering these questions in the next chapter.

Discussion Points

° List as many group tasks as you can that might encourage people to understand and apply the ideas in this book.
° Draw up a chart of the various techniques described in this chapter according to aims, tutor's role, special skills, etc.
° What would you look for as evidence of success for each of the techniques described? Why?

7

THE TUTOR'S JOB

Whatever theory or research evidence makes sense, its translation into practice is a complicated and tentative process. Our good intentions are often difficult to put into effect even where we know what is necessary to achieve them. In the process of realising our aims we may find ourselves stuck in patterns of communication and interaction which fail to realise the full energy and potential of a group.

To write about the practice of skills in groups is in some ways self-contradictory in that it is making 'content' out of 'process'. Nevertheless, in this chapter, I propose to offer some specific ideas about what the tutor, and in turn the students, might positively do to enhance the effectiveness of group learning. In some cases the tutor may choose to keep a low profile and merely respond to the ferment of discussion at suitable times. I shall call initiatives of this kind <u>tactical</u>. While many of the variables affecting behaviour are ephemeral and even capricious there are on the other hand some which the tutor can influence, if not control, by decisions taken before the group actually meets. I shall call this kind of action <u>strategic</u>. 'Strategic' therefore refers to planning the overall structure and content of group teaching where 'tactical' refers to the handling of events as the discussion itself progresses. In acting strategically (for this purpose), our knowledge and understanding of group dynamics and of the characteristics of the particular group may suffice. For tactical purposes however the more elusive qualities of skill and sensitivity are demanded and these cannot be acquired without some training, practice and reflection.

STRATEGIC CONSIDERATIONS

As the organiser of a group meeting or a series of
meetings, the tutor has an opportunity to influence
the course of events in at least three areas of
decision: group size, group membership and the physical conditions in which the group meets. The tutor
might also wish to plan for possible exigencies and
prepare a small list of questions to ask himself
such as 'What am I trying to achieve and what do I
have to do to achieve it?' (see Chapter 5) and 'What
courses of action should I be prepared for?' (see
the previous chapter for some possibilities).
     Though we often tend to make such decisions by
ourselves, there is a lot to be said for drawing
on a friendly colleague's help to check out our
thoughts. If this can be done happily and on a
reciprocal basis, then so much the better. Care
taken in the preparatory work can reap many later
rewards and pre-empt several of the common problems
of learning groups.

Group Size

The number of students in each group has a profound
influence on the kind of interaction that can be
attained. The smaller the size the greater is the
likelihood of trust, close relationships and conson-
ance of aims among members; these advantages may
however be offset by the lack of variety, and the
greater probability of a 'poor mix'. In the larger
group, though a better mix and a more favourable
student/staff ratio may be achieved, a sense of
competition, and a greater differentiation of role
might be expected to occur. Not only does the
opportunity for each member to contribute diminish
in inverse ratio to the number of people in the
group, but the discrepancy in level of participation
between high contributors and low contributors is
disproportionately greater. There are thus quite
significant differences too in the style, frequency
and length of spoken contributions, not to speak of
non-verbal behaviour, in groups of three to six
compared with those of 12-15 students.
     If time-tablers and course tutors have not
already determined the size of group for us, we
might ask ourselves the following set of questions:

          'What is the optimum range of group size
          socially and educationally for a given set of

aims and tasks?' (assuming we can predict
these).
'What, apart from educational aims, do I hope
the groups will achieve socially?'
'What mix of sex, nationality, age, etc. do I
want to have?'
'Do I intend or need to be present as tutor
with all the groups all the time?'
'What limitations does the meeting room(s)
impose on the total group size and the kinds
of activities possible?'
'How does it all fit into the scheme for the
whole course?'

Figure 7.1 may give some indications of the dimensions to be taken into account.

Although decisions about group size may be
predicated upon several variable factors, more often
than not the tutor will be stuck with two fixed
ones: the total number of students and the room in
which they meet. However, with a little initiative,
we can, whether with 6 or 96 students create a
variety of group sizes for different purposes. For
instance, it is possible by pairing the students in
dyads, to encourage the sharing and development of
half-formed or tentative ideas, the airing of
anxieties, or merely to provide a break in the
pattern of participation. A fuller range of tasks
and consequent changes of the communication pattern
in groups is offered in Chapter 6.
In many ways the size of total group most
amenable to a variety of aims and techniques is
20-30. In recent years this sort of number has
achieved popularity in management and teacher
training as the most suitable for the workshops.
Workshop formats allow a variety of group techniques
to be practised. Apart from the universal facility
of organising dyads, they provide for either 3-5
groups of 6-18 with or without a tutor, or plenary
sessions; workshops thus combine the advantages of
small and large group experience.

Group Membership
The way in which students are assigned to groups
likewise depends on the purposes, both educational
and social. As a general rule a heterogeneous mix
of students in each group provides the best chemistry for interaction and achievement of task. Such
qualities as age, sex, nationality, personality

137

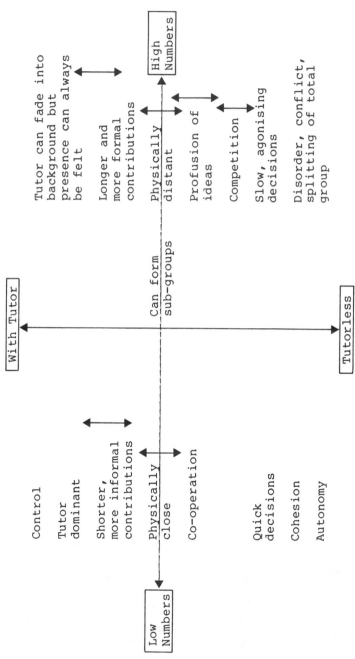

Fig.7.1 Characteristics of Groups in Relation to Size and Tutor's Influence.
The short arrows indicate possible variations of that characteristic on the chart.

can be taken into account. One procedure for
accomplishing effective mixes is as follows:

> Divide the total number of students by the
> possible number of groups to estimate the rough
> size of each group.
> Decide on criteria which might be used to
> differentiate one student from another, e.g.
> sex, age, background, expressed interest, exam
> results, nationality.
> Go through all the notes and assign a code
> to each according to these criteria A, B, C,
> etc.
> Then, starting with Group 1, take one person
> from each of A, B, C, etc., until this group's
> complement is made up. Repeat this if the com-
> plement is more than the number of qualities.
> Do the same for the other groups. Finally,
> check that each group has a similar mix and
> adjust if not.

Intellectual differences may also be taken into
account. If the main purpose of discussion is to
solve problems or to clarify or elaborate matters
which have already received attention, then there
are both commonsensical and research reasons
(Amaria, Biran & Leith, 1969) why it may be wise to
mix the better progressed or more quick-thinking
students with those who are either behind with their
work or slower thinking. Provided the given task
demands co-operation, the former will find themselves teaching the latter. In this way we can
'kill two birds with one stone': the quicker students learn the subject matter better themselves and
the slower ones are provided with the opportunity
to query misconceptions without embarrassment.
Suddenly there are as many 'tutors' as students!
It would be a mistake however to think of group
composition solely in terms of individual qualities.
Of equal concern is the sociometry or likely pattern
of emotional links among the members (where these
can be known beforehand). In every group personal
likes and dislikes for fellow members soon begin
to grow and can have an important influence on the
way the group functions. Again, research and common
sense tell us that people tend to agree with the
individuals they like and disagree with those they
dislike, even though both might express the same
opinion.
Cliques may present another problem. There
are good reasons for separating groups of students

who have such close affinity with each other that they form an exclusive sub-group which could easily destroy the cohesive fabric of the larger group. On the other hand there may be pairs or threesomes who somehow trigger or inspire each other in more productive ways. The tutor needs considerable skill and sensitivity in watching out for cliques and taking appropriate action, which, though an extra chore, can deflect so many subsequent problems.

If the choice of group partners is to be left to the students (as happens often with projects) it is advisable to adopt a schema which allows them to find partners with whom they prefer to work yet avoids the risk of some feeling left out or not chosen. A sociometric device suggested by Stanford & Roark (1974) is as follows:

> Give each student a card and ask him to write his name in the upper left hand corner. Then ask him to list two members of the class with whom he would like to work. If a student can think of only one or wants to list more than two, that is perfectly acceptable.

The cards are then handed in to the tutor who uses the information on the cards to assign students into groups containing at least one colleague for whom they expressed preference.

Even with preparation like this the tutor may need to be alert to the dangers of friends falling out or of exclusive cliques developing as the life of the group develops. What the tutor might subsequently do about such happenings is suggested later.

The beauty of the workshop format described on page 136 is the facility it offers for varying the mix of people and affinities in groups while still allowing for planned changes of group membership both for the sake of variety and in order to monitor the progress of each group (though any such decision must be tempered by knowledge of the disruptive effect of breaking up groups).

Physical Conditions

It is in the physical arrangement of chairs that many of the most basic yet influential problems in group discussion can occur. Who sits where and at what distance from whom will affect the social roles and relationships pursued by members. The cardinal rule is, if you want full and democratic participation, play down any prior differences of role and reduce the likelihood of their becoming firmly established. A closer sense of sharing in a common task is thus more readily achieved.

A starting point in organising the physical arrangements is to ask:

- What associations does the room have in the minds of the students?
- Is it the tutor's room, a classroom, a 'neutral' room?
- Is the room a regular venue, is discussion vulnerable to noise or interruption?

Then it may be sensible to consider the seating arrangements:

- Is everyone equally spaced?
- Does anyone have a special position, e.g. behind a big desk; at the head of a table?
- Can everyone make eye contact with each other?
- How possible is it to rearrange the groupings of chairs and tables?

It is remarkable how often tutors maintain an evidently dominant position for themselves by sitting behind their desk, with students grouped round in front, without being conscious of the effect it has on participation. The diagram opposite indicates some of the layouts commonly used in tutor-centred discussion groups. I leave the reader to make judgements on the level of participation and the sort of communication pattern likely to occur in each case.

Now although an awareness of the effects of the physical position of students and tutor may be highly desirable, there may nevertheless be a limit to the amount of self-conscious juggling of furniture that a group of students will be prepared to undertake. Sometimes there is a sense of 'why can't we just stay as we are?' and perhaps the tutor should bow to this feeling rather than make a self-conscious effort to 'structure the environment'. If the configuration of chairs and tables is strange to the students, the tutor may have to explain the rationale, particularly when the students themselves are invited to help in the operation. An obsession with re-arranging the furniture can indeed unsettle students.

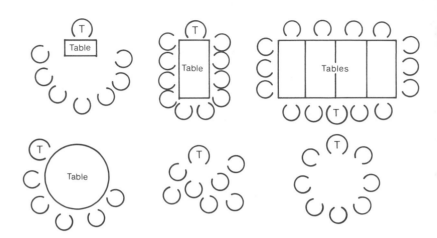

Fig.7.2   Optional Arrangements of Furniture in the
          Classroom

        Even in such an apparently 'impersonal' task
some sensitivity to the underlying feelings of
students may be necessary.   Would it be better to
say:

        'I'm not happy about these tables - I feel they
        get in the way.   Could you move them?'

or

        'I expect it'll make you feel a bit exposed but
        I'd like to try a more open arrangement for the
        group?'

        There are, of course, no easy answers.   At a
recent class with a group of students who were
accustomed to my moving the tables out of the way
and the chairs into a circle, a fascinating but
tense discussion about an unrelated issue developed
as we stood by the door on the way into the room.
        This led in turn to an enthusiastic switch
of interest by the students into an unexpected field
of study.   In my judgement the cliff-hanging conversation about what they might have been missing would
have collapsed had I then killed the moment with:

        'Look, before we sort this out, could we just
        rearrange the furniture?'

        The physical scenario of teaching is something

which requires careful handling and its effects are not always predictable. As with all manoeuvres connected with group study however, the need to reveal reasons and to be attuned to the resulting feelings can not only make things easier but also be of unforeseen benefit to the learning process.

Planning What to Do

It is never easy to decide in advance what will catch the imagination of a group of students or to anticipate what kind of learning might occur through a one or two-hour session. To some extent, the learning may be gauged by the level of subject matter implicit in the prior reading. Nevertheless, to rely on a factor external to the dynamic of the group and its stage of development might have a stultifying effect. Both theory and research inform us (page 35) that both the evolving dynamic of a group and the intellectual growth of students (pages 42-45) require that the sophistication and the spectrum of aims and tasks should change and develop both within each meeting of the group and as it progresses through a course.

The choice of aims and tasks will be largely predetermined by what is feasible for a particular group and its physical environment, and also by its state of preparedness. Prior reading is a clear case in point; group discussion frequently falls down or lapses into a mini-lecture as a result of inadequate preparation by the students. If this sort of thing is likely to happen, it is sensible for the tutor to have some alternative strategy in readiness. Here are three possibilities:

1. Have copies of a few seminal paragraphs, discussion points, or critiques related to the text which the students can quickly read in the group (for the tutor to adumbrate what the students have not read puts the tutor in a lecturing role).

2. Discuss with the students why the work has not been done and perhaps agree a firm contract henceforward on preparatory work.

3. Cancel the meeting on the grounds that nothing useful can take place until the students have fulfilled their part of the (implied) contract.

As we saw in Chapter 5, specifying aims in group teaching carries with it several hazards, mostly because of the unpredictability of the outcome. Nevertheless, depending on the overall purpose of the group meeting, there are good reasons for improving our capacity to understand the tutor's job better through a process like the one shown in Fig 7.3. It indicates how we as tutors might take time out to anticipate, monitor, reflect and revise procedures.

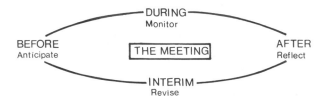

Fig.7.3   Monitoring Strategy for Group Tutors

As with all cycles, one can engage in the process at any point, though logically one might be expected to start at 'BEFORE'. The proposed activities under each stage are:

Before - consider what you want to achieve (aims)
        - decide on how you might do so (techniques/tasks)
        - write some notes on these to refer to after (read up any notes on previous sessions)
        - try to anticipate incidents or developments which might occur (start with 'the worst thing that could happen is...')
        - imagine what you might do to meet such eventualities
        - decide how you might monitor what happens in the group during its progress

During - monitor what is happening; this will at the very least require you to set yourself slightly apart from the discussion at times, even when you are directly involved

- ask yourself how your intentions compare with what you observe happening
and what that implies
- whenever the opportunity occurs take
'time out' either by yourself or collectively to take stock of progress

After - jot down notes on what you did and
what you didn't do that you wished
you had while the memory of them is
still vivid
- check back with the notes you wrote
before the session
- review the session if possible with
a colleague - and in any case jot
down further notes on what you want
to do differently next time
- look at any other information you
have gleaned, e.g. video or audio-
tape, questionnaire, informal chats
with students outside

Interim - mull it over
- read books like this one!
- revise as you see fit
- prepare new material

While this model can be viewed as a 'macro'
cycle of thought processes and experiences, most
reflective tutors will be carrying out a series of
'mini' cycles in which the process of anticipation,
decision, action and assessment are quickly, if not
subliminally, rehearsed during the group session.
A more representative diagram might therefore
be:

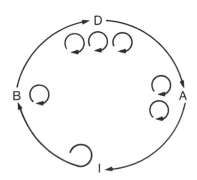

Fig.7.4. Modified Strategy for Monitoring

This whole procedure may strike the busy tutor as far too self-conscious and elaborate for practical purposes. Yet it is merely making explicit a process of thinking that commonly exists at a subliminal level which, because it is conducted unconsciously, is prey to the vicissitudes of emotional blocking and denial. In other words it is an attempt, as is much of this book, to apply academic canons and procedures to our everyday practice: and we are notoriously poor at doing just that!

The practical value of any of these catechisms is probably as great as those of a more religious intent: they depend on some commitment to the faith and on a kind of dedication to the task. Yet they do require honest checks against first-hand experience. A 'meta'-cycle might therefore be added - a check on the whole procedure and its revision or replacement according to personal needs.

The simplest adaptation might be to reduce the 'catechism' to two simple questions which though self-evident are most helpful to ask oneself prior to each meeting with a group of students:

What do I want to achieve?
What do I need to do in order for that to happen?

It is to the second of those two questions that we now turn in looking at the tactical aspect of tutoring.

TACTICAL CONSIDERATIONS

<u>Roles</u>
As soon as tutor and students encounter each other at any meeting, mutual sets of expectations about personal behaviour begin to hold sway. As explained in Chapter 6 the tutor, whether he likes it or not, is invested with some of the authority of the institution as an organisation inasmuch as it defines the rules and requirements of courses for the students, and this is compounded by his authority as judge and assessor of the students. In this sense the tutor will be an authority figure no matter how he may try to minimise it. However one must distinguish between being 'in authority', being 'an authority' and being 'authoritarian'. As tutors we are <u>in authority</u> for the reasons described above and because we have ultimate responsibility for the

time and space boundaries in the meeting; that is we (usually) are deferred to over questions of starting and finishing, and who may join or leave. We will also be perceived as an authority on account of our expertise in the subject matter. When either of these aspects of authority are challenged there is a possibility that we will fall into an authoritarian style of leadership in order to preserve the only image or role we are able to conceive of ourselves. What sort of threat such a challenge poses depends on either our point of view or on how we personally experience the problem. Fears of losing control or (at the level of unconscious fantasy) of annihilation, are common in such situations.

The virtue of acquiring a repertoire of options is again evident. The authority role is not the only one available to us. We can adopt one or more of several roles according to how we define the need and the educational aims. The following roles constitute a convenient classification rather than a set of mutually exclusive categories.

Leader/Instructor: the traditional role which is easily acceded to through the preconceptions of both tutor and students but which frequently leads to dissatisfaction on the part of both. Typically, the tutor initiates proceedings and demonstrates control over content and process with a short statement or summary and then tries to draw out students' thoughts, periodically linking them together and redirecting the content of discussions as appropriate. Often the tutor's task in providing the initial stimulus is taken by a student, but in a sense only as an 'alter ego' for the tutor. There is a great danger with this role that the students may become over-dependent and feel constrained by what the tutor demonstrates as acceptable knowledge, ways of thinking and academic standards. In educational terms, at least, the tutor may thus establish an authoritarian or autocratic atmosphere. Sometimes students behave as if this atmosphere existed even though they would hotly deny it.

Neutral Chairman: a variation of the leader/instructor role in which the tutor controls procedure but does not contribute to the content in any determining way. It is thus possible for him to create a 'democratic' atmosphere (see page 33).

Facilitator: a difficult role for the 'traditional' teacher in that it involves careful listening and eliciting rather than giving of one's own knowledge. Both tutor and students may find this regime difficult and even painful to adapt to. It should not be supposed that the facilitator role represents a 'laissez-faire' style of leadership: rather is there a sense of shared or developed responsibility for learning. It usually requires that the tutor be student-centred, helping students to express what they understand by respecting them for what they are rather than what they 'should' be. (See page 17)

Counsellor: if the personal or social needs of the students demand it, or if a tutorial is designated for such purposes, the tutor may wish to draw out some of the students' emotional problems on the grounds that anxieties shared can be both relieving and reassuring, and it may be valuable feedback for the tutor. The tutor may also have some tentative suggestions for tackling the problems. Small, more 'intimate', groups are of course preferable for these purposes.

Commentator: the tutor sits outside the perimeter of the group and comments from time to time on the dynamic of the group interaction or on the kinds of arguments being used by members. In this way, though students may be aware of the tutor's presence and influence, they are not constantly using him as a reference point or focus of attention in discussion. (See also pages 124-6)

Wandering Minstrel: where the total group is split into sub-groups (as in a workshop) who are working on a set task, the tutor can helpfully infuse his influence by circulating round the groups:

(a)   to check their adherence to the task and identify any teething problems
(b)   to help them out of any unproductive patterns of thinking or interaction they have got into
(c)   to pick up trends in the discussions for use at any subsequent plenary discussion

In this way the tutor may perform several roles in his travels according to what is currently taking place in any group he happens to drop in on. Again, the tutor's authority is in general evidence but should not be obtrusive within the groups.

Absent Friend: many of the best virtues arise from necessity: tutors find it necessary to absent themselves from the group for reasons of nature or administration and are often suprised at the intense buzz of conversation which greets them on their return. It is an interesting test of the effect of one's authority to make a video tape before, during and after one's temporary absence from a group. The essence of this 'role' is physical withdrawal from the room, and this applies equally to situations where sub-groups have been formed as to the integral group. For instance, it is not unusual for a tutor to sense that his presence is causing some sort of 'stickiness' in the group, especially where students are being asked to make a decision which requires them to reveal some of their doubts and uncertainties. There is a danger nevertheless of the group(s) disintegrating unless a task (implicit or explicit) is generally agreed for the duration of the tutor's absence.

The choice of role for the tutor may be determined by:

(a) the declared aims and objectives of the meeting or the course
(b) the kind of task undertaken

or

(c) a summary assessment of the dynamic of the group

Clarification of the role can help polarise activities more purposefully than is typically the case when the relationship between students and tutor is tacit and obscure. Several of the roles could be combined and varied over time. With a project group for example the tutor may first act as a chairman, then as a facilitator, followed by consultant and, because of the students' withdrawal to work on their project, an absent friend.

Now it may well be argued that as competent tutors, we are in and out of these roles continually and the above discussion merely confirms established modes. That is possibly so, but as I have proposed before in Chapter 4, the muddled and often uneasy nature of some teaching relationships demands clarification at times in order to make the transactions more straightforward and explicit. Students can thereby reorientate themselves to what the tutor is providing and adopt a personal approach which matches that of the tutor. On top of that, the polarising of the relationship in such ways can enable the achievement of higher order aims, especially in the area of autonomy, peer co-operation and learning about learning.

While the spelling out of roles may seem in general to be valuable there may be occasions when, for good reasons, the tutor may wish to leave things obscure; when for instance, the aim is to examine the students' response to the tutor in the traditional leader role in order to dig out some of the deep-seated assumptions they may have about teaching and learning. Richardson (1967) describes the resounding silence which frequently followed her proposal to the group of students that they decide for themselves the form and content of the discussion. She claims it is important to discuss this reaction on the road to achieving a better comprehension of crucial relationships in the group and particularly the most problematical one, that of authority.

If we look again at this question of authority in the group, it may now be apparent that some aspects of it are an unnecessary encumbrance to the creative tutor and that he might be wise to divest himself of them. Though he may find it difficult to avoid representing the institution and be ultimate arbiter of standards, the tutor may nevertheless be able to frequently shed the role of subject expert (necessity may demand this in the case of project work) and even more often that of controller of processes and procedures in the group. In other words, through open negotiation in the group, the leadership role may be shared among the members. Hill (1969) proposes a set of roles and functions which enable this 'devolution' to take place. The lack of satisfactory experience of democratic discussion makes it difficult for students to adopt such roles readily and accordingly he proposes a list of criteria through which one might gain a common understanding of what effective discussion can be like. These criteria are that:

1. a happy, non-threatening atmosphere prevails

2. learning is accepted as a co-operative exercise

3. learning is accepted as the object of discussion

4. everyone participates and helps others to take part

5. leadership functions are distributed

6. material is adequately covered

7. members attend regularly and are prepared for the discussion

8. evaluation (assessment) is accepted as an integral part of the discussion group

This list corresponds in many respects with the University of East Anglia 'contract' (see page 244) but does not mention the central issue of assessment. It does nevertheless clarify certain functions which group members may perform, when the occasion seems to demand it, in order to assist group process:

1. initiating - starting the discussion, proposing new ideas, activities, resuming it after a lull;

2. giving and asking for information;

3. giving and asking for reactions;

4. restating and giving examples;

5. confronting and reality-testing - restating others' messages and checking their examples;

6. clarifying, synthesising and summarising;

7. timekeeping and holding groups to discussion plan;

8. encouraging participation by others.

Readers will notice the similarities with Knowles' list of functions for group maintenance and task (page 30), though here the maintenance roles are somewhat underplayed. Obviously, these functions are not required at all times or in equal measure in a group. Indeed, as Knowles remarks, if a function is performed inappropriately it may interfere with the group's operation. But it can be helpful when a group is working unsatisfactorily to pause and consider which of these functions might be lacking and to remedy the situation before moving on. Whether the functions should be allocated to individuals or shared and used as necessary by the group as a whole is a moot point and will depend on the skill of its members. What is fairly certain is that members should be discouraged from playing just one role at every meeting, lest they become stereotyped in it. If possible, roles should be re-allocated as and when individuals feel able to perform them adequately.

One might expect the competent tutor to realise all these behaviours in the leadership role, yet the value of sharing them round the group can be immense as then students are able to learn the skills for lifelong participation in groups. These positive or helping functions could, however, be of little use if due recognition were not also given to some of the 'negative' behaviours which Hill lists as:

> Aggressing (being aggressive)
> Blocking
> Self-confessing
> Seeking sympathy
> Special interest pleading
> Playing around
> Status-seeking
> Withdrawing
> Dominating

(Compare again with pages 31, 32)

The appearance of these behaviours in individuals tends to be irritating to other members. They may be tackled most constructively through regular reflection on, or evaluation of, group process, but, always bearing in mind the need for a consistency between them and the group task.

Rules

Where roles described the positions taken by individuals in a given context, the context is defined by rules. Rules are needed:

> 'to transform experience into a meaningful, orderly and predictable social world, and establish expectations about the behaviour of things that populate the world.'
> (Worsley, 1970, p.355)

Rules, except in particularly formal settings (e.g. committees) are internalised, implicit and generally unstated. Nevertheless, it is usually clear when they are broken: 'foul' is called and sanctions operated to bring the 'miscreant' back to order.

In general, the rules of everyday interaction do for groups as long as they appear to be productive, or if they evidently maintain a stable set of relationships. Yet from our understanding of some of the unconscious processes to which groups regularly fall victim, it is apparent that many of the unexpressed needs of members are satisfied only through somewhat destructive behaviours.

Everyday rules are often more ambiguous than many would like to believe, and there is often hidden disagreement about them anyway. It is the very fact that such ambiguities and confusions are hidden that leads some tutors, and more especially 'growth group' facilitators, to propose explicit ground rules for discussion.

Many of the problems that students feel in expressing themselves in groups stem from either uncertainty about what the 'rules of the seminar game' are, or from their feeling overly constrained by assumed rules to do with authority and competition. For instance, it is frequently assumed that it is the tutor's job to fulfil most of the roles listed on pages 29,30 and it is not for the students to propose objectives, topics, changes of direction, or procedures. Often there is also a rule or norm against expressing one's inner feelings or against interrupting anyone making a presentation. Several of the rules of behaviour in seminars are drawn by students from their school experience and have no great relevance in tertiary education. It is sometimes important therefore for a tutor to formulate with the members of his group some explicit ground rules which, though they may appear more constricting in some ways, can generate a sense of freedom as students begin to understand what is and is not 'OK' with the added knowledge that they are free to propose changes if they wish.

Making rules explicit can therefore help students avoid distracting pressures and better concentrate on the learning task. Such 'ground' rules may be:

(a) that existing implicit rules are changed or revoked, e.g. students may initiate and redirect discussion.

(b) formalistic - for example: no-one speaks a second time before everyone else has spoken once; comments begin with 'I' (I believe, I imagine, I have read, etc.); the tutor speaks only in answer to direct questions; no evaluative comment may be made, etc.

(c) meta-rules - everyone takes responsibility for the process (see Hill's list on pages 150-151); 'time out' may be called at any time to review progress and efficacy of the rules; all rules may be changed by a consensus.

It is clear that the more rules of this kind that are introduced, the nearer the discussion gets to a game (see page 117) and many students may take legitimate exception to that as a regular feature. However, there is a lot to be said for encouraging a group to explore its own implicit rules and to consider which of these it means to keep and which change in an explicit manner. It would be folly to suggest that a group should (except perhaps in Social Psychology) be constantly preoccupied with rules and their formulation but it may be sensible to examine occasionally what rules exist and to experiment with one or two changes in order to determine whether any improvement in the group climate takes place. These rules will naturally affect the tutors' role and vice versa. These two elements of social interaction are indeed complementary and it is this which makes their exploration in groups a fascinating pursuit.

Leadership Interventions

'Of a good leader, when his task is finished, his goal achieved, they say, "We did it ourselves"' (Lao-tse).

(a) Encouraging interaction

For several of the reasons already described, students are often strangely inhibited in discussion and at best seem prepared to make only rather formal contributions. As one student, quoted in UTMU (1978) remarked:

'People ask questions and this stimulates the group. I feel we don't mind if a friend asks a question, but if a lecturer asks you, you dry up. A member of staff will always have the answer at his fingertips. I've always resented making an idiot of myself.'

Students who are remarkably talkative outside classes are often reluctant to contribute to group discussion when a tutor is present, and we have already noted how a tutor absenting himself from the room quickly stimulates a resurgence in conversation among the group, even on academic topics. What can a tutor do while present which might induce a similar sense of open discussion among students without abdicating his 'proper' role as leader? The necessary skills or behaviours are not difficult to acquire, though it may not be easy to produce them always when most wanted. They are nonetheless worth including in one's repertoire even if one does need to perform them self-consciously in the first instance.

i.   Glancing Round the Group: It is generally considered rude not to look at somebody when they are talking to you. Yet to do so as a group leader will quickly create the sort of communication pattern illustrated on Fig 2.1 (a). It is not easy to pick up the habit of scanning the group both when we are talking and when students are contributing. Though we will want to catch the eye of a student as he talks from time to time we can, by looking around, encourage him to follow suit and so cause the whole group to give him more attention, thus discouraging the common tendency for discussion to drift into a series of one-to-one duologues.

ii.   Looking for Signals: If, when one student is talking, we glance round the group, we will find ourselves picking up cues from others who are puzzled, or anxious to check something. As the contribution ends, we will be in a better position to draw in some of the less vocal students.
   Often the cues are no more than an indrawn breath, a snort of frustration, a shifting of position, or a puzzled frown. To have noted them and to be seen to have done so, is usually helpful to us in deciding what to do or what not to do at the next stage in the proceedings. We will also be better appraised of the group climate. In fact we may even be contributing to a more positive climate through the very act of glancing round the group.

iii.   Being Ready to Use Non-Verbal Communication: Sometimes when it may be difficult to interrupt a discussion without sounding critical or punitive, a non-verbal intervention can work wonders. On some occasions, this might consist of catching a student's eye and giving him an encouraging smile or inviting him to speak by raising your eyebrows. On others, the connection may be through gestures – an extended palm to suggest 'Would you like to come in now?': - or using two hands to indicate 'What does everyone else think?'. Of course, these non-verbal signals are the natural partners to verbal invitations but are generally less intrusive and just as productive. Two non-verbal gestures which are not often used but seem to work effectively are the 'traffic cop' signals designed to bring students into a discussion and to block them out. (See Fig 7.5)

iv.   Bringing in and Shutting Out: The above gestures (Fig.7.5) highlight two complementary purposes. In order to encourage a student to talk, it may be necessary for the tutor to invite him or her into the discussion, either verbally or non-verbally. By the same token, it is sometimes necessary to exclude more vocal members or to stop them before, as often happens, both their less vocal

156

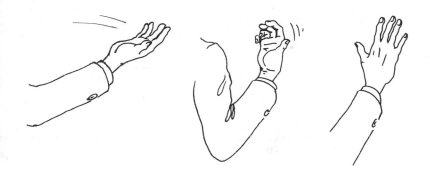

Fig.7.5   Hand Signals for Bringing in and Shutting
          out

colleagues and they themselves have become fed up
with what they are saying: This becomes a sort of
'rescue operation'.

A non-verbal way of expressing these injunctions
has already been described. However, very often a
student is not actually conscious of his real
environment when talking or when waiting to talk,
and a verbal stimulus is also needed. For example,
when a student silently smiles or raises his eyes to
heaven one might interject: 'What are you thinking,
John?' or 'You smiled, John'. The latter is usually
more threatening than the former but has usually the
desired effect of drawing a student into discussion.
       However, the opposite problem may prevail:
how to shut out someone who constantly talks or
interrupts. Provided we can do it supportively and
straightforwardly:

        'Could you just hold it there Brian - it would
        be interesting to know how the others respond
        to that.'

or
        'Let's put that on ice for the moment, Gill,
        while we hear what everyone else has to say,'

the student should not feel unduly put out. The
problem is rather on the tutor's side, as it is

enormously difficult to consciously interrupt someone in the sure (but often erroneous) belief that
one could be hurting their feelings, and we may
well feel that the risk is too great to take in a
group of students. Should this be so, the solution
might be to practise these skills within the safer
company of colleagues in a 'practice' group. (See
Chapter 10)

v.   Turning Questions Back: Of the many tempta-
tions open to the unsuspecting tutor, one is
the supplicant question which places us on our
authority pedestal: 'Can you tell us what you know
about...?' or 'What should the answer be?' or
suchlike.

The simple solution is, of course, to turn the
question back with: 'Well, what do you think?' on
the grounds that:

> (a)   the student probably has an inkling of
> the answer anyway or he would not have
> asked the question

and

> (b)   it is usually better to get students
> to formulate their own ideas in the first
> instance.

There is of course a danger that this simple tactic
could become an undiscriminating habit. There are
many occasions when the tutor may be the only person
present who could possibly know the answer to a
particular question, or where a refusal to answer
could slow down proceedings. The judgement in all
these situations must be based on a recognition
of the dynamic and the learning needs of the group.
    A very useful and more comfortable variation of
'turning questions back' is to redirect or deflect
them. For instance the question from a student:

> 'I don't understand what the author is trying
> to say. What does it all mean?'

could be met with

> 'Well, what does anybody else think?'

or

158

'Does everyone else have the same problem?'

or

'Do you have _any_ ideas about what it means?'

vi. Supporting and Valuing: Thus far we have considered some very quickfire, though not always easy,
tactics for the tutor in a leadership role. However
it is easy to overlook an important ingredient of
effective group discussion: the creation of a
feeling of security and belonging; an atmosphere of
trust and openness where people are valued for what
they are so that they have no need to fear making
a fool of themselves. Now this is easily said, but
not so easily done in the thick of a hectic term's
work where teaching and assessing become an almost
undifferentiated continuum. The temptation to
correct discussion contributions in the same way
as one might write comments to an essay is great.
Perry (1970) describes how tutors typically view
the discussion as 'an opportunity to develop
initiative and scope in their own thinking', at
least initially.

> 'No sooner do the students get started,
> however, and some error or inexactness is
> voiced, than the older form of responsibilities
> imposes on the tutor the imperative of
> 'correcting'. In the time where this tendency
> gets in motion, three to five corrections of
> this kind appear sufficient to defeat the
> students' initiative for search and flow of
> their exploration. The initiative for conver-
> sation then falls back on the instructor who
> then finds himself in a monologue or lecture,
> with the sensation of being somehow trapped,
> compelled, by powerful forces, in himself and
> the students, to do what he had never intended
> to do.'

This is not to say that the correction of
'errors' is an unacceptable sin. The question is
not one of 'whether' but rather of 'when' and 'how'.
To reject or correct the first contribution a
student makes would generally be counterproductive.
Apart from inhibiting expression, as in the above
quotation, it is likely to lock the students into
the first four stages of Perry's scale of intellectual development (see page 42-3). Nevertheless

some kind of corrective action may be called for;
but this can be achieved in a less inhibiting and
intellectually more elevating way:

> 'Is that <u>really</u> so?'
> 'Could you think about that again?'
> 'Let's just look at that more carefully.'
> 'How does that tally with what you said
> before?'
> 'Would anyone else like to comment on what
> George just said?'
> 'Uh-huh!'

and so forth.

Students will doubtless pick up that they have
said something irrelevant or inconsistent but be
encouraged to discover their own way out.

vii. <u>Checking and Building</u>: Students (not to speak
of tutors) are not always as lucid as they would
wish to be when formulating ideas for the first
time. Some of the most imaginative contributors to
a discussion may find it difficult to express their
half-formed ideas clearly at first. Lest the whole
group continue in a state of confusion the tutor can
quickly check for understanding by simply asking:

> 'Let me check that I understand you. Are you
> saying...?'

and the student is often grateful for the clarification. What the student <u>does</u> say may well relate to
a line of argument pursued earlier in discussion or
contradict something he has said earlier. In each
case, the tutor can help to make links with comments
such as:

> 'That ties in with what you were saying before
> - it sounds as though you have a coherent view
> of it.'

or

> 'Does that contradict what you said a few
> minutes ago?'

or

> 'So it would be fair to say that whilst you

160

disagree with the functionalist view, you have
not yet...'

Ideally, it would be preferable if the students
were left to make the interpretation for themselves:

'How does that connect with what you said
before?'
'Is Julie being consistent there?'

Sometimes the tutor may go further in putting
several emerging themes together and formulating a
new coherent picture of the topic under discussion.
But again how much better it would be to allow the
students to do so for themselves!

viii. Re-Directing: The sense of initiative required
of a tutor in acting on the physical environment,
which we discussed on pages 140-143, is just as
valuable when it comes to changing the social
interaction. Again it is a matter of knowing when
it is important to act and when the prevailing
climate is too good to destroy. It is never easy,
especially when the tutor has a planned schedule of
discussion, to decide whether students would be
glad of a change in the direction of the discussion
or would feel cheated of a rewarding pursuit. Yet
sometimes it _is_ necessary to take command and say:

'Hang on to that but let's switch our attention
to another aspect...'

or

'I think we've reached the point where we could
turn our attention to...'

More often than not, it is difficult to be sure of
the climate and also of one's own motives. A safer
way of approaching the problem may once again be to
test the group:

'Are you ready now to...?'
'Do you think we've worked on that one for long
enough now?'

It may be even more valuable to check the process as
well as content:

'Could we stop at this point and check whether

161

we're going about this the right way?'

This intervention is almost identical with the basketball term '<u>time out</u>' in which teams take a break from the game to review progress and discuss tactics.

There is nothing unusual about all these leadership interventions. They are practised quite frequently in everyday life but are somehow forgotten in the culture of a discussion group. We must however use them with discretion, not in pursuit of our own needs, but in response to what our growing awareness of the group process tells us.

Asking Questions

Supposing a tutor were to open discussion with:

'Do you think the assassination of Archduke Francis Ferdinand was intended as a precipitating factor for World War I, even though none of the schemers, if schemers they were, could have had any notion of the consequences in terms of both the extent of hostilities and the degree of suffering that resulted?'

Pause. Ten seconds' silence.

'Let me put it another way. On the evidence we have, was the War a typical example of intentional cause in international conflict? Or was World War II a better one?'

Pause. Another ten seconds' silence.

'Did nobody read the papers I asked you to look at last week?'

What, if anything, went wrong here? Were the questions too complicated? Did the tutor wait long enough for an answer? What sort of answer did he want? This imaginary dialogue (based on two real transcripts) is intended to demonstrate at least one of the common traps in asking questions: posing a multi-part, highly-academic and leading question at the start of a session, not waiting long enough for a response and then rephrasing it as another question. We all do this sort of thing from time to time and we usually wish we could 'unask' the question rather than becoming more deeply enmeshed through our own wish to appear clever. Yet having got ourselves into this fix perhaps we could learn from this tutor by waiting a little longer for a response, using our 'third ear' to reflect on the way the question came out, and possibly checking with students:

'Do you want me to re-phrase that?'

or

'Was that question too complex/obscure/involved to answer?'

Questions serve at least three purposes in discussion: to test the students' knowledge, to clarify information, and to stimulate students into expressing ideas and constructing arguments. Very often the same question can satisfy all these purposes, though that will depend on the group climate and any underlying message in the question. There is perhaps a further purpose served by questions. That is the opportunity it gives the tutor, or anyone else in the group, to make a link between what they and the others are thinking. The choice of question will depend very much on when it is put and the purpose of the discussion. If, however, we take the above three purposes of questioning we can look at the different types of questions which relate to each and leave the decision as to their practical application to the reader.

Testing Questions: These will mainly begin with words like 'what', 'how', 'where', 'when', 'which' and will therefore be essentially convergent as they are intended to elicit specific information. They are concerned with checking knowledge, and the answers are generally predictable.

'What is the best catalyst for...?'
'Which critics have described <u>Godot</u> as a comedy?'

With comprehension:

'How do you justify that...?'

With application:

'How do you predict that would work in...?'

163

'What relevance does that have in...?'

With analysis:

'What qualities do these have in common?'
'What would happen if...?'

With synthesis:

'How does that connect with...?'
'Could you summarise what we've discussed so far?'

and with evaluation:

'Which do you think is best?'
'How do you feel about that?'

Such questions are clearly linked with Bloom's taxonomy (see page 71) and the accompanying list of verbs might prove a helpful reference. However, they can, as part of a <u>probing</u> exercise (Hedley & Wood, 1974) be combined in a way which is searching and vigorous.

<u>Clarifying Questions</u>: Whether a question is defined as a clarifying or as an elaborating one will often depend on the expression on the questioner's face and what has preceded the question. However these sorts of questions could be used to clarify:

'Can you rephrase that?'
'What did you mean by...?'
'Can you give me an example?'

Where the last question fails we might follow it up with:

'Might this be an example...?'

and provide one of our own.

<u>Elaborating</u>: Elaborating questions are essentially a gentler way of enquiring than the other questions we have discussed. They are concerned with helping students express themselves more fully, both in thought and feeling:

'Can you tell me more?'
'Could you elaborate on that?'

'Uh-huh, what else?'
'How does that make you feel?'

Reflecting and selective reflecting (see page 18) while not strictly a form of question, have an important place here. For example:

Student: 'I've been thinking that, if you take the phenomenological argument to its limits then you end up with nobody helping others to make sense of their own world. There would be no point in teaching, for a start.'

Tutor: 'No point in teaching.' (Reflecting)

or

Tutor: 'Take the argument to its limits.' (Selective Reflecting)

It is easy to see how, with a little inflexion, these 'reflections' could sound like quite threatening questions. It is essential therefore that they are said in a neutral tone as though one was ruminating over the particular phrase.
There are also questions which are intended to rouse the curiosity or the imagination. For example:

'I wonder if that really would happen?'

or

'If you were in that position, what would you do?'

Often questions like these are best kept ambiguous, though this could be very threatening for a new group.
Let us not forget, too, the principle of personal relevance mentioned already in the section on communication. A question like:

'How did it seem to you?'

or

'What did you like about it?

is much more acceptable as a starter than:

'What is your assessment of Y's Theory?'

It is clearly not in the best interest of discussion that the tutor should spend most of the time asking questions: this would quickly set up a focal pattern of communication. The more students can competently take over the task of asking each other questions the more responsibility they will be taking for their own learning. However, it is quite properly the tutor's job to explore and probe further into students' understanding of issues. The UTMU booklet offers the following counsel to tutors who want to avoid getting stuck with unproductive questioning processes.

- Try to have some idea of the mental processes students are going through, and adjust your questions to the way they respond rather than thinking up good questions beforehand as though the quality of a question was independent of the time, place and person involved.

- Try to avoid questions which suggest one answer is expected more than another, e.g. 'Do you think Wordsworth had a great influence on Coleridge?'. Rather ask: 'What sort of relationship do you see between the works of Wordsworth and Coleridge?'

- Try to avoid playing the game, an elaboration of the above, in which you invite the students to guess what is in your mind, as in the children's party game 'Hunt the Thimble'. If you do not want students to arrive at a predetermined answer or you have your own favourite solution, it is probably better to draw out a range of possible answers from students and then encourage discussion of their merits. This often produces ideas which you had not previously thought of. You may then reveal your own list for comparison.

- Try to ask questions which give informative answers. Avoid verbal checklists: 'Did you calculate the mean?', 'Did you subtract the mean from each reading?' Rather ask: 'Tell me exactly what you did.', followed by 'What about...?', 'What else?', 'Uh-huh?'.

- Ask questions which elicit responses at the higher end of Bloom's Taxonomy, (see page 71) e.g. 'Could you put those ideas together for us?', 'How does that theory compare with the other?', 'How important do you think this scheme is?', 'How do you feel about it?' or 'How committed do you feel to that?'.

- Be very cautious about showing approval and disapproval in evaluating answers. Sometimes it may help reticent students to have their one and only contribution approved, but disapproval is likely to change what a student is willing to say. An honest attempt to contribute should be welcomed. If you feel a comment is irrelevant to the discussion (remember it may not be irrelevant to the student concerned or to the other students), you may respond with 'That's very interesting - could we come back to it later once we have settled the issue of...?'. It is important to recognise that the apparent irrelevance of a comment may be an indication that the student is feeling out of depth or has had to wait so long to speak that the contribution has become out of date.

- Once you have asked a question be prepared to wait for an answer. Short silences are not necessarily a bad thing - they often get students talking more freely in the long run once they know you require (and appreciate) an honest answer to an honest question. If every question is greeted with silence then it might be of value to discuss with the group why this may be so.

- If you find you do not get the answer you want, consider the possibility that the answer a student gives may be the answer he or she wants, or that you have asked the wrong question!

Sometimes it can be useful to encourage individual thought about a question by asking students to write some brief notes which might then be compared with a neighbour's. As well as allowing students to stand back from the discussion for a while it can encourage participation by quieter members. Notes may sometimes be transferred to a board or overhead projector so that they may be shared more easily.

Remember you can often ask questions with little more than the raising of an eyebrow (if you can do it!). Facial expressions are frequently a more direct and less threatening means of querying someone's contribution.

Discussion Points

° What prior planning is done in order that the groups to which you belong run successfully?
° What assumptions lie behind the various interactions, roles and rules described in this chapter? To what extent might students employ them?

LEARNING GROUPS IN CONTEXT

THE LEARNING MILIEU

Although the institutional setting in which a learning group occurs may not be seen by the group itself to have a significant influence over their deliberations, it is evident that students can be profoundly affected by aspects of institutional life outside the formal curriculum. Parlett (1977) contrasts the educational foreground of lectures, tutorials, courses, examinations and so on with the relatively unchanging background of buildings, traditions, local customs, geographical features, etc.

> 'While students are concerned - inevitably and properly - with attending to the foreground, much of what they do and think about while in the institution is governed by the background. That this is ever present, "taken as read", and rarely examined systematically is no guarantee it is educationally insignificant in its long-term impact.'

The view that a department has of itself is a kind of foreground which may conflict with the background of learning norms among students. Indeed the more loudly trumpeted the self-image, the more likely is the presented picture to be a false one with consequent disillusionment for students. Self-image is often revealed at induction talks designed to orientate students to their studies. Parlett reports one department that adopted a tough and austere image, warning the students of the hard work ahead, that some would fail and that the control of knowledge and its dissemination lay firmly with the department. Another conveyed a more open attitude to learning; the department chairman talked about University as:

'a time during which you should take a critical look at yourselves and rethink things - it should be a most stimulating time.'

and later broke the meeting into small groups to discuss the course. His caution was 'Don't let the work get on top of you'. A third department set the tone by immersing students in their work from the start with experiments involving measurements of each other, while staff circulated and instructed students on techniques.

Nevertheless, it is more than possible for student norms to prevail in spite of staff intentions. Students can be reluctant to discuss academic matters outside the organised class - there is often a taboo on it. Further, there may be strong disinclination among students to follow what they agree are desirable educational goals but which conflict with more immediate pressures to do with assessment. In physical sciences for instance, some students are likely to look for 'correct' answers to tutorial problems rather than engage in a wider intellectual discussion even though they may accept this as valuable to their development in a more professional sense.

Many of these features of student life become part of the folklore that is passed on from one influx of students to another. Folklore can, as Parlett suggests, support the status quo all the more powerfully when the departmental sub-culture becomes insulated from the wider culture of the institution and the outside world through the self-confirming nature of its academic ideology and the:

'progressive retrenchment of certain ideas that all within the organisation adhere to and take for granted, and which are not exposed to any bracing challenge from the outside.'
(Parlett, 1977)

Students also draw comparisons between experiences of different groups and between the learning milieu in different departments and these often serve to underline the prevailing folklore.

The Physical Environment
Whatever the intentions of a curriculum or the

motives of individuals, the physical arrangement
of teaching rooms, staff offices, corridors, social
and domestic amenities and constraints of the timetable will partly determine the pattern of communication and relationships in an institution. To
some extent, powerful drives such as the need for
personal affiliation can mitigate many of the
physical barriers - distance for one. However,
where the desire to learn is (as it often seems to
be) a less than powerful drive, physical proximity
and frequency of encounter can have a marked
effect. The nearer one lives to somebody, the
greater the likelihood that chance meetings will
occur and even where they do not, their likelihood
may also exert a strong influence. Of course, the
very fact of meeting does not ensure that effective
communication will occur; nor does the lack of
meeting mean that it will not! Festinger, Schachter
& Back (1950), quoted in Smith (1973), reported in
a study of friendship patterns in Massachusetts
Institute of Technology, that students whose rooms
were relatively inaccessible had fewer friends and
those whose rooms were more accessible had more
friends and they tended to be from nearby. However,
this does not presuppose, as Smith has pointed out,
some similarity of interests between the students.
    A similar situation exists where the proximity
of a 'significant' person or object causes a person
to attend to them more readily than another at a
greater distance. People are always more alert to
immediate demands. It is likely, therefore, that
frequent casual encounters with tutors and group
colleagues will serve as a regular reminder of
agreed tasks and a spur for new ideas for the group.
The frequency of group meetings will determine the
extent to which the group ethos will prevail over
other priorities.
    To some extent the total size of the institu-
tion will also affect the sense of group identity
because the likelihood of chance meetings is
lessened both with physical distance and with a
larger population. It would seem likely that the
anonymity and the sense of alienation that may grow
in bigger institutions would push people into small
(and perhaps deviant) affinity groups and discourage
participation in organised group activities. This
hypothesis is supported to some extent by Barker
(1968) who found that with the increasing size of a
school, students tended to become audience rather
than participant in many of the school activities.
    In the same way, it is probable that the

physical shape of the environment will influence the nature of casual interaction. A building designed as a set of rooms leading off long corridors limits encounters to hasty exchanges in the corridor or specially arranged meetings in designated places, neither of which promotes spontaneous communication. A conveniently situated open area or refreshment facility can offset this sort of environmental drawback to some extent, but there is no substitute for rooms arranged round a central area with refreshments immediately available.

It is as if the problems of communication and relationships in the environment echo those experienced in the learning group. Size, physical layout, personal proximity and so forth all play their part. One might even hazard a guess that the style of interaction present in a learning group could be influenced to a large extent by its general environment. The implication of these notions is that whether one is thinking of the learning group or its environment, physical arrangements must be taken into consideration if the kind of educational and social relationships we desire are to occur.

EDUCATIONAL MATTERS

The design of a course, or curriculum, involves many value judgements about styles and techniques of teaching and learning and the order in which they should occur. Ideally these judgements should be subsumed under a general educational style or philosophy agreed by the teachers and even the students. However, the limits imposed on educational procedures by logistics, such as disposition and availability of rooms, frequently make the reality of curriculum development a resigned failure. More often than not, educational ideals are decimated by timetables which organise course programmes into a fragmented collection of learning experiences for the student and give a similar sense of disconnectedness to the teachers.

However, it would be unfair to place the blame for this kind of course entirely on timetabling committees. Teachers themselves are prone to equally myopic tendencies in at least two ways. One is connected with course content or subject matter, which is frequently regarded as a sort of academic territory to be established and defended against the encroachment of other warring tribes of academe. The second is the way in which the subject content is transmitted and the apparent need to control its dissemination and boundaries. It is normally the teacher who determines what is to be learned, and how, and what counts for an acceptable standard of learning. However, beneath all this there may exist a hidden curriculum; one in which the teaching is geared to the interests and levels of achievement of only the brighter students to the neglect of the majority whose main, and perhaps only, concern is to qualify competently and get a job. What Stenhouse (1975) describes as:

> 'Official policies which tend to encourage those (school) teachers who turn away from the practical and vocational realities of their pupils and turn to higher things'

acquire even more significance in tertiary education where the power of abstract reasoning, in which many otherwise able students are not proficient, is highly valued. Tutors usually define reality and 'acceptable' knowledge in discussion groups and can quickly and firmly establish norms about the kind and level of knowledge that may be discussed. Many of these norms are determined by the style of tutor intervention. Sometimes, the style can be inhibiting; for example, where tutors open a seminar with a learned introduction or where their eloquence sets too high a standard for students who are still struggling to put their half-formed ideas together, never mind express them.

On the other hand, tutors can equally well set standards whilst still drawing students into the the discussion. They can, for instance, pick out what they consider loose or 'incorrect' thinking and reflect it back either to the contributor or to the whole group using some of the interventions given in Chapter 7 and in Rudduck (1978). To employ them skilfully requires plenty of practice.

In their capacity as both leaders and organisers of learning groups, tutors are involved in mediating the values, requirements and ultimately the authority of the institution which, willingly or not, they will be seen to represent. They also have the quasi-administrative role of passing on and collecting organisational information: small groups provide an effective means of ensuring that some of the more difficult administrative guidance is given and properly understood. How a tutor carries out the administrative/organisational function can be crucial to the relationship established with a group. However, there is one organisational role which can have a much more critical effect on the atmosphere of the group; that of assessor. Whether the concern is with setting exams, marking essays/lab work, or in appraising contributions to the discussion group, the tutor's authority can be seen by the students as all-pervading because of the typically absolutist, unilateral nature of assessment. It is a, perhaps unfortunate, fact of academic life that both tutors and students frequently collude in a sort of protocol or game, the rules of which may be expressed by: 'You are too old or free to be controlled by my openly asserted authority but I know you know I'm your assessor, though I'm going to pretend that I'm not'. The anxieties surrounding assessment affect many seminar groups:

> 'The seminar, ideally, is a place where people can take risks with ideas. Risk-taking is more likely to occur in a secure structure and the security of the seminar is sometimes threatened for students by uncertainty about assessment. Are they being assessed? And, if so, on what? The obvious conclusion, in the absence of any explanation of the assessment procedure, is that they are being assessed on their spoken contributions (frequency? length? or the elusive concept of quality?)' (Rudduck, 1978).

The tendency of some seminar tutors to maintain power by preserving the ambiguity of their assessment role can therefore create a group atmosphere which is both counter-educational and uncomfortable. As Rudduck explains:

> 'The shadow of assessment is likely to make the enquiry more teacher-oriented than it might if there were no assessment or if the rules of assessment were made clear to the students'

There is, of course, an essential tension between the two roles of mentor/facilitator and that of assessor. This is particularly so where continuous assessment takes place or where students' seminar performance is appraised. In such cases as Richardson (1967) describes:

> 'The responsibility for assessment has to be recognised by teacher and student alike as

part of the fabric of the personal relationship between them; there is no longer any way
of externalising it.'

Richardson's approach to the problem when working
with student teachers was to bring the subject of
assessment out into the open and work through the
anxieties which the duality of her role implied.
It was apparent to her that student behaviour
changed both when essay titles were given and when
essays were due to be handed in. The complex of
behaviours, developed in school, to handle the
student-teacher's hopes and fears about assessment
in classroom revealed itself in an uncharacteristic
rivalry for the tutor's approval and a mutual
sense of embarrassment and secretiveness about
what they were learning in preparing their essays.
After the problems of assessment had been openly
discussed within the group, the atmosphere changed
dramatically to one of cheerfulness and buoyancy,
and the group acquired a 'personal commitment and
intellectual enjoyment not previously evident except
in one-to-one sessions'. Yet again the value of
self-disclosure (see page 53) as a trigger to a
more open climate of communication seems to have
worked.

At the University of East Anglia, the 'assessment problem' has been tackled in one subject area
(Moral Philosophy) by the drawing up of a learning
contract in which the assessment function of the
tutor is openly described. For example:

It is important to make explicit that <u>nothing
you do (or fail to do) in the small group meetings will be assessed for grading purposes</u>.
Grades for the course will be determined by
two essays...

Although grades will be determined by the above
essays <u>no grade will be given unless you keep
a record of the work done for and in the small
group meetings</u>. This record will consist of a
loose-leaf folder containing:

Accounts of your work in the sub-group.
Accounts of the themes and arguments
raised each week in the small group meetings.
Three summaries of your own, developing

175

> views, to be written at the end of weeks
> 3, 6, and 9. (Rudduck, 1978)

In this way, what happens in the groups becomes a necessary part of the assessment procedure yet is not itself assessed. How effective this procedure was at UEA is not reported.

This section would not be complete without some reflection on the pervasive influence of a more traditional assessment procedure, the 3-hour unseen examination. The mounting anxiety which increasingly afflicts the group discussion as the 'exam season' approaches is familiar to most tutors, and there is often little they can do to offset it, except to recognise it and perhaps take 'time out' to discuss its nature and possible remedies. Like most anxieties, its effect is to cause regression among the student population to the point where many of the higher level aims cannot be realised. Students become increasingly concerned with picking up bits of knowledge to tuck away under their belts and are unwilling to engage in the more open-ended and creative kind of discussion which may have prevailed before.

Where the tutor is also the examiner or, as is even more likely, has sight of the exam papers, students may take up various stratagems to reduce their anxiety. Miller & Parlett (1974) discerned three groups of students in their study of the effects of examinations at Edinburgh University, the cue-seekers, who actively sought to pick up hints about exam questions and tried to make a good impression on tutors, the cue-conscious who were equally aware but not active in their approach, and the cue-deaf who believed that only hard work achieved success and that any impression they made on tutors would have no effect on their marks. How these practices affect the quality of interaction in group discussion is not reported; one could make an inspired guess without much difficulty. However, there was a clear indication that tutors become involved in an equivalent set of behaviours - hinters, tantalisers and non-hinters, depending on whether they are anxious about students not doing well in their subject, want to relieve unproductive student anxiety, or like to play a one-sided power game. As in most interactions involving anxiety, a collusive pattern of behaviour between students and tutor can easily develop. All this activity can be seen as part of what Snyder (1971) calls the 'Hidden

Curriculum' - strategies which students resort to in order to survive.

GROUPS AS PART OF THE CURRICULUM

Let us now look again at the legitimate framework of learning in which tutors and groups are engaged. As we have already noted, the amount of time and physical space available for discussion groups can have a profound effect on the kind of learning which takes place. There is a world of difference, for instance, between the small group of eight students working intensively with a tutor for three hours, with a 20-minute coffee break included, and a science 'tutorial' in which 20 students assemble for one hour in a room with fixed benches or large tables arranged in rows. It would be blinkered however, to view small group teaching in isolation from the rest of the curriculum. In physical sciences, as indicated in Chapter 5, there is a tendency to view small group work as an added extra, a means of improving students' understanding of lecture material for instance, rather than as a coherent mode of learning in its own right. Part of the problem is the enormous load of information in the syllabus which science and engineering lecturers believe must be transmitted (though how much is actually learned is a different matter). Yet whatever view we may take of the students' role in learning it is evident that knowledge, to be learned effectively, must be processed, its meaning incorporated into the students' patterns of think-ing, and ultimately communicated by the student in a coherent and acceptable form. If the syllabus is taught as an accumulating sequence where each stage of learning is dependent on the previous one, then it is essential that the students learn pro-gressively and not terminally: they must integrate their understanding as they go along rather than through a 'flash in the pan' revision at examination time. Group discussion is an invaluable aid to this kind of continuous learning. If it is to be used the course must be tailored to accommodate it as as an integral feature.

Timetabling Group Discussion
Bligh (1976) suggests several frameworks for the inclusion of group work in the formal timetable. Some of the groups are planned to occur within

lecture periods, some between; yet others are linked to practical classes. Whether or not several groups can operate concurrently will depend upon the number of students, tutors and available facilities. For example, within a large hall with moveable furniture, any number of small groups could be formed before, during or after a lecture.

In a terraced lecture theatre, however, any sustained small group discussion would probably have to be left till after the lecture. Some possible arrangements for the integration of group discussion are shown in the following diagrams:

(a) within a time-tabled lecture session.

		Mins.
Review previous work in pairs	I	5
Lecture	II	20
Buzz Groups on lecture so far on set question	III	10
Feedback to Lecturer	IV	5
Lecture	V	15
Interval before next class	VI	5

Fig.8.1 Integrating Group Discussion into the Lecture

In this sequence, the following educational points may be observed:

1. A link is provided between the previous session in the subject and the present one with the initial review (I). This may be done in pairs or two students could be asked to present a report.

2. The lecture periods (II, V) are short enough to maintain maximal attention (see Bligh, 1972).

3. The students have a chance (III) to process the knowledge, clear up misunderstandings and enjoy a change of activity.

4. The lecturer can make a rough check on what the students have learned (IV).

5. There is space at the end to minimise the amount of interference between the learning from this session and that from the next.

This sort of structure for a lecture session requires both careful planning and firm but sensitive direction by the tutor, particularly in making decisions about when to change the learning activity. It also demands about two hours to make it really effective. A more profitable and extended version of the above scheme is shown in Fig.8.2.

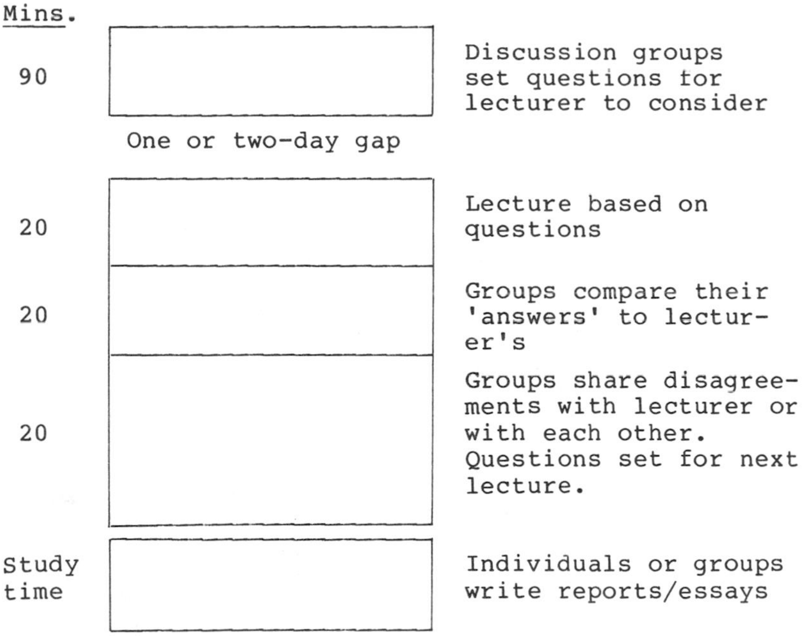

Mins.

90	Discussion groups set questions for lecturer to consider

One or two-day gap

20	Lecture based on questions
20	Groups compare their 'answers' to lecturer's
20	Groups share disagreements with lecturer or with each other. Questions set for next lecture.
Study time	Individuals or groups write reports/essays

Fig.8.2   Sequencing Lectures and Group Discussion

Figure 8.3 demonstrates a combination of group and individual work for practicals which carries over the distilled learning from one session to the next.
This arrangement primes students for a collective encounter with the lecturer. It makes a

179

clear contrast to the kind of lecture that ends in a throwaway comment like: 'Oh, next week we shall be looking at the application of complex numbers to space frames,' as might occur in physical science, or a lengthy and un-annotated booklist in social science.

The permutations of these arrangements are considerable and each tutor would have to work out a plan according to the aims and logistics of the course. In some cases, alternation and linking of lecture and discussion can be tightly organised as a total strategy for the whole course. In others, given some leeway it can be incorporated within an otherwise standard timetable.

			1st Part of
2nd Part of 1st Practical			2nd Practical
		Study	
90 minutes	45 minutes	Time	45 minutes

Groups do experiments	Paired Groups share findings and discuss critically	Individuals write up reports	Paired groups appraise reports in dyads and discuss as a whole

Fig.8.3 Combining group and Individual Work in Practicals

In looking at ways in which sequences of group work may be organised within a fairly traditional curriculum we should not forget that there are many courses or parts of courses where there may be much more freedom to experiment and to provide for varying degrees of self-direction in the groups. Some schemes of this kind are described in the second part of this chapter but for the sake of contrast it is worth mentioning here three other approaches.

One is the kind of group project, already discussed on Pages 109-10, which is scheduled so as to allow students to learn, as the project evolves, the knowledge and skills required for its successful completion. This they do by using the staff as

individual consultants on certain topics, having
lectures arranged in response to emerging interests,
and attending training sessions in teamwork, creative thinking and report writing. Another approach
is described by Fransson (1976) as 'group-centred
instruction'. In this, though there is a curriculum
to be followed, the organisation of learning lies
with the group who may determine how, within certain
guidelines, they wish to use their tutors. The
tutors in turn make certain demands of the groups,
instances being the writing of diaries, assessment
discussions and questions which demand co-operative
work. The third approach is the scheme in operation
in the medical faculty at McMaster University where
the students learn clinical work in groups, frequently with simulated patients. Their formal
assimilation of knowledge mostly takes the form of
library study in response to the practical problems
presented to the group. Groupwork is considered
sufficiently important for each student to be presented with learning resources on groupwork - e.g.
'The Small Group Tutorial', obtainable from the faculty of Medicine (See also Neufeld & Barrows, 1974).
Schemes like these make special demands of the
students and tutors in overcoming the various constraints, habits and norms of the educational
institution of which they are part. Any evaluation
of success must therefore take into account the
influences of the total learning milieu which may
include implacable opposition by colleagues and by
some of the students for whom the dispersal of
authority may be extremely unsettling. Nevertheless, more traditional schemes of teaching, it
seems, are often followed purely because they
fulfil mutual expectations - college is, after all,
the place where eminent people are supposed to give
lectures, and demonstrate their expertise, and
where students congregate to gain benefit from
them. The problem is that teaching on the one
hand, and learning on the other, are likely to
follow two different rhythms. When one is active,
the other is frequently passive, whether we take a
short or a long-term view. Accordingly, if we want
to establish a curriculum which balances democratic
learning principles with academic expertise we will
need to take firm and continuing checks and measures
to ensure success.
Within any curriculum, some aims may have
priority over others at different times, and an
important but often neglected job of the course
tutor is to organise and monitor the teaching and

learning so that some sort of coherent experience may emerge. Sensitive group tutors can plan their own unfolding patterns with the group but there may be wider considerations to be dealt with. One of these occurs on the modular or unit system of course design where students can often experience a sense of 'bittiness' in their studies. (Nuffield Group, 1977). Some institutions have attempted to achieve a degree of integration across the modules by scheduling a 'synoptic study' session into the timetable. In the synoptic study students might discuss relationships between the elements, apply the separate knowledge to a particular focus (e.g. Science and Society) or solve integrative problems. A somewhat less conventional but nevertheless valuable task would be to discuss the experience of learning in each module and to explore ways of enhancing it - though this might be politically risky without the full agreement of the tutors teaching the modules! Nevertheless, some sort of small group experience would seem vital in the unit or modular system to give students the possibility of developing a sense of social identity and a feeling of belonging and commitment to the intellectual life of the institution. Parlett & King (1971) report an attempt to overcome many of the fragmenting effect of an orthodox timetable in which students of Physics worked on 'Concentrated Study' - the full-time study of a single subject for a month with no competing academic demands. This curricular innovation provided enormous scope and freedom for varied and spontaneous group work. At Worcester Polytechnic Institute in the USA (ASEE, 1976), students take part in a project-based unit of seven weeks' duration in which they work exclusively on their project.

One aspect of student experience of higher education which does not appear to have received much attention is that of multiple group membership, often coupled with a complex of tasks. What looks on paper a well-coordinated and reasonably demanding course can be experienced by the individual in a very different way. Unfortunately, the day-to-day experience (not to speak of the hour-to-hour experience) of the student is not often examined by course designers. The constant need in a traditional course programme for a student to switch attention across specialisms, and align himself to different groups of people, can be either an inspiring stimulus or a muddling burden, depending on the student's capacity to cope with a variety of demands or, in less fortunate cases, to defend

against increasing bewilderment and anxiety by
opting out and possibly failing.

Whatever kinds of group activity are formally
organised, informal peer grouping will inevitably,
and quite properly, occur. There are, as Newcomb
(1967) says, diverse motivations for students
to subject themselves to the influence of peer
groups: some, for example, have strong tendencies
toward conformity, while some others seem to be
compulsively deviant. Both can find support from
like-minded groups. Some need to be dependent on
authority whereas independence is essential to some
others; although the latter may seem to be immune to
peer-group influence, the fact seems to be that they
need it as much as the others but tend to find it
in smaller and more selective circles. For some,
membership in high prestige groups is the crucial
thing; positions of 'leadership' or dominance, or
perhaps just prominence, are required by still
others. Some students become group members because
of the interests and attitudes for which the group
seems to stand, while others appear quite willing to
adopt the norms of any group that becomes important
to them for other reasons. Many of these and other
motives can be combined in the same person as he
finds different kinds of satisfactions in multiple
and doubtless partially overlapping groups. The
effects of peer-group membership will vary with
such motives and with the degree to which they find
satisfaction through affiliation.

It is clearly not the task of tutors to become
involved in maximising or otherwise determining
peer-group affiliation and influence; to do so
would be intrusive and could deprive students of
essential opportunities for change and development
not available to them in the organised curriculum.
It can however be enormously helpful for tutors to
understand something of the nature of students'
extra-curricular concerns and their motives for such
involvement. Information of this kind could be
quite valuable in forming judgements about what the
course may be failing to offer any student, particularly where most of his or her energies appear to
be diverted from the educational programme. What is
more, there is always the possibility, if there is
no overlap between the values of peer groups and
the learning group, that peer group norms entirely
divorced from intellectual concerns will develop.
For some students this may represent a necessary
and welcome relief from the considerable demands of
the legitimate educational culture. For others it

could represent a disturbing influence, a constant doubting of the values of the learning group. It is probable that, as Newcomb suggests, this sort of isolation will occur where there is a feeling of anonymity within the learning groups either because of large numbers or a lack of concern for the students at a personal level. If this is so it serves to underline the worth of aims in learning groups directed to personal development, self-esteem and a sense of belonging.

SOME CASE STUDIES IN GROUP TEACHING

In this section we shall see how various academic teachers in institutions both in the UK and abroad incorporated principles of group learning into 'real-life' teaching schemes.

The vast majority of these Case Studies are selected from the contents of the six Nuffield Newsletters, published from 1973 to 1976. The Nuffield Group for Research and Innovation in Higher Education visited several universities in the United Kingdom and compiled their reports on the basis of interviews, concentrating on larger departments with a substantial undergraduate intake. Their survey was by no means comprehensive or representative and it included a wide range of approaches and issues apart from small group teaching. The Nuffield Group based their original selection on criteria such as the applicability of the descriptions in other contexts, that they are less familiar, sometimes ingenious, and are likely to cater for the interest of teachers looking for ideas as solutions to some of the problems. They were also concerned about the potential for transfer to other institutions.

The Nuffield Group also drew attention to the fact that most of the contributions were drawn from science and technology. They put this down to the possibility that these faculties were at the time of their study beset with more obvious problems:

'the swing away from the popularity of their subjects among university applicants, the marked decrease in graduate employment opportunities, the logistical problems of integrating practical and theoretical work and so on.'

The following selection from the Nuffield work is limited to those descriptions of small group

teaching which address themselves to some of the
problems and issues already highlighted in this
book. They are grouped, as far as the variety of
approaches allows, according to the aims and
purposes they serve. However within each is a
wealth of information to do with tasks, techniques,
sequencing, links with other learning, context and
assessment. There are no appraisals save those
provided by the contributors. The events were
between eight and thirteen years ago. In some
cases the schemes did not prove viable and were
discontinued.

Developing Particular Skills

There has lately been a recognition that higher
education is not just about knowing, understanding
and analysing (see Bloom's categories) but also
about communicating, applying, interpreting, evaluating and even 'softer' categories of behaviour.
These skills do not develop merely by talking
about them or recognising them, but by practising
and incorporating them into one's behavioural
repertoire. Small groups can offer both the safety
to take risks in trying and testing new behaviour;
they also give the tutor a greater certainty that
everyone is participating. They therefore aid
learning in more than a superficial sense.

Language Teaching and Communication Studies:

The Department of European Studies at Brighton
Polytechnic provided courses on 'communication
skills' for science, engineering and building
students, who spent two or three hours a week
for one year studying this subject. The first
part of this course was devoted to basic
aspects of communication such as identifying an
audience, choosing media, and defining content,
combined with learning some practical skills
such as operating closed circuit television
cameras and using recorders. In consultation
with their tutors the students then chose a
topic related to their own degree course: the
tides, cosmetics, x-rays and radio astronomy
are some examples. Students worked in groups
of three, preparing a script and making a
fifteen-minute television documentary. This
was criticised and improvements were suggested
The final part of the course was devoted to
making a television presentation on a different

topic; this second presentation was included in work to be assessed for the degree.

The Purpose and Content of Practicals: The purpose and content of laboratory work has become a major area of concern for many science departments. The work is not only time-consuming and expensive but to many students the repetition of experiments and the re-verification of established theories appear tedious and irrelevant. Greater weight, it is agreed, should be given to the imparting of skills and techniques. The first-year practical course in the Department of Organic Chemistry at Leeds was reorganised with this aim. Experiments were grouped together and planned to illustrate either a technique or an underlying principle. Students worked in groups of five to six under the supervision of a laboratory demonstrator; they were provided with detailed written instructions of the experiment they were to carry out and with a statement of the aim of the particular exercise. Each student in the group performed a different experiment but they later came together with the demonstrator to discuss their results and determine the general principle or practical implications involved. Each student was required to write his report in the context of the broader area of experimentation covered by the group.

Simulations, Case Studies and Games: A course in the Department of Mechanical Engineering at Nottingham entitled 'The Engineer in Society' made extensive use of discussion, role-playing in industrial and other situations, and specially designed games. Some of the role-playing sessions were videotaped to facilitate an analysis of communications problems (e.g. in lectures, interviews and committees). The objectives of the course were to broaden the interests and outlook of the undergraduates; to interest them in the social history of engineering; to consider the responsibilities and communications problems of engineers; and to give them an introduction to management techniques useful to engineers in industry.

The Study of Environmental Planning and Pollution: The School of Environmental Sciences at the University of East Anglia had a course option on 'Environmental Planning and Pollution' (EPP) for final year students. The course lasted three terms and involved eight hours' teaching a week. The first three weeks mainly comprised lectures and seminars in welfare economics. The remainder of the course was in two parts. For two terms the student elected to do five out of eighteen options in areas in which staff have special competence. These varied from year to year, but the 1971 programme included such themes as the principles of conservation; coastal erosion and protection; water resource development; atmosphere pollution; recreation pressures; and the national parks. The remaining four weeks were devoted to case studies to which students could apply the skills and knowledge acquired in the earlier part of the course. Examples of case study areas might have included: analyses of the documentation for the Tennessee Valley Development Project; the development of Foulness; or the problems of North Sea exploration and development.

Teaching methods varied over the course: in addition to seminars and case studies there were field studies and role-playing exercises which were found particularly successful in areas of controversy (such as the problems of flooding in the study of water resources). Fifty per cent of the assessment was by examination and the remainder by course work. There was latitude for negotiation between tutor and student on the type of course work assessment preferred.

Group Studies and Texts in Language Learning: Language courses are often defined largely in terms of the final examination papers, in which students are required to translate from and into the foreign language, to write prose, and to take an oral examination. A typical approach to teaching language in preparation for these examinations is through the weekly production and correction of translations and prose exercises. Final results and examiners' reports have indicated some deficiencies in this approach, and in particular the failure of a number of students to acquire either the necessary language skills or the ability to read and study literature critically.

To meet these shortcomings the Language Centre and the Department of French at Birkbeck College, London adopted a less conventional approach involving students actively in the learning process and concentrating on the development of an understanding of what language is and how it may be used. Each week, for three hours in the first year and one hour in the second year, students learnt to understand and use the language by a direct and intensive study of spoken and written texts in French. The sessions were reinforced by small group discussions of fundamental questions related to the aims, objectives, methods and techniques of language learning. These small group studies and discussions, in which students shared experience and understanding, were sometimes tape-recorded, transcribed and used as a basis for further discussion and course development. There were plans to make videotape recordings of small groups at work. Two teachers were usually present at each group session.

Since the introduction of this alternative approach, the students' standards of performance in the language improved significantly in relation both to previous year groups at Birkbeck and to examination performance in London University as a whole.

There have been several attempts to base learning processes on a more careful consideration of what a physicist, or an engineer or whatever, actually does - the professional processes (q.v.Parker & Rubin, Page 80) - or indeed what a student has to do in order to succeed. Traditionally it has been assumed that these skills and qualities are automatically acquired through contact with the education process - learning by contagion. These few examples serve to illustrate that not everyone believes this and that students can benefit from a special focus on what they need to be able to do - their competence skills.

Training Students in Specialised Skills: The Department of Physics at Birmingham introduced a new component in the first year course.

Once a fortnight students met for one hour in groups of about fifteen with one member of staff, to engage in group activity designed to help them acquire specific professional skills. Even during the experimental stage, these sessions created considerable interest within the department. Starting with the question - What skills are required by a physicist ? - a series of problems were prepared which related to such areas as: the communication of results; the ability to translate (for example from graphs to words); the ability to formulate problems in mathematical terms; the design and explanation of experiments. Students tackled these groups of four while the staff member circulated to give advice as required. Each session normally ended with a review during which each sub-group reported to the group of fifteen. Student participation was lively, partly because any one group was left alone for much of the time with a specific task to perform.

Small Group Work in Biological Sciences: During the first two terms of their first year, students of Biochemistry and Microbiology at Kent University attended twenty sessions, at which small groups of students carried out, with staff supervision, work designed to develop basic skills. They dealt with topics such as the working out of pH values, radiochemical activities and the handling of bacterial growth equations. This type of session was interspersed with a second kind in which attempts were made to develop awareness of general scientific methodology in biochemical studies and closely related areas. The group would be told, for example, that dead fish had been found floating on a local river; they were asked to devise a strategy for investigating the episode. Experience gained at this stage was thought to be of value in helping students to make more use of tutorial periods and of work in group projects in later years of the course. As part of their studies in biochemistry, second year students were required to work on three published research papers in, e.g. the field of nucleic acids. They read the papers and worked over a period of three weeks on a number of questions which arose from the

189

data in the papers and the overall philosophy of the research described. They worked in small groups during this exercise but presented their results individually. The method was found to stimulate interest and also served as a good discriminator of student ability.

<u>Syndicate Studies for Engineers</u>: The stimulation of creative talent within a group of engineering students formed an important aspect of the final year course for the four-year sandwich honours degree in electrical and electronic engineering at City University. Students learned, through studying in syndicate groups, how to collect, evaluate and communicate information. Major features of the syndicate method of study are that it encourages active participation in critical appraisal and creative design or specification, and offers students the opportunity to undertake direct responsibility for decision-making.

The syndicate approach, which was first introduced into the course about five years ago, involves groups of from six to ten students in studying a subject of common interest in some detail: each member's activity was expected to contributed to the knowledge and understanding of the group as a whole. The subjects chosen for syndicate study, although specialist in nature, often had wider implications - they included, for example, such topics as surface transport systems and medical electronics. One staff member acted as guide, consultant and assessor to each syndicate, but did not deliver formal lectures. The study period ended with a conference at which students read papers and the work of each group was subject to general discussion.

The syndicate weighting in marks was the equivalent of one written paper: staff members who did not participate in the syndicate acted as additional assessors.

<u>Role-Playing and Simulation in Politics</u>: First-year students at Lancaster University who chose, as one of their options, a Part 1 course in Politics, could participate in a 'cabinet decision-making game' and an international crisis simulation. The rules for

these exercises and the briefs for those
taking part were developed by academic staff
in the department. Normally about ten students
(members of a seminar group) took part in the
cabinet game, and a group of up to sixty took
part in the international crisis game; they
were allotted roles which they were expected to
play in accordance with the brief provided.
There is room here for a great deal of initiative and the various outcomes would be largely
determined by the way in which the parts were
played and by the members' reactions to each
other. The cabinet game was a regular part of
the main course, and the international crisis
simulation has been voluntarily undertaken over
a weekend.

Platform Discussions in First Year English:
Firstyear undergraduates in the English Department at Manchester University were introduced
to literary criticism and analysis by means of
platform discussions between members of staff
in the department. Following a lecture on a
given topic the students were asked to read a
relevant text. Aspects of the text were then
discussed by members of staff before a student
audience. Students were encouraged to interrupt this discussion and to participate in it.
The idea was to demonstrate the approaches to
analysis and criticism which students would be
called upon to use in their studies of literature. The technique also had a socialising
function, since first year students were able
to meet with and listen to several members of
staff at each session. Platform discussions
were seen as a useful introduction to seminar
work because, with these discussions, students
could see the range of opinion possible on
literary topics and learn something of the art
of deploying knowledge in argument.

A variant of the skills' development theme
is that of encouraging the questioning of basic
assumptions particularly in respect of the
subject(s) students are studying.

Debating Controversial Issues in Physics: In
the third and fourth year of the Physics
sandwich course at Brunel University, an

191

attempt was made to create a greater awareness
of controversial issues in physical science.
When this approach was originally tried in the
first and second years, it was found that the
critical questioning of certain basic concepts
and assumptions proved disturbing to many
students: the decision was therefore taken to
delay the process until students had been able
to acquire a greater background of knowledge
and experience. Given active encouragement by
the staff, many issues for discussion were then
raised by the third and fourth year students.
In particularly interesting cases, a debate was
arranged involving two or more lecturers as
well as the students themselves. On occasions,
basic differences of approach towards a
problem were highlighted by lectures involved
with separate parts of the course. The conflict
often resolved itself into a question of integrating separate areas of knowledge or gaining
a perspective by contrasting one set of
assumptions with another. For instance, in
atomic or nuclear physics, the relationship of
micro (or localised) systems to the main
(macro) system with which they are intrinsically associated can provide conceptual
difficulties for many students: it was found
that such difficulties could often be resolved
by exposing them to open discussion.

This scheme was not without its problems. After a
few years it was evident that the genuine spontaneity demanded of the lecturers in a public encounter
where professional integrity could be at risk, meant
that few were willing to participate, with a consequent loss of spontaneity. After a year of
experiment, the scheme became somewhat artificial
and was discontinued.

Videotapes and Group Discussion: One of the
courses offered to students in the School of
Environmental Studies at University College,
London dealt with Perception and Communication.
It was voluntary, non-assessed and primarily
for first year students. One and a half
hours a week was timetabled for a series of
programmes dealing with basic aspects of
perception and communication. Six twenty-
minute video-tapes - designed to show the

importance of an individual's assumptions, expectations and attitudes in communication, the effect of context, and the essentially egocentric nature of perception - were prepared by Dr M.L.J. Abercrombie. These were intended to stimulate students to question previously held assumptions and attitudes and thereby come to a clearer understanding and command of their own processes of seeing and learning.

In the first term the videotapes were used as a prelude to group discussion. In the second term discussions on the main themes were continued; but were linked where possible to the projects on which the students were working. Films were shown where relevant to the specific topic under discussion; and some lectures were given on more specialised problems of communication (for example, communication on building sites).

Evaluation indicated that some students welcomed a course which, though academically relevant, was voluntary and earned no examination credit. It was also found that students welcomed the opportunity the course provided to get to know one another and members of staff, and the way in which it helped them to express themselves.

For source of video tapes see ULAVC (Page 308)

Getting the Most from Lab Work
Laboratory work typically occupies a lot of student time and institutional resources, yet is often a source of incipient boredom to both staff and students. Why this should be in an area replete with possibilities for discovery learning, scientific purpose and the application of theoretical knowledge is a matter worthy of research in its own right.* Suffice to say that several academics have seen the potential of making the laboratory experience more stimulating and have found ways

*Perry (1968) recounts a 'brilliant freshman scientist who was so disgusted with "cook book" laboratory exercises that he took to playing variations on themes and finally provoked his instructor into blurting: "See here, there'll be no more experimenting in this laboratory."'

of linking it to the rest of the curriculum in a congruent way where previously it existed as a misunderstood extra. One of the more popular features seems to be the conducting of experiments in groups followed by comparison and mutual criticism between groups. Within this format there is potential for students to develop experimental skills, a co-operative approach to study and the ability to communicate what they have found out.

New Approaches to Chemistry Teaching: The Chemistry Department at City University instituted a number of different approaches to the teaching of inorganic chemistry to meet the changing attitudes of students and changing employment prospects for chemistry graduates. The overall aim was to promote self-motivated, intellectually independent people through a study of chemistry.

There was, for example, a team approach to practicals. Divided into groups of four or five under a member of staff, each student was given a different but related experiment. On the completion of the experiment each student wrote it up and spoke about it in a seminar at which the group discussed and criticised the work done. Discussion with, and criticism by, their peers was found to generate a great deal of initiative and energy among the students.

(This scheme was later discontinued because it was difficult to transfer the sense of commitment to other staff.)

Laboratory Seminars in Physics: In the first year programme at Brunel the customary three-hour sessions of experimental laboratory work were augmented by small group 'laboratory seminars'. Each group of six students worked with a tutor on a particular theme (for instance, insulation) and considered possible applications of various physical concepts, principles and techniques. Students were encouraged to discuss any aspect of the theme which they considered relevant; the discussion was as far as possible kept open-ended. Experimental work was introduced or developed in whatever way appeared important. All members of the group

were expected to work on the design and construction of the experimental equipment and
were expected to keep an up-to-date log book
and to write reports. The main aims of the
laboratory seminars were to encourage a co-
operative approach towards the solution of
problems and to give students greater confidence in their ability to communicate.

Learning About Experimentation: A new approach
to laboratory work was adopted in the Engineering Department at Brunel University. All
first-year students attended a self-contained
course in experimentation which ran over two
terms. The aim was to provide an intellectual
challenge through experimental work. The
experiments served not only to illustrate or
amplify physical laws but also provided student
experience in the clear formulation of experimental objectives, the planning of an experimental programme and the unravelling of laws
from data.
    The laboratory periods were of three
hours' duration and two such periods, one week
apart, were devoted to each experiment. Students worked in two and threes: members of staff
(there was one tutor to every ten studens for
the experimentation course) discussed progress
and problems with each group during each
session. The course was supported by a series
of six lectures (subsequently videotaped)
covering such areas as the approach to experimentation; dimensional analysis; curve fitting
and technical report-writing. Students were
provided in advance with a full explanation of
the course, together with detailed suggestions
for keeping their notebooks. The notebooks and
each report were carefully scrutinised, the
marks forming part of the overall asessment.

A series of three videotapes entitled
'Experiment in Experimentation' is available from
the Television Centre, Brunel University.

Rather than allowing students random progression through their practical work, some departments
organised a clear sequence in which the evolution
of skills was closely linked with a series of group
tasks.

Linking Seminars to Laboratory Work: The Physiology Department of the Nottingham School of Medicine devised a system of laboratory work and related seminars which allowed students to participate in a number of experiments without increasing the total time spent in the laboratory. For the experiments students were divided into, say, six groups of eight. These groups carried out related but not identical experiments, and each member of the group wrote up the work in a form that was easily communicable to his colleagues. For the seminars, the students were divided into another six groups, so that each new group contained at least two members of an original group. Thus each student in the seminar not only presented, or helped to present, the report of his experiment, but also heard reports of about two other experiments.

For further information see Short & Tomlinson (1979).

Reorganisation of Laboratory Work: In the Department of Physics at Birmingham, the old laboratory 'circus' system, where all the equipment was set up in several laboratories through which everyone passed, was abandoned and replaced by a more structured 'unit laboratory' system. For instance in the second year there were three 'unit laboratories' concerned with transistor electronics, electrical measurement methods, and optical physics; students spent three successive periods of five weeks in each laboratory, followed by a further seven to eight weeks on a substantial project. In each of the laboratories a member of staff set up a linked sequence of laboratory and seminar work with a group of 12-14 students. Staff developed the work in their own way: for example one unit might start with very simple problem experiments, leading on to a group discussion of the lessons learned and perhaps the introduction of certain principles concerning the techniques used. These ideas were further developed by assigning more complicated problems to individual students who might report back to the group in subsequent seminars. The sequence possibly ended with

short open projects involving use of the ideas
developed.

There were certain advantages noted. An
individual staff member had a more definite
and personal responsibility for the progress
of a group. Students also had the benefit of
working in small groups on a connected set of
ideas linking experiments with the development
of theoretical understanding. It was found
that student effort and attendance improved.

The following innovation was the direct result of an
evaluation of the traditional style of laboratory
work.

Systematic Course Revision in Electrical
Engineering: Until 1973 the first year
Electronics laboratory course in Electrical
Engineering at the University of Salford was
organised on mainly traditional lines. Students followed a set pattern of structured
experiments, guided by detailed instruction
sheets. However, it seemed to some of their
teachers that, since many students were
clearly unhappy with this approach, the
problem should be investigated.

First, a research fellow in the department undertook a preliminary survey of staff
and student views of the course; this was
followed by a detailed questionnaire aimed at
discovering their perception of the aims of
the course and the relative importance of the
aims perceived. At the same time, a sample
survey was made of twenty university departments of Electrical Engineering in order to
find out about significant recent changes in
first year laboratory work patterns elsewhere.

The information obtained in this way led
to a restructuring of the course with the aims
of reinforcing lecture material; creating
greater interest in the subject; and providing
the opportunity for students to become familiar
with sophisticated equipment. Students worked
in pairs through a series of experimental
problems of increasing difficulty. No
direction sheets were provided, but lecturers
spent more time in the laboratory and were
available to help where necessary. The
experiments gradually became more open-ended
as the course proceeded; by the end of year

they were, in effect, small projects involving problems of design and the construction of equipment.

The power of assessment can be used to advantage, too.

A Lecture Course with Discussion Groups in Biology: One of the courses available for second and third year students in the School of Biological Sciences at Leicester University was concerned with development and differentiation. It was run jointly by two lecturers, one from Genetics and one from Biochemistry, and 20 to 30 students took it each year. Like all other courses in the School, it consisted of 33 lectures and 50 hours allocated for practical work. However, no practical classes were run and the time was used instead for a series of group discussions and for free time during which the students were asked to prepare for these by reading prescribed material. Groups for discussion consisted of eight to ten students and each group met about nine times for a period of two to three hours. Topics were announced a few weeks before and were closely related to the lecture course. Extensive reading lists were issued. Each discussion was supervised by one of the lecturers, who took a fairly active role in questioning the students and encouraging them to talk freely, to question one another and to be clear and precise. Much of the prescribed reading consisted of published papers and the emphasis in discussion was often on the interpretation of experimental data, on techniques available for testing ideas, and on the nature of the experimental evidence for material prescribed in lectures. In other discussions, the object was to clear up confusion resulting from the vague use of terms such as differentiation and to discuss the general principles and aims of the course. In these discussions also, the students were encouraged to think in terms of what can be tested.

The discussions were popular and although the students initially felt that the amount of prescribed reading was too great, most of them learnt to extract information more quickly and precisely and many of them claimed to have read

far more during this course than in any other.
There is evidence that many became more
critical and questioning in their reading,
learned to think in terms of testing ideas
experimentally, became more careful in their
use of words and developed confidence in their
ability to cope with complex material.

In the School of Biological Sciences,
part of the final mark for each course was
based on an assessment of course work. In
this course, the students were assessed on
their performance in discussions, but were
asked to write a 2,000 word review of a group
of papers relevant to some aspect of the
course, and in this it was hoped they would
use the skills learnt in discussion. A wide
choice of topics was provided about six weeks
before the article was to be handed in. The
reviews were assessed for breadth, thorough-
ness, clarity, understanding of the published
papers, and critical comment.

There is a possibility that laboratory work may
be seen as an end in itself or as an educational
enclave. At least one attempt has been made to
link it with the rest of the curriculum, however.

Integrating Laboratory and Lecture Courses:
The Chemistry Departments at Cardiff and
Chelsea were collaborating in an experimental
project in which the section of the first-year
physical chemistry course dealing with reaction
kinetics was being run as an integrated activity. Some students in each university were
taking this 20-hour course which was largely
self-paced and had a workshop focus. Time
previously used in carrying out experimental
exercises was used for a wide diversity of
activities with particular emphasis on the
handling of data. Students would, for example,
measure a rate constant as part of a group
experiment on activation energy, work out their
results and bring them to a group meeting for
discussion and evaluation. Each student would
then use the group's collective findings in
his final calculation of activation energy.
The lecturer's function was to develop the
conceptual framework of the subject (with the
help of notes issued in advance), to promote
discussion and to supervise the performance of

experiments and calculations. The course was
assessed in both departments by a three-hour
paper which included a question on data
handling. This common course provided an
opportunity to examine the effectiveness, in
two institutions with similar course aims, of
carrying out and discussing an experiment on a
group basis, linked with the issuing of data
for calculation, notes and questions, as
against requiring every student to carry out
the given experiment himself. The implications
for both staff and students, of such redistri-
bution of time and effort in practical work
were then studied.

See also Magin (1982).

Making Learning 'Real'
Science and engineering teachers are lucky. They
have in the laboratory a ready-made, self-contained
formula for students to try out their academic
learning in practical tasks. The equivalents to the
laboratory in the Social Sciences are case studies,
games, simulations, role-plays and so on, where
students can experiment by applying their own skill
to problems within a controlled environment.

Case Studies, Business Games and Field Work
in Business Studies: Case studies, Feasibility
Studies and Games may be used as an end in
themselves or as a focal point for illustrating
and bringing together various parts of a course
otherwise studied separately. This latter
approach was used at North East London Polytechnic in a four-year sandwich degree course
in Business Studies. The selection and use of
case studies was carefully planned beforehand
and the activities formed an integral part of
the teaching programme. For instance, a course
on marketing used several case studies both in
industrial and consumer marketing at the end of
each series of lectures, to illustrate and con-
solidate the theoretical areas dealt with and
to highlight the practical problems involved.
The behavioural science part of the course used
similar exercises to demonstrate, for example,
decision-making or group dynamics.
     An integrated deterministic model of the
game (non-computerised) designed specifically

for business studies undergraduates was used to highlight the decision-making aspects of business under imperfect information. This game also formed the basis for a study of group dynamics.

In the final year, students paid an intensive study visit to one of the Common Market countries. They analysed in detail beforehand the structure and operations of four or five firms in an industrial area and, from this work, they prepared questionnaires which were sent to the firms several weeks before the visits. They spent one day at each organisation and interviewed a wide range of personnel. Evenings were used for discussing their findings. A report was eventually submitted to each of the firms visited for its comments. Visits were made to the industrial complexes of Rotterdam, The Ruhr, Zurich-Baden-Winterhur, Turin-Ivrea and Lille-Roubaix-Tourcoing.

Simulation of Historical Events: The word 'seminar', in the context of the University of East Anglia, was used to denote both a total course and a one-and-a-half-hour meeting between one or two teachers and eight to fifteen students. In the seminar course on 'Religion, Science and Philosophy in Post-Restoration England', the class was asked in three or four of its individual meetings to simulate a relevant historical event: a parliamentary debate or the trial of a Quaker would be two examples. An outline of the exercise was given to the class in advance, and a video-tape was usually made of at least one of the simulations. Although Professor J.R. Jones, who took this seminar, commented that the performance primarily suits the more extrovert student, he found that the experience of collective presentation, interlinking the imaginative and the factual, helped the majority of students better to understand the salient historical issues involved.

Providing a Variety of Experiences
The expanding body of research evidence (Entwistle, 1976), which shows that students vary in the ways they learn (see pages 39 to 44), makes it apparent

that a variety of learning experiences can help the day-to-day needs of individual students and can cater for the differing needs of students 'across the board'. It can also serve to create different and unexpected understandings of subject matter.

Varieties of Small-Group Teaching: A number of alternative ways of using classes (the major small-group teaching unit at the London School of Economics) were explored by Mr M.J. Reddin in the Department of Social Administration. He was concerned to see how the method and organisation of teaching should vary according to the needs and interests of individual students and teachers, the aims of any particular course, and the kind of material to be presented. The possibilities investigated ranged from the traditional formal paper read by a student, to sessions where the introductory presentation of a topic was split between two to four people while others in the group, having undertaken specified reading assignments, acted as 'resource consultants'. In a contrasting session students would be provided with an 'unseen' case study and with no more than a few minutes' preparation (and with no source materials), would be asked to argue the case for applying a particular policy.

Problem-solving exercises constitute a third small-group strategy; two major forms have been used. The first was deliberately open-ended (e.g. 'You have been asked to design and introduce a system of child allowances in the UK...'). The students were positively encouraged to build an 'ideal' system; in fact, rules could be imposed on the exercise prohibiting consideration of presumed budgetary or cultural constraints. Other exercises, (following this example), then imposed a series of closely defined constraints which could have demanded modification or compromise in relation to the 'ideal' starting point proposals. An alternative approach, more conspicuously practical in its initial focus, was the presentation of specific human 'dilemmas' which required individual professional decisions to be made for immediate action. The aims here were to make the participants articulate the criteria for their chosen course of action and try to identify the degree to which such criteria were 'subjective' or 'objective'; to try to get the students to assess how far their criteria changed over time, particularly whether their formal education at the university affected their views; and to get them to discuss the implications of the specific policy choices.

A Course on Scientific Communication: An optional course in the General Studies programme at Surrey University, 'Science Teaching and Communication', included a component designed to stimulate a more critical attitude towards the way in which forms of scientific communication (usually dealing with aspects of the social responsibility of scientists) are presented. Students were provided with copies of newspapers or journal articles to be read before they attended the weekly discussion class with the course tutor. Each session began with an introductory talk or film appropriate to the content of the article; the class then either had a discussion as a whole or broke up into groups of four or five to discuss and criticise the style, content and implicit values of the communication. In the latter case, each group later presented the main points of its discussion to the whole class and important aspects of the exercise were drawn together by the tutor. Students were, in addition, required to write their own critical appraisal of a selection of the materials studied in this way.

Autonomous Learning

Group discussion, while potentially more democratic than lectures, does not of itself guarantee student participation in the choice, pacing and direction of study. That, in a sense, is a separate 'deal', and its negotiation is one which requires of the tutor careful and judicious handling.

Student Participation in Course Planning: A second year option in the Sociology of Industrial Societies was available to all students at Lancaster University with a basic knowledge of Sociology. On this course, the tutor did not lay down the units or topics to be covered. Instead, students were asked to put forward their own ideas for areas of study relevant to the general theme as it appeared in the course outline. These were discussed in the first seminar; the group then agreed on a structure for the course. Based on a series of themes drawn from the list of those suggested, individuals or small groups of students undertook to study, in depth, two of the topics which were chosen, as far as possible in accordance with their particular interests, and, after a number of individual consultations with the course tutor, presented two project reports for assessment.

No lectures were given, but most students attended the group seminars, which only in the early part of the course were led by the tutor. As the course continued, students organised their own project work and presented their own papers. Each lead at least one discussion related to his own special interest(s).

At these sessions students were encouraged to criticise each other's work, and to make suggestions for the improvement and furtherance of the projects under review. Project work counted for 50% of the assessment on the course, the other 50% being awarded on a written examination. Alternatively, a student may normally have developed one of his projects into a full-scale dissertation to replace all other forms of assessment on the course.

Student Planning in a Dip.H.E.: The two-year Diploma at North East London Polytechnic aimed to share responsibility with the student for planning his own programme. The course began with a six-week planning period during which the student worked out his objectives for the course and negotiated with his tutors the form which his study would take over the two years. Negotiations were formalised in a contract which was available, if necessary, to the validating board for the programme.

The programme for all students comprised work centred on regular sessions in which they aimed to develop co-operatively the skills necessary for the fulfilment of their objectives. In addition, the student carried out special interest studies under the guidance of a tutor who could have been in any subject group in the Polytechnic.

Assessment was entirely based upon course work. Profiles of strength and weakness, agreed by the student, were drawn up at the end of each term and certified copies of these documents were made available to the student on completion of the programme, whether or not he was awarded a diploma. To qualify, the student must have done satisfactory work in Special Interest Studies and in a group 'set situation'.

The course clearly appealed to the mature student; about half were over 25 years of age. A recent study has shown that about 80% of the students in the second year of the course would like to complete an extra year in order to obtain a degree. They also expressed a strong preference for continuing to study in the same way as at present.

The NELP course leads us into the whole philosophy and practice of project work and raises at least three crucial issues for partners in the learning process: what is worth learning, what sort of guidance can you provide and how do you assess? Nowhere do these issues come to light more than in group projects. Should the group take collective responsibility for everything or should there be a division of labour? How does that question affect decisions about whether to assess relative contributions or the team as a whole.

Planning, Conducting and Assessing Group Projects: Many university departments may hesitate to include group (as opposed to individual) projects because of the obvious potential difficulties of assessment. However, students in the Department of Building Science at Liverpool have for some years undertaken this kind of work. A major topic area is chosen towards the end of the second year; a recent example is the building of the new arts library. The full brief, as given to the architect for the actual building, is given to each student. On this basis, rough sketch plans are prepared by individual students. One of these plans is selected for further development and students then collectively decide the main feature of the proposed building (for example, heavy concrete building or frame with curtain walling). At this point they break up into small groups of two or three to study one or more of such detailed sub-areas as project management, foundations, structure, heating and ventilation, cost planning and design and contract documents.

Tutors work closely with students. There are regular committee meetings of the whole group, run by the students, and reports are written both jointly and invidually. The project mark accounts for about 25 per cent of the overall assessment, and course tutors have experienced no major problems in assessing the contributions of individual students to the work of their groups.

The Nuffield Group summarises some of the approaches to assessment in group project work:

'The most serious difficulty in assessing project work is, however, assessing the individual students whose work has been done in a group. The decision in favour of group projects is taken, in spite of this, for what seem to be two main reaons: lack of apparatus or space to enable each student (or at most a pair) to work alone; or because there are positive learning advantages to be gained by group work. In the latter case, syndicate type working is common. For example, a group of chemical engineering students will work jointly on designing a continuous flow reactor, but within the project each student will have a specific task to perform; in effect, individual students carry out projects within the group project. Where syndicate working is not possible, a total mark may be awarded to a project and students may be allowed to distribute this between them. Even when no such total responsibility is given to students it is helpful to consult them at an early stage before decisions about the sharing out of marks are reached. In group project work, very close supervision is essential if the supervisor is to gain as detailed a picture as possible both about the specific contribution of each student and about the working of the group as a whole'. In seminar work, the relative contributions of students are more visible and there are schemes for assessing these which at the same time

underline some of the purposes or preferred
activities in group discussion.

> Stimulating Student Participation in Seminars:
> A method of involving students more actively
> in seminar work was developed in the Department
> of Building Science at Liverpool. One topic
> was chosen each week and allocated to a student
> who was to write a paper and distribute it to
> the group two days before the seminar. Another
> student read the same source materials and
> chaired the seminar. The writer opened the
> discussion by elaborating on his paper; the
> chairman's task was to draw attention to rele-
> vant issues omitted in the paper to stimulate
> group discussion. The course tutor played as
> far as possible a non-interventionist role but
> would attempt to correct misconceptions and to
> sum up at the end. Seminar performance was
> assessed as follows: writing of paper, 40 per
> cent; presentation of paper, 20 per cent; 20
> per cent to contributions as chairman, and 20
> per cent to participation in the discussion in
> other seminars.

Perhaps there is a case, which this points to, for
ensuring that group project work is more visible to
the tutor, at least for review meetings. An example
of how this can be achieved with such meeting and
a positive spur from the assessment procedure is
described below.

> *Cross Referencing in Group Projects: With
> project work there is always a residual worry
> that what students gain in depth of knowledge,
> they lose in breadth. At Technion University,
> Tel Aviv, Israel, in Mechanical Engineering,
> the students do project work in pairs. Every
> fortnight 5 pairs meet to review progress.
> One student in each pair takes the role of
> presenter and the other of scribe and critic.
> Presenter A would describe progress while his
> partner jotted down notes as; critics B2, B3,
> B4 and B5 questioned him. Presenters A2, A3,
> A4 and A5 would then take their turns. At the
> next meeting the roles would be rotated.

*Based on a discussion between the author and
Ferdinand Zawistowski of Technion University. This
item was not part of the Nuffield Study.

Students do all this in the knowledge that 50% of their project assessment will be based on their understanding of one of the other projects at a viva voce examination. The rub is that they are not told which project it will be until they walk into the viva!

*Peer Tutoring in Engineering: There is traditionally a heavy emphasis, in first year engineering and science courses, on learning basic information through lectures. In addition the students can feel very isolated in their first experience of higher education. At Imperial College, in 1976/77, an attempt was made to tackle both issues for the Fluid Mechanics element of the 1st year Civil Engineering course. Lectures were replaced with Open University texts and supplementary notes; the focus of learning was the laboratory experiment done in groups of six to eight students, who were instructed in experimental procedure by a prepared video film. Following the laboratory work, the groups moved to a classroom where they compared their results and conclusions one group with another. When not involved in lab work the group tackled problems, some of them more conceptual than numerical. Here the procedure was to split each group into sub-groups with slightly different phenomena in the same conceptual area. Their task was then in turn to work out their answer or explanation and teach it in whatever way they chose to their companion sub-group. Two tutors circulated offering guidance where necessary. The idea was for the students to extend this 'peer-tutoring' approach to their out-of-class learning and more particularly to their examination preparation.

Sessions on numerical problems were conducted with two of the larger groups in a different room with another tutor as chairman. Each group was given two problems; one to solve and the other to discuss. Following this, one group, each member taking turns, explained their solution to their problem while the other group checked for understanding. The tutor took opportunities to draw out general

---

*This item was not part of the Nuffield Study, but part of an evaluation study I conducted from 1978-80.

principles and clarify problem-solving strategies.

At the end of the course, though 3 months before the sessional exams, a one-hour mock exam was set. Students then each marked and commented on a partner's script with the aid of a set of model answers. Some students found the lack of authority and structure in this course stimulating. Others found it unsettling especially because it took place at the beginning of their college career.

The idea of replacing lectures with other sources of information of course brings to mind the possibilities of structured or step-by-step discussion and the use of video tapes and handouts, and in many ways this could be seen as a firm step in the direction of more student-centred learning.

Background Notes and Course Booklets for Students: The Department of Veterinary Anatomy at Liverpool has given considerable attention to the provision of background notes for undergraduate courses. A complete bound set of course notes and diagrams was prepared and these were available to students for the cost of the materials used - about £1. Each student also received a detailed syllabus showing how the course developed week by week and when and how tests would be administered and marked. Formal lectures for 'covering the course' and giving out factual information were thus largely obviated, and replaced by informal lectures which were combined with spontaneous questioning and discussion. These lecture-discussions were used mainly to analyse difficult topics with the aid of over-head projector transparencies and films.

A similar approach was adopted in one of the lecture courses in the Department of of Chemistry at Liverpool. The objectives of this course were analysed in some detail, and summary sheets, specifying the ground to be covered at each stage, were provided for students in booklet form at the beginning of term. Supplementary lecture material and question sheets related to the objectives were also made available; tutorials were based on the question sheets and thus directly linked to the other elements of the course.

New Teaching Methods and Approaches in Chemistry: For several years Professor Kettle of the University of East Anglia experimented in lectures with ways in which to teach 'group theory' to chemistry undergraduates in the early part of the course. An opportunity in 1972 to try out a seminar approach indicated that seminars were more effective in isolating students' conceptual difficulties and in enabling students to move at their own pace towards an understanding of the subject.

A seminar course was designed which circumvented mathematical difficulties and which concentrated on helping students to understand the concepts of symmetry at their own pace. A series of about twenty ten-minute video tapes were prepared. Video tapes were to be shown at appropriate points in each seminar; the video tapes to be interleaved with structured discussion periods. The next video tape would then only be shown when a pre-defined goal was achieved in the discussion (the goal to be known only to the seminar leaders). On each tape there would be a discussion of the points covered in the previous discussion period illustrated with models. The video tape would then raise questions aimed to take the seminar to the next conceptual stage. It was planned to use post-doctoral workers as seminar leaders. The teaching of the whole course would be discussed with them and detailed course notes indicating the logistic path of the course would be prepared and issued to them in advance. Notes would also be given to the undergraduate students.

For the first term of the first year of this course an introductory laboratory programme was designed which introduced students to the handling of models and to carrying out problem exercises. The course was first taught in this way in 1972 to 1973. It was later developed to use peer-teaching procedures.

Part of one of the seminars on Symmetry Theory can be seen on the video tape of group discussion 'Short Extracts', one of a series available from the University of East Anglia.

There are two other aspects of group projects

which demand attention: the specification (where such direction is relevant) of stimulating tasks and the possibilities for interdisciplinary learning. Often the most exciting experiences for the student are to get outside the four walls of the institution and get involved in the 'real' world.

The inhibitions of the learning milieu are not to be underestimated: the prevailing culture of academic learning and its assessment within the walls of the institution can be very constraining and a sense of both freedom and social purpose can soon be experienced when students encounter unfiltered problems.

Social Responsibility and the Curriculum: A number of university departments are experimenting with curricula embodying some 'social action' component. An example is provided by the Electrical Engineering Department at Imperial College, where third-year students were given opportunities to integrate their technical and non-technical studies through a choice of projects on such themes as medical electronics, safety for shipping in the Channel, electric cars - past, present and future. Students worked in teams of five or six with a staff supervisor who acted as observer and consultant: each team had an allocation of £10 for incidental expenses. Each group tended to develop a division of labour as students began to explore their relative skills in terms of making outside contacts, contributing to 'brainstorming' about the plan and scope of the work, drafting the report and so on. Much help was given by the library staff to students needing access to non-technical literature and information. The scheme in general succeeded in arousing the active involvement and interest of both students and staff. The group project represented just over 8 per cent of the final-year degree work.

Although the programme was originally limited to electrical engineering students, the plan was gradually to extend it across department, faculty (and even institutional) boundaries and hence build up a central bank of suitable project themes exploring social issues related to a number of different academic disciplines.

Law in its Social Context: A number of law
schools have responded in the early 70s to a
growing concern of students in the social
aspects of the subject. The Department of Law
at the London School of Economics experimented
with a variety of possible approaches. One of
the most successful was the organisation of a
one-week group project after the first-year
examination. The project (which usually
attracted the participation of more than half
the annual intake of 70 or so undergraduates)
was planned to involve field surveys on various
aspects of the functioning of the legal system:
examples included a study of the awareness of
tenants of their rights under the rent acts; an
enquiry into the incidence of legal representation in magistrates' courts, county courts,
rent tribunals and rent assessment committees
in London; a review of the extent of compliance
with the laws of consumer protection of window
advertisements in retailers' shops. The tutor
collated and published the results of the
students' field-work in appropriate journals.
The main benefits to the students were in terms
of their participation in a published study
early in their legal training, their experience
in taking part in a substantial piece of
research, and their opportunity to see for
themselves the law in action.

Other activities included a free legal
advice service for anyone at LSE (where some
twelve law students, assisted by a faculty
member, regularly manned an advice session
twice a week), and the planning, as a third
year option, of a 'clinical programme' involving a practical experience of professional work
assessed for credit on a pass/fail basis and
based on the experience of similar programmes
in the USA.

To some extent the following scheme served not
only to realise inter-disciplinary aims but also
took students out of the immediate influences of
their own departments.

Collaboration Between Specialist Engineering
Students: An experimental final-year group
project, involving students from each of the
main engineering departments at Queen's

University, Belfast, was organised in 1973.
Engineering students at Queen's took a common
first year, after which they chose a special-
isation in Aeronautical, Civil Electrical or
Mechanical Engineering. This project was devised to see whether students, having specialised, could fruitfully work together again on
a common area, in this case, personal rapid
transport. The students, who were supervised
by a member of staff from each of the departments involved, met and reported on their work
weekly, and more general planning meetings were
held every month. Each student was responsible
for a specific part of the project, and, with
the help of the staff, an overall timetable and
flow-chart were devised at the outset. At the
end of the year, each student submits to his
department an individual report, on which he
was assessed. A general report on the scheme
also went forward to the Faculty Board.

A Special Combined Studies Programme: The
Science Faculty at Leeds has made considerable
effort, to provide, for students in combined or
joint undergraduate courses a sense of identity
and manageable workloads. The planning, co-
ordination and day-to-day administration of the
now numerous joint courses (some of which cross
faculty boundaries) were the responsibility of
the Combined Studies Department, with a full-
time Director, an Assistant Director, seven
lecturers from different departments (each
working one day a week for the Combined Studies
programme) and its own ancillary staff. All
were housed in the Combined Studies Centre
which comprised offices, a common room, seminar
rooms and the students' study room. A Combined
Studies Society provided social activities and
also organised the election of students to
staff-student committees. These served three
groups of students: those concerned mainly with
biological subjects; those concerned with mathematical subjects; and those involved in other
science subjects. Although the committees, on
which students are in the majority, had no
executive power, they are recognised as having
an important advisory function. They met regularly under the chairmanship of the Director;
the meetings were called and the agenda drawn
up by an elected student secretary.

Designing Courses

The idea of using small group techniques for curriculum development may fall strange on the ears of those of us brought up to accept an atmosphere of individual and separate responsibility for the content and process of courses. Yet our aims in designing courses are very similar to those of an interdisciplinary seminar. Similar techniques might therefore be beneficial.

A Syndicate Approach to Curriculum Development:

At Sussex, a first-year core curriculum in molecular science chemistry and some courses for those specialising in chemistry were developed by a number of working-groups. These groups were called syndicates, and consisted of three members of faculty drawn from differing areas of the subject. There were seven syndicates at work at one time. Since the beginning of 1972, the syndicates have worked on the formulation of course objectives, and have now produced detailed lists of objectives for each part of the course. The syndicates selected and produced relevant materials, and devised appropriate forms of assessment. When the courses were in operation, the syndicates continued to review and evaluate them.

Group Planning of Courses:

The Department of Chemistry at University College, London, adopted a team approach to the development of their new first-year chemistry course. This course, on 'The Molecular Basis of Chemistry', aimed to show how the chemist relates experimental observations on matter in bulk to models at the atomic and molecular level, and how the interplay of the chemist's observations with conceptual models allowed the latter to be refined and developed.

The course, a compulsory precursor of all further main chemistry courses, consisted of approximately 70 lectures and 70 hours of laboratory, seminar and library work. It was divided into five main sections. In planning the content and teaching materials, the group of five lecturers responsible for teaching the course for the first time in 1973 to 1974 divided into pairs: one pair was made responsible for each of the five sections. Where possible, as a matter of deliberate policy, no lecturer worked on a topic with which he was especially familiar.

In collaboration with the London University Audio-Visual Centre, the group prepared a number of slides and filmstrips with accompanying notes and audio-tape discussions, so as to provide the students with a wide range of learning materials. Since no suitable textbook embodying this approach existed, specific and general reading notes were made available together with outline notes on each lecture. In the first year all five members of the team attended every lecture. In the two years that it ran it was a great success, especially where we the class divided into small units, each with a group leader for programmed seminar, practical calculation and problem classes.

Evaluating Group Work

Although we shall be looking at this aspect in greater detail in Chapter 9, the following description could serve as a reminder that the best laid plans of staff and students for group learning may come to nought without a built-in means of reflection and self-appraisal.

Analysis of Video-Taped Tutorials: During the academic year of 1971 to 1972 a number of physics and mathematics tutorials in the School of Mathematical and Physical Sciences at the University of Sussex were video-recorded and subsequently discussed by a small group of faculty (twelve). Each tutorial contained one member of faculty and about five students, and by using a wide-angle lens the sessions were usually recorded in the normal surroundings of the tutor's room. The group started meeting for about 1 1/2 hours on a weekly basis during the Spring Term of 1972 (until the end of the Summer Term) and was concerned with attempting to find a more adequate language to discuss learning and teaching within the tutorial situation. Interaction analysis and discussion of the tapes led to more general discussions on the nature and purpose of tutorial and small group teaching within the Sussex pattern and an attempt to agree on some basic objectives. It appears to those concerned that the recording and subsequent analysis of tutorials may be useful not only for faculty but also for students.

Handling Change

The foregoing case studies include a cross-section of several different but inter-related elements: subject area, tasks, techniques, organisation, planning and evaluation - all within the context of various aims and purposes. There should be sufficient reference points for readers to recognise or identify with similar concerns in their own institution. The case studies are in the main not so much a description of problems but of solutions to them. If any of them seem to fit your own concerns and inspire some sort of action, that is all to the good, but beware! Colleagues might not share your analysis of the problem any more than your proposed solution. Your understanding and handling of a wider group process may be well and truly tested in your attempts to introduce even small changes to the system. Further reading might be a good idea. See for instance Huberman (1973), Havelock (1973) and Bennis, Benne & Chin (1968). But don't let opposition to change undermine your enthusiasm!

Postscript

Two excellent source books on how to improve lectures, seminars and tutorials are now available. See Gibbs, Habeshaw & Habeshaw (1984) in the Bibliography.

Discussion Points

° What external influences are there on the work of groups you belong to? In what ways do they affect what happens?
° What principles of learning in groups seem to be evident in the various case studies? Draw up a classification chart.
° Discuss the differences between the ways members of your group relate to each other inside as opposed to outside the seminar/meeting. What seems to determine these differences?

EVALUATING GROUPS

Whenever two or more people interact they are in some sense evaluating one another. Teachers do it of students, students of teachers, each of their own colleagues. The trouble is that, when others make judgements about us, we usually feel threatened and undermined; it is taken as an attack on our self-esteem. There are, too, understandable doubts among teachers about any evaluation which attempts to judge complex phenomena in simplistic terms. Teachers, as Miller (1975) remarks, are:

>'sceptical that the intricate network of their experience, which contributes to their concept of themselves as a teacher, can be encompassed in some kind of measurement which is either meaningful or helpful'.

Yet even if a suitable kind of measurement were available the probability is that most teachers would find 20 good academic reasons why their self-image should not come under scrutiny.

The major part of this problem is possibly that a sense of being judged is likely to create a defensive reaction. In the view of Gibb (1961), a defensive climate results from the sort of communication which displays evaluation, control, strategy, neutrality, superiority, or certainty. Supportive or co-operative climates, on the other hand have the following qualities: description, problem orientation, spontaneity, empathy, equality and provisionalism. Each of these corresponds to its equivalent defensive quality taken in the same area. Thus it is more supportive to say, 'Just then, it seemed as if you were having difficulty with students who wanted to go their own way in the discussion.'

(provisionalism) rather than, 'You can't control discussions!' (certainty). (c.f. list on pages 54-55)
The way in which evaluation is handled is clearly of great importance if the results are to be accepted and acted on positively. A lot of the threat can be taken out of evaluation if as much initiative and responsibility as possible rests with those being evaluated (E) as in the following approach:

1. E says how he feels.

2. E describes what he noticed about, what he was conscious of, in himself during the interaction; what he noticed about the others. The others then describe what they noticed about E.

3. E names as many positive things as he can about what he did. When E has finished, others name positive things.

4. E names the negative points about what he did but is asked to translate these into problem questions thus:

   'I let Pat go on too long' becomes 'How can you stop someone going on too long?' to which E's answer might be 'By saying, "Hold it there Pat, I'd like to hear what other people think about that before you go on"'.

   Once E has exhausted his list of negative points, the others propose theirs but convert them into problem questions.

5. E finally says how he now feels.

(E need not be just the tutor. It could refer to any student or to the whole group.)

The value of this approach is that, in first requiring a description of events, it is less threatening to E and should develop a greater awareness among all concerned of process as it occurs. Then, in commenting first, E can anticipate the potentially hurtful things others might say or might feel inhibited about saying. Last, in having negative points converted into problems, a constructive future-orientated view is encouraged.

The timing of evaluation is important too. We do not like to hear something critical of ourselves, either when we feel vulnerable (e.g. when something has just gone wrong and there is an audience watching) or when it is too late to do much about it (e.g. at the end of a course). A 'formative' evaluation, that is one done in order to achieve useful changes for those involved, is generally less threatening and of greater learning value than a 'summative' one, completed at the very end of a course.

Who initiates the evaluation, who conducts it, who processes the results and how, where it is done, who else is doing it in parallel - all these questions may also be of consequence in determining how efficiently an evaluation is carried out and, more importantly, how conscientiously its results are implemented. Yet, where evaluation is seen as more of a regular process in which all group members view themselves as contributors and take responsibility for outcomes, there is more chance of change through co-operation. Five minutes set aside at the end of each meeting to review how things went, are therefore likely to be of greater benefit to all concerned than any formal externally applied procedure.

Evaluation as Learning

It will be apparent to anyone using these techniques that they are not merely a way of evaluating group work but also give individuals the chance to reflect on their own behaviour in groups. In this sense they comprise a creative source of learning, one that informs both individuals and the group as a whole about their part in its work and suggests ways of improving the group performance. As Cox writes in UTMU (1978):

> 'Significant developments in the evaluation of teaching will not come from staff thinking about their own courses, or from students as consumers expressing their judgements about the courses which are provided for them, but by an integration of evaluation into the learning process so that an important part of the students' learning is in fact coming to understand his own strengths, weaknesses, inhibitions, and styles of thinking and working in relation to the varieties of constraints and opportunities presented by the course.'

Evaluation, whether it be of individual students, the group, the tutor or all of these, is likely to improve the prospects of training and improvement:

1. if it enhances the experience of teaching by creating a climate of openness and honesty where there might otherwise be a sense of secretiveness and mistrust,

2. if it is organised as a co-operative act in which both teacher and students articulate their experiences and both learn from it,

3. when there is no question of its being used for promotion or other public purposes, except where this has been clearly opted for,

4. where it is organised at stages in the life of a group rather than at its con- clusion and all concerned can have the opportunity to develop and change for mutual benefit.

As Miles (1981) comments, group members feel better about evaluation when they see the specific methods as clear and sensible, and that it is an integral part of a training programme and feeds directly into improvements.

Some Evaluation Methods for Small Group Teaching
The method or technique that one chooses to evaluate group work must, of course, be established and agreed within the context of the group and the overall climate of the learning situation. The consequences of unacceptable evaluation can be disastrous. Before evaluating, questions like:

'Who is it for?'
'How is it to be used?'
'How honest can we be?'

have to be faced and answered.

1. Observation: Though the observations of an eval- uator external to the group may to a certain extent be invalid and superficial, a collection of such views, provided they are to do with the group as a

whole and do not refer to the behaviour of individuals, can form a useful basis for appraisal of the groups' success. The fishbowl technique can therefore be a useful device in this respect.   In this, one group arranges itself concentrically round the other and the outer group acts as observer, and evaluates.   This relationship is reversed to allow the second group to be observed.

2. <u>Diaries</u>: Whenever the life of a group extends over a period of time, members can derive great benefit from keeping diaries in which they can record:

(a)   what ideas, concepts, principles and information they learned.
(b)   what they learned about their own ability to discuss, agree and express ideas, as well as their own contribution to the group process.
(c)   how they saw the group as a whole.

Rainer (1980) offers a host of ideas on diary writing.   If these diary comments can be shared in the group even on a selective basis, many helpful insights can be gained by students and tutors alike.

3. <u>Reporting Back</u>: At the beginning of each group meeting, 5 to 10 minutes may be allocated to one or two members who report back what happened, and what they gained from, the previous meeting.   For this to work the rapporteurs for the following week must be selected at the beginning of each session so that they are alerted to the task in good time. As with most forms of open evaluation there is an incidental spin-off: a sense of continuity between one meeting and the next.

4. <u>Checklists</u>: Any group is, of course, free to determine its own criteria and marking system for evaluation of its own performance.   On pages 230-236 are five Schedules for use in study groups and workshops.   They are valuable as triggers for discussion as much as for a thorough evaluation. They may be used by the group itself or by another group in a 'fish-bowl' arrangement (see above).

5. <u>'Do it yourself' checklist</u>: Using the 'snowball' technique, (see pages 92 & 93) (individuals --> pairs --> fours --> eights) individuals are asked to write down a maximum of three statements worth

221

making about the group/class/course, and these are
successively pooled and refined in sharing them
with a progressively larger number of colleagues.
Finally the whole group is asked to draw up a list
of statements (which must be shorter than the aggregate number produced if any real discussion is to
occur). These are written on a board or newsprint
on public view. Each statement is then given a 3
or 5 point scale from 'strongly agree' to 'strongly
disagree' and everyone marks their rating for each
statement with a blob (to make the weighting or
preferences more visually apparent).

e.g.: I think this
group has wasted
all but the last
half hour.

SA	A	N	D	SD
●●●	●		●● ●	● ●

Fig.9.1   Statement Ratings for Group Evaluation

The great virtue of this technique is that everyone
contributes and the results are immediately visible.
The group can thus quickly discuss some of the
salient features of the ratings, particularly those
where close agreement is apparent and those where
there appears to be a fairly equal balance between
opposing views.

6. Interviews: Whilst one-to-one interviews for all
students are hard to justify in terms of time and
energy spent they can be of unpredictable benefit,
both in what they can reveal of the less-than-
conscious experience of students and tutors, and in
the way they help students to integrate their
learning; interviews require participants to reflect
intensively and comprehensively. One-to-two interviews are more economical but not so confidential,
while one-to-group interactions can reveal to the
interviewer a lot about how effectively the group
operates. Who conducts the interviews is of course
a problem, though, given an open and trusting
relationship between tutors, there is no reason why

one should not interview members of another's group. It is not our purpose here to learn interview techniques but it might be helpful to indicate to budding interviewers some of the sorts of questions which might stimulate revealing answers (though they may not all be suitable for every situation):

How did the group go for you?

What did you like best about it?

What did you like least about it?

What sort of things, apart from content, do you believe you learned from it?

How would you describe the climate of the group?

How would you describe this group, as distinct from any other you've experienced?

Any suggestions on how the tutor might improve the handling/the work of the group next time round?

Anything you would like to have said to the tutor at the time but preferred not to?

What else stood out for you?

Questions of this kind are usually sufficient to provoke a wealth of comment on group experience. With the additional use of 'eliciting' questions, (see pages 164-165) there should be little problem in getting a comprehensive picture of what went on.

7. <u>Pass-round questionnaire:</u> Each student is asked to divide a sheet of paper into three areas to cover:

'Things you found most valuable, and why'

'Things you found least valuable, and why'

'Ideas for improvements'

and to write responses to each. Once completed,

each sheet is passed round the group and read quietly in succession by each student. When the sheets have circulated to the last person before returning to their author, students are invited to read out or recall any comments they agreed or disagreed with or which stood out in any other respect. Finally the authors receive their sheets back and add any further comments to their sheet before it is collected for processing.

8. Self-made Evaluation: More sophisticated groups may be asked to split into two or more sub-groups, each of which has to devise a technique of evaluation which it will use on the other sub-group(s), and then to administer it. It could choose from one of the above techniques or create an original one. Whether the self-made evaluation is set up as a regular monitoring task throughout the life of the group or is organised only at the end is a matter of choice, but it does have the enormous virtue of being good fun and thus raising spirits at the end of a course when they are typically at a low ebb.

9. Video Playback: Provided the group can be recorded in its natural setting, video recording and play-back can serve to alert everyone in the group to behaviours and events which they may have failed to notice at the time they were recorded. A consultant from outside the group can be brought in to start and stop the play-back at the behest of the group and to ask facilitating questions about the interaction:

'What was going on there?'

'What were you thinking/feeling at the time?'

'What effect did that have?'

'What did you fear might happen?'

'What was your strategy?'

'What do you think he expected of you?'

and so on.

Alternatively the playback could be sprinkled with questions such as on the checklist on pages 226-7.

Managing the Evaluation

It is easy for an evaluation of group work to
resolve itself into a critique of the tutor rather
than of the whole group. Certainly, the tutor
will, in most cases feel, responsible if things go
'wrong' but, recognising the mutual nature of human
interaction for being what it is, we must avoid the
temptation of judging the success of a group in
terms of the tutor's skills alone. This notion
becomes more compelling when we understand the
value of the students themselves learning about
their own group skills through the process of
evaluation.

Evaluation works best if it is seen as a
continuous process engaged in by all those who contribute to the setting up and participating in the
group. Many of the evaluation methods or instruments included in this chapter can be used equally
well for training purposes. The choice of which one
to use may depend on the preferences of the group,
the style of its operation or the kind of problem
that seems to beset it. The group may choose to
develop new instruments and methods more responsive
to their immediate situation. Whichever approach we
use, we must be aware of the sorts of bias to which
evaluation may be subjected, particularly the wish
to please (or displease). For this to be revealed
for what it is, the 'results' of the evaluation must
be processed through discussion in an open climate
where support and challenge can create the possibility of change, (see Smith, 1980). The way in
which results are presented is therefore of the
utmost importance; this may be another matter to be
determined by consensus in the group.

Please turn to next page for checklists for use in
evaluating groups.

CHECKLISTS

Observation of Discussion (From UTMU, 1978)

Objectives

1. What was the purpose of the discussion?
    Was it clear to the participants?
    Did they accept it?

2. Is the teaching method appropriate for these
    objectives?

Setting

1. The room itself - what associations does it
    have?
    Does it encourage intimacy and relaxation?

2. Seating - are the chairs comfortable? All the
    same?
    Draw a plan of their arrangement. Note empty
    chairs, distances between participants, promin-
    ence of any one group member including the
    teacher.

Role of the Tutor

1. What role was dominant? - facilitator,
    chairman, instructor, etc. (See pages 146-149
    on the Role of the Tutor.)

2. Was it clear, accepted, appropriate?

3. What kind of questions were asked - open,
    factual, personal reactions, critical, appropr-
    iate to the level of the students, loaded...?

4. What proportion of the time did the teacher
    talk?

5. What techniques were used to involve group
    members?
    What use was made of praise and encouragement?

6. Were students discouraged from participating -
    how and why was this done?

Evaluating Groups

Roles of Individual Students

1. What interpretations (if any) can be made about individual students' characteristic behaviour? What observable effects do they have on relations within the group (including the tutor)?
2. What role does each student have (e.g. leader, playboy, passive observer, clarifier, consensus taker, reconciler, etc.)?
    Are these roles temporary, changing or permanent?
    Are they sought, accepted or thrust upon them?

Dynamics

1. Length and frequency of each member's contributions.

2. What status does each group member have? (N.B. the teacher is a group member.)

3. Is the group harmonious or competitive?
    How were conflicts dealt with? Denial, avoidance, repression or made explicit and worked through?

4. What emotions or motives are aroused? e.g. Do questions produce fear, curiosity, laughter ...?
    What are the goals of group members?
    Do they coincide with the teacher's objectives?
    How much commitment?

5. Did the group stay formally as one group or did it split up for different phases?
    What effects were produced by the changes or lack of change?

6. What rules appeared to prevail, what behaviour is appropriate in the group, e.g. order of speaking, not disagreeing with tutor, avoiding specifics?

Group Behaviour Questionnaire

Instructions: Answer all questions with the names of two group members. Base your nominations on interactions in the group. Be sure to choose two people for each question. Do not include yourself.

1. Which members can most easily influence others to change their opinions? _____ _____

2. Which are least able to influence others to change their opinions? _____ _____

3. Which have clashed most sharply with others in the course of the meetings? _____ _____

4. Which are most highly accepted by the group? _____ _____

5. Which are most ready to support members? _____ _____

6. Which try to keep themselves in the limelight? _____ _____

7. Which are most likely to put personal goals above group goals? _____ _____

8. Which have most often introduced topics not directly related to the group task? _____ _____

9. Which have shown the greatest desire to accomplish something? _____ _____

10. Which have wanted to avoid conflict in group discussions? _____ _____

11. Which tend to withdraw from active discussions when strong differences begin to appear? _____ _____

12. Which have sought to help in the resolution of differences between others? _____ _____

13. Which have wanted the group to be warm, friendly and comfortable? _____ _____

14. Which have competed most with others? _____ _____

15. Which have done most to keep the group lively? _____ _____

16. Which would you choose to work with? _____ _____

17. With which have you talked least? _____ _____

Fig. 9.2

Reprinted from: J.William Pfeiffer and John E.Jones (Eds.), A Handbook of Structured Experiences for Human Relations Training, Vol III, San Diego, Ca: University Associates, Inc., 1974. Used with permission.

Evaluating Groups

Statements for Evaluation of Group Function

1. Members of the group have agreed upon and understand the specific goals for the group

2. Members of the group have agreed upon and understand the ground rules for the group activity

3. The group has responded to the feelings or moods expressed by its members

4. The group has listened to and responded to members' ideas and comments and expressed recognition of contributions

5. All members of the group are involved and have participated in the discussion

6. The atmosphere of the group has been friendly and open, encouraging members to express criticisms or ask questions which expose themselves

7. The group leader encouraged discussion by group members before presenting his own ideas to the group

8. The group leader has synthesised related ideas and summarised concepts that the group has been discussing

9. The group leader has determined if all group members have reached agreement about a particular point or are ready to move on to something else

10. The group has confronted a member who was hindering the group in achieving its task such as undue arguing, going off topic, etc.

11. The group has been able to discuss areas of differences between members such that it does not avoid conflict nor does it allow the discussion to become destructive

12. The group leader did not dominate nor did the group defer unduly to the leader's recognition of contributions

13. The group has evaluated its progress toward its goals during and at the close of the session

14. At the end of the session the group has decided on its specific task and work required to be done for the next sesssion

COMMENTS

Fig. 9.3

(From 'The Small Group Tutorial' McMaster University Educ.Monograph 3, 1972)

229

Evaluating Groups

Analysing Group Activity

Please rate each aspect in terms of the description of each end of the scale by circling the most appropriate number.

1. Degree of mutual trust

   High suspicion   3 2 1 0 1 2 3   High trust

2. Degree of mutual support

   Genuine support for each other   3 2 1 0 1 2 3   Everyone for themselves

3. Communications

   Guarded, cautious   3 2 1 0 1 2 3   Open, authentic

4. Group Objectives

   Not understood by group   3 2 1 0 1 2 3   Clearly understood by group

   Group is committed to   3 2 1 0 1 2 3   Group is negative towards
   objectives   objectives

   Low attainment of   3 2 1 0 1 2 3   High attainment of
   objectives   objectives

5. Handling conflicts within group

   We deny, avoid or suppress   3 2 1 0 1 2 3   We bring out conflicts and
   conflicts   work through them

6. Utilisation of member resources

   My ideas, abilities, knowledge   3 2 1 0 1 2 3   My ideas, abilities, know-
   and experience were properly   ledge and experience were
   drawn out and properly used   not drawn out and not
                                        properly used

7. Suitability of group method

   Group method suitable for the   3 2 1 0 1 2 3   Group methods unsuitable
   objectives   for the objectives

GENERAL COMMENT

Fig. 9.4

Evaluating Groups

Group Behaviour

Observer's Sheet

BEHAVIOUR									
Initiating									
Clarifying									
Seeking information									
Giving information									
Integrating									
Consensus testing									
Encouraging/ supporting									
Mediating									
Standard setting									
Compromising									
Gate keeping									
Releasing tension									
Expressing group feelings									
Being open									
Dominating									
Manipulating									
Blocking									
Belittling									
Distracting									
Splitting									
Excluding									

Task — Positive (Initiating through Consensus testing)

Maintenance — Positive (Encouraging/supporting through Being open)

Negative (Dominating through Excluding)

These terms are explained more fully on page 232

Fig. 9.5

Evaluating Groups

Initiating Proposing tasks or goals; defining a group problem; suggesting a procedure for solving a problem, suggesting other ideas for consideration.	**Clarifying** Clearing up confusion; indicating alternatives and issues before the group; giving examples.
Seeking Information/Opinion Requesting facts about a problem; seeking relevant information; asking for clarification, sources of interest etc.; asking for suggestions & ideas.	**Giving Information/Opinion** Offering facts, providing relevant information; stating a belief; giving suggestions or ideas.
Integrating Putting related ideas together; building on others' contributions; summarising ideas at end of period of discussion.	**Consensus Testing** Sending up 'trial' balloons to see if group is nearing a conclusion; checking to see how much agreement has been reached.
Encouraging/Supporting Being friendly, warm and responsive to others; listening attentively; accepting and respecting others and their contribution.	**Mediating** Attempting to reconcile disagreements; getting people to explore their differences.
Standard Setting Expressing standards that will help group achieve worthwhile goals; applying standards in evaluating progress of group.	**Compromising** Offering to compromise own position, ideas, status, admitting error, disciplining self to help maintain group.
Gate Keeping Seeing that others have a chance to speak, bringing in and shutting out, keeping discussion open to whole group.	**Releasing Tension** Draining of negative feelings by making a witty intervention, diverting attention from personally embarrassing matters; triggering laughter.
Expressing Group Feelings Sensing mood of group, relationships within group, feelings of others and expressing them.	**Being Open** Revealing feelings/inner thoughts; expressing disquiet, frustration, satisfaction etc.

The above group behaviours explain the terms included in the Group Behaviour — observer's sheet on page 231. They may also be used as behaviour cards in a group discussion.

Fig. 9.6

Evaluating Groups

Discussion Points

° What are the principal risks in evaluation for
  (a) the evaluator and (b) the person(s) being
  evaluated? What happens to the risks when these
  two are one and the same?
° Choose one or more of the evaluation measures to
  review the work of your group(s). What makes the
  one(s) you choose more useful or valid than any
  other? How might you administer it? How did it
  work out?

TRAINING METHODS AND ACTIVITIES

The natural offspring of evaluation is learning and change. Without these consequences the task of evaluation would be sterile. The primary concern of this chapter is to consider ways in which improvement in group behaviour can be effected. There are three possible approaches:

The Practice Group: in which a small number of people (tutors and possibly students) come together to study group process either in a workshop or a regular series of meetings within a risk-free environment whose boundaries are sacrosanct.

The Teaching Group: Seminars, tutorials, etc. in which the focus for learning about group process is the tutor/student group itself with all its thorns and roses.

The Task Group: for example, a staff working party or conference planning team who may, apart from their primary task, wish to learn about how to work more effectively as a team.

Each of these naturally has its own merits. Each could complement the others as part of an integrated programme; and starting with one might well lead to the development of others.

Practice Groups
Readers of this book will by now be well aware that group processes embody a complex web of attitudes, understandings and behaviours. Some of us learn to function effectively within this web quite early in life but, for most of us, it appears

there is a great deal of <u>unlearning</u> to do: shedding some of the expectations and stock responses we have developed over years of parenting and school- ing, and acquiring new ways of listening, perceiving and acting in groups. Changes of this kind involve considerable personal adjustment and many might argue that this is too much to expect of adults, especially those in a teaching role. Yet, as Miles (1981) has pointed out, if the group itself is used as the learning medium, more change is possible than many of us are inclined to think. The various exercises included in this chapter are all based on small group activity. They assume that the small cohesive group is the most effective medium for personal understanding and growth in group skills, whether it results from a regular meeting of committed tutors or as one of several sub-groups in a large-scale workshop.

The exercises are based on one further assump- tion: that participants are committed to improving learning in the groups of which they are part. This does not mean there is no value in one or two antipathetic members taking part. Far from it; one or two cynics may contribute hugely to the creation of a realistic group process and may also cause their colleagues to take less for granted. Yet if, for whatever reason, their purpose is persistently negative, their presence can destroy the fabric of the group.

Whereas academic discussion in seminars often deals with content divorced in time and space from what is occurring within them, 'practice' groups have to focus much more on the 'here and now' experience of their members. Just as there is no way in which one can comprehend group dynamics without seeing it in action, so it is virtually impossible to become aware of one's own effect on a group, or to develop new skills, without part- icipating in the dynamics of a group committed to these tasks. In order to develop more effective group behaviours, the learner must have the chance to learn from doing, exploring, trying out and from observing others.

For this to happen, the group must operate in a climate where there is a degree of mutual trust and tolerance and where participants feel free to take risks in admitting failings and anxieties and in experimenting with newly-learned behaviours. One of the most revelatory processes in practice groups is seeing ourselves as others see us. In some cases this can arise when others describe how they saw us. However as the feelings of safety and trust grow in a practice group, it becomes increasingly possible for members to reveal their own observations about themselves and each other. Though this trust may grow quite naturally in a well-run group, there are helpful exercises in developing it. One of these is the Johari Window interaction (page 53). Nevertheless, an atmosphere of trust does not develop easily and it is often safer at first to employ distancing mechanisms (for instance video tape or role play). It is less threatening to learn about one's own behaviour in a group by watching and identifying with others in an enactment whether those others are:

(a) unknown people on a prepared video tape

(b) the group members themselves detached in time through the playback of an interaction video recorded shortly before

or

(c) a role play in which members may (semi-legitimately) claim they were not being themselves.

Such devices, though always to be valued, become less and less necessary as the degree of trust develops, excepting always that a particular problem may generally or individually pose too great a threat for live confrontation, or that it is the only way of bringing an external scenario like a laboratory within the scope of the practice group's immediate experience.

Finally, it is important to stress that the central concern in practice groups is to examine the social rather than personal behaviour. How people relate to each other has precedence over what goes on inside them (though the latter is of definite consequence). The practice group is 'usually less concerned with the inner reasons for why someone does something and more concerned with how he does it, what the impact is on others and how he can improve what he does to become more skilful' (Miles, 1981). A person may, in the course of such a group, gain vivid insights into some of his inner problems, especially in the way they may hinder his effectiveness in relating to others, but this is incidental to the primary concern of the group.

Planning   Once a practice group has been launched or even before, someone will have the responsibility of preparing and planning, whether that person is a designated or a self-appointed leader.   There are various concerns he or she will have to address, each of which may affect the quality of learning in the practice group.   Among these are:

(i)   Assessing own motives

(ii)   Making judgements about the institutional context:

    (a)   what attitudes and interests in group learning exist

    (b)   what priority participants are likely to give it

(iii)   Deciding:

    (a)   who should plan

    (b)   who should participate

    (c)   timing and physical arrangements

    (d)   roles of leader(s)

    (e)   evaluation strategy

(iv)   Organising the content (a sequence based on psychological rather than logical criteria is usually more effective)

(v)   Choosing ways of maintaining continuity between activities or separate meetings

Above all, the programme for a practice group should be amenable to change in response to members' developing needs and interests.   Ideally it should be planned and monitored by them in the way described as a Peer Learning Community (Heron 1974).

Leading   The role of leader in a practice group (if of course it is relevant at all) need not be unlike that of the facilitator described in Chapter 7 but with a ready reprertoire of techniques and skills to demonstrate, in response to issues that arise in the group.   As leaders we must also be prepared to face considerably more challenge to

our position than academic tutors, with their
legitimated authority, might expect. We should not
be put off our stroke by this, but rather see it as
an opportunity for further 'here and now' discussion
of the way a tutor might handle critical incidents.
For instance if an incident arose in a practice
group the leader might ask 'How would you handle
this if you were in my position?'.

As practice group leaders we may expect to be
confronted with the following sorts of problems:

1. Initial attack or challenge to our
   authority, or worse still: withdrawal

2. Being 'trapped' by anxiously dependent
   members - 'Tell us what the tricks of the
   trade are; how you would do it?'

3. Conflict over expectations and aims,
   especially where there are involuntary
   members

4. Resistance to change - 'This is irrelevant, it doesn't apply to us', 'What's
   the theoretical justification of all
   this?' or long abstract discussions

5. Frustration - people feel they are not
   getting what they want from the group

6. Revolt, where a group wants to go its own
   separate way (fight)

7. Cosiness - 'Aren't we a lovely group?' -
   which probably means that the conflict and
   pain necessary to learning and change are
   being avoided (flight)

8. Low points, where spirits are flagging -
   can occur at any time but almost always
   at the end when members are likely to be
   somewhat depressed that the life of the
   group is at an end.

In tackling these problems the leader will
have to draw on a range of skills, techniques and
strategies, be _alive_ to the need to maintain continuity and momentum, and be flexible in allowing
reasonable changes of direction and alternative
courses of action. Wyn Bramley's book 'Group
Tutoring' (1979) is full of practical hints on this

sort of problem and merits close reading.

Teaching Groups

The opportunity for risk-free experimentation is of course much less in a normal tutorial or seminar group. It is not easy to stand aside from the tutoring task (though opportunities for role play of a different kind might arise) and we might risk undermining our credibility if we were to expose our failings (and feelings) to general scrutiny. Nevertheless if evaluation can be viewed as a learning as opposed to a judgemental procedure, then the possibilities are boundless. Any of the evaluation techniques described in the previous chapter could be used provided always that it is used as a basis for developing more effective behaviours and processes in the group, and that it is conducted as a whole-group task rather than as one polarised between tutor and students. Whether this work is done on a planned basis, or activated by critical incidents and crises as they arise, will depend on the kind of course being followed and the relationship between the tutor and the students.

Task Groups

Both tutors and students are frequently called upon to work on specific tasks with a view to developing some kind of end-product. Staff working parties and student project groups are examples of these and there are close parallels between them. Yet rarely do either tutors or students reflect on their teamwork skills in their work together, or seek substantial improvement in their skills as the work progresses. This is understandable when we consider how unusual the demand for co-operative behaviour in a general climate of rivalry and competition must appear to members of a task group. Increasingly, however, the need for improvement in this basic management skill is being appreciated in negotiating problems in teamwork. Two successful approaches to learning teamwork studies 'in the saddle' are:

1. to give team members a short induction in which they practise various training exercises (those on pages 250-268 for instance), in anticipation of problems to come; this could be followed by a shorter session in the middle of the project or task as a checking and topping up exercise

2.   to encourage the group to use simple evaluative measures, checklists, or diaries, and to meet at prescribed times to discuss teamwork problems and make explicit what they are learning from their handling of them.

In the case of student projects, where assessment has an important place, there is a danger that the competition for marks will initiate open discussion of co-operative strategies. In this case it may be a good idea to require in addition to the project report, a commentary on process issues in the project and what students learned from them. This commentary would be a necessary part of the final submission but would not be assessed. The checklist on page 268 is of especial value with small groups of this kind.

TRAINING ACTIVITIES

The following examples of training activities are not in any sense a cookbook for improving group skills. Leaders or tutors will need to adapt them to meet the immediate requirement in the light of their own abilities and the situation in hand. It would probably not be wise therefore to use the activities without reference to the rest of this book. Readers will no doubt develop their own variations and create new exercises which make more sense in their particular setting.

The activities are designed for work with groups or sub-groups of no more than eight members, possibly in a workshop format. The aggregate number of sub-groups should not exceed four or five.

In selecting any particular activity a tutor or leader might check that:

(i)   It is appropriate to the interests and mood of members at the given time

(ii)   It has relevance to their teaching/task needs

(iii)   Learning occurs at different levels

(iv)   Learning can readily be transferred or carried beyond the confines of the learning environment

    (v)   The skills required for running them lie within the tutor's competence.

What may be acceptable, relevant and feasible by the end of a series of activities may be less so at the beginning. The beginning in fact requires special attention and it is usually sensible to start with some warm-up or introductory activities. The first two exercises described on the following pages are of this kind.

Paired Introductions   Commonly in groups, individuals are invited to introduce themselves as a way of getting started. It is hoped thus that everyone will become more open and friendly towards each other and that defences will be somewhat lowered. Yet frequently people are either reluctant to say much about themselves or ramble on at an inconsiderate length about their own background and interests. Interpersonal boundaries often remain untouched. A procedure that appears to be much more successful in breaking the ice socially is as follows:

    (i)   individuals interview their immediate neighbour in the group for two or three minutes about their background, interests and what they hope to get from the group or workshop, and are in turn interviewed by the same neighbour.

    (ii)   each person then introduces their partner to the group (in no particular sequence) preferably 'as the spirit takes them'. A time limit of two minutes or so is imposed on each contribution.

    (iii)   any person who feels something important about them was left out by their partner may repair the omission at the end.

    (iv)   Everyone may be asked to reflect on the experience and to consider whether they might use it with their own academic groups.

This complete procedure should be explained to everyone before they embark on it.

<u>Walking Interviews</u> With a larger group it is often desirable to encourage a level of mixing which seated positions do not allow. Walking interviews encourage people to mill and ask questions of each other that they might not otherwise consider. The procedure is:

> (i)   members are invited to write down one (or two) questions which they would like to ask every other member of the group.
>
> (ii)   they then mill around, locate a partner to put their question to and themselves answer questions from. (There is an explicit proviso that anyone may refuse to answer any particular question without any consequence.)
>
> (iii) when a reasonable degree of mixing has been achieved, the group may be reassembled and asked:
>
>> (a) whether any general patterns of information emerged.
>> (b) what specific items of interest people picked up.

Several other 'ice-breakers' may be found in Pfeiffer & Jones (1973 to 1984), Davison & Gordon (1978). See also Card Exchange.(pages 275-6).

<u>Prepared Video</u> The tape or film of an unfamiliar learning group is ideal for this activity. Such a tape is 'Short Extracts', obtainable from the Small Group Teaching Project at the University of East Anglia. This shows edited excerpts of groups in different subject areas at various stages in the development of discussion. One procedure for using this tape is to play it with the leader in control of the stop/start switch but with everyone permitted to signal when they want it stopped. In the following step-by-step discussion (see page 91) the leader asks questions about the group on the screen such as:

> - What sort of atmosphere has been created? and how?
> - What expectations does the tutor appear to have? What expectations do the students appear to have?

- How would you describe the manner of the tutor? What effect do you think it has?
- Have you any comments on the physical layout, numbers, apparent statuses? How do these affect interaction?
- How would you describe the tutor's relationship with the group?

The most suitable points to ask these questions, and others which will certainly arise, will be evident in the screened action as it evolves. The timing is a matter of judgement, bearing in mind what is to come. The leader must therefore view the tape beforehand.

At certain critical points on the tape, such as when the tutor asks the group a question or a student aims one at the tutor, more specific questions may be asked:

- What do you anticipate will happen?
- How would you respond if you were the tutor/ a student?

at which point participants could be asked to role play in pairs what they might do. Then, after the tape has been played forward to reveal what eventually did happen:

- What did you think of that?
- What other ways could the tutor have gone about it.
- What would be going on in your mind if <u>you</u> were the tutor?
- How do you see the discussion developing now?

and so on.

At other times it may feel right to ask questions which search for the emotional underlay of the discussion:

- How do you think the students/tutor feel?
- What is going on?

or, for the intellectual life of the group:

- What do you think the students are learning?

and whatever answers are forthcoming:

- Anything else?

in order to press for less obvious issues.

The University of East Anglia Small Group Teaching Project has six other video tapes:

'Boxes'
'Inorganic Reaction Mechanisms'
'The Waste Land'
'Why be Moral?'
'Kyd's Spanish Tragedy'
'Art and Popular Imagery'

<u>A Contract for Small Group Discussion</u> (Rudduck,1978). Discussion of this document is almost guaranteed to unearth all sorts of assumptions and values in small group teaching.

The Evidence

1.   A contract designed by a seminar leader to contain the effects of his authority.

Moral Philosophy

(Please read twice and note any obscurities.)

During this term we shall be doing more than Moral Philosophy; we shall be conducting an exploratory experiment in small group learning.

(i)   Hypotheses: most small group work, as at present conducted in this school* (perhaps in the university as a whole), obstructs the intellectual independence of students and leads them to depend on the faculty leader. The faculty leader, in turn, finds intellectual and emotional security in using his authority and expertise to dominate the small group situation. Minor frustrations apart, this set-up satisfies both students and faculty; but it may be educationally disastrous.

(ii)   Phenomena Consistent with This Hypothesis:

1.   The Faculty leader introduces, imposes and forces discussion back to his own agenda:

*School, i.e., Department of the University.

(a) he takes note and pursues only those student remarks which can be used for or bent towards his ends

(b) his questions often have, as their only point, the eliciting of an already anticipated answer (for instance, they seldom express genuine puzzlement)

(c) tensions arise when the expressed purpose of the small group (free discussion) clashes with the faculty leader's hidden agenda

2. In the shadows of the leader's agenda (either explicit or hidden), the students:

(a) spend much energy in trying to guess at the leader's agenda (the guessing game)

(b) try to get the leader to produce his agenda in a series of mini-lectures

(c) are reticent in producing remarks which cannot clearly be seen to fit the supposed agenda

(d) direct all or most of their attention to the leader's remarks and little to those of each other (particularly true of the brighter student)

(e) get many of their psychological rewards anticipating or fitting their remarks to what they take to be the leader's goal. Punishments accrue insofar as they fail in this task.

3. Many students do not feel the intellectual or social need to prepare for small-group work. They can be assured that the faculty leader will take the burdens of keeping things going:

(a) watch for the use, by students, of the weapon of silence; and for the faculty leader's response

(b)   notice how preparation for small-group meetings tails off when students realise that the leader will ensure that the relevant arguments, the important theses, the critical appraisals are covered regardless of volume and relevance of student contributions.

(iii) Towards an Alternative Method: If the hypothesis under one is correct, then there should be some arrangements which help small groups to break the stranglehold of the faculty leader and generate some intellectual autonomy amongst students. The following strategies are directed to that end and they constitute the explicit conventions under which we shall work this term.

1.   Coverage of material: With the institution of examinations in the background, it is inevitable that students should worry about covering the group. If this worry is taken into small groups then it is my impression that discussion can suffer; both students and faculty regard the small group as a means of extending coverage, consolidating information, reinforcing lectures. The leader enters the room with an agenda to be forced through, and the students attend with note-pads at the ready. To combat the demon of coverage, we shall test the following moves:

(a)   small group discussions will not be geared to the subject matter of preceding lectures

(b)   coverage of material will be achieved by a set of nine or ten lectures (Monday of each week), arranged to deal chronologically with moral philosophy from J.S. Mill up to the present time

(c)   each student will be required to take one of the following texts and study it in depth - hopefully, in co-operation with one or two other students. An essay will be written on this chosen text or on some aspect of it. (List of several introductory texts.)

2. 'Follow-up' lectures: At the end of each week, the course is timetabled for a second lecture. This is designed to allow me to follow up questions and issues raised by the small group meetings of the week. If there is nothing worth following up, or if we decide to use the hour differently, then the lecture will not be given. This is the only lecture time explicitly associated with the small group discussion material; the first lecture of each week is not designed to provide grist for the small group meetings.

3. Agenda for Small Group Meetings: The agenda for each week's seminar meeting will lie in the hands of the students. Each group of twelve will divide in half and each sub-group of six will take it in turn to sort out the week's agenda. Each sub-group will need to meet together (and with me) in the week before their week of responsibility to warn the others of the reading required for the following week's meetings. I will try to ensure that the necessary directions for the following week are duplicated for all members - and, if possible, the necessary reading. In week two, the other half of Group A will repeat the process, thereby deciding the agenda for week three.

Two things are worth stressing. Firstly, that the sub-groups really are free to choose any topic falling under the head of 'Moral Philosophy'; they may decide to extract themes, arguments and assumptions from the manifesto of the Gay Liberation Front, or they may prefer to chop up an article by A.J. Ayer. Secondly, by the end of about the fifth week everyone ought to be picking out patterns of, and relationships between, various problems. By that time each group ought to be in a position to string together small group discussions so that their results are cumulative and connected.

4. Conduct of Small Group Meetings: it would

be a mistake to think that small group meetings run on a student agenda are likely to be more informal or more comfortable. It will be an explicit convention that the sub-group in charge of the week's meetings does not present a sub-group lecture to the other members; the object of the exercise is that everyone should be prepared to contribute to the topic in question. The sub-group which has decided the agenda is obviously in a better position to guide and help the discussion, but its members have no more obligation to contribute than anyone else. At all costs we must avoid the phenomenon of a passive audience sitting through a class paper.

5. Recessive Faculty: It should be clear that our small group meetings are explicitly designed for student-control; my own role will be recessive and consultative. As the groups (hopefully) gain internal solidarity it will be easier for me to enter the discussions without fouling up the pattern. Most of my time in seminars will be spent trying to identify the emerging themes and arguments of the discussions so that I can write them up for the second lecture of the week; any questions I ask should be requests for clarification.

6. Assessment: It is important to make explicit that nothing you do (or fail to do) in the small-group meetings will be assessed for grading purposes. Grades for the course will be determined by two essays.

   (a) An essay on some one text, part or aspect of a text, chosen from the list under (1)(c). Due in: Week 6.

   (b) An essay on the title 'Why Should I be Moral?' (Reading list to follow). If you wish to choose some other title then please see me first. Due in: Week 9.

Although grades will be determined by the above essays, no grade will be given unless you keep,

Training Methods and Activities

A Contract for Small Group Discussion Quotation Continued

week by week, a record of the work done for and in the small-group meetings. This record will consist of a loose-leaf folder (35p at the Bookshop) containing:

> Accounts of your work in the sub-group
> Accounts of the themes and arguments raised each week in the small group meetings
> Three summaries of your own developing views, to be written at the end of Weeks 3, 6 and 9.

These folders must be given in at the end of the course and, in addition, I will try to collect a few each week (from Week 2 onwards) to comment on. (They will, of course, be returned the following term after the final collection.)

7. Evaluation of the Course: We shall need to meet periodically to discuss what is going wrong and how we might put it right. I will try to arrange such sessions in Weeks 3, 5 and 7. If any individual student has problems, then I am available at any time to discuss them - timetable permitting.

Consultants' and Assessors' Game
A structure which can be adapted to serve many different purposes.

Preamble: The Consultants' and Assessors' Game provides a framework in which a variety of problems can be examined and solutions proposed. The participants, instead of talking around issues in an open-ended way have to make proposals to a panel of assessors. The class is split into two or three teams who take the role of consultants or experts with the task of providing a solution to a relevant problem. Their solution or proposal is presented to an assessors' panel which is composed of one or two representatives elected from each group and their job, in addition to making the final adjudication, is to set criteria for the acceptability of the proposals or solutions. The whole exercise should last 1 1/2 to 2 1/2 hours.

Aims: To experience working as a team on an agreed task within a limited time-span. To produce proposals or solutions on a given problem and to subject them to critical scrutiny. To study some of the interpersonal behaviour and reactions arising from inter-group competition and perceptions.

Number of Participants: A minimum of ten and a maximum of 25. All should have a reasonable level of experience in the field covered in the task (see Organiser's Instructions, paragraphs 2 and 3).

Time Required: A minimum of one hour, but preferably 2 1/2 hours. (The smaller the total number participating, the less the amount of time needed.)

Materials: Whatever the teams require for the presentation of their proposals. Newsprint or OHP transparencies with pens will probably suffice.

Physical Setting: A room large enough to accommodate the teams and the assessors' panel without undue sound interference; otherwise, separate rooms for each team: also, a room (may be one of the above) in which the formal presentations of the teams' proposals can be made.

Training Methods and Activities

Organiser's Instructions

1. Explain the goals of the exercise and describe its structure by using the following diagram.

Assessors' Panel

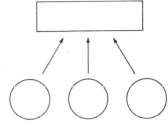

Consultants' Teams

Formulate criteria
Supervise presentations
Make assessment

Formulate separate proposals

Make presentations to Assessors Panel

2. Either announce a preselected problem or task to be worked on by the teams, or invite everyone present to suggest and agree one. The task should be one which the participants are competent to work on and which allows for a variety of solutions (for example, the design of a bridge or a study skills' course, the formulation of a new law or a research submission).

3. Agree with participants on sufficient background information to define the context of the problem. It is important to remember here that definition of too much detail:

(a) is time consuming,
(b) can stifle a lot of creative thinking,

and
(c) can detract from the central task.

For example, if the task is to design a study skills' course the teams will doubtless need to know how many students there are in the institution, what subject areas are studied and possibly how much money the team have got; but other questions such as how long the course should be, how many tutors are available, whether any members of the team are to be tutors, when the course should be held and so on, may be left to the teams to decide within the ambit of their proposals.

4. Having negotiated the task, form two or three teams (not more than 8 in each) and set them up

Organiser's Instructions (Cont'd.)

    in separate working areas.

5.   Now distribute the Consultants' Team Instruction Sheets.

6.   After about 20 minutes, remind each team to elect two members who will jointly comprise the Assessors' Panel. They will not <u>represent</u> the views of their original team so much as take them into account in determining criteria.

7.   Once the Assessors' Panel is composed, find them a suitable place to meet. Give them the Assessors' Panel Instruction Sheet.

8.   At this stage the teams sometimes want a clearer definition of role, e.g. are they lay pressure groups proposing a new law or are they architectural consultants competing for a tender? If it helps to sharpen their focus this should be encouraged. It may be one team wants to imagine they are students and the other lecturers in proposing a new course. So be it, as long as it neither inhibits the production of imaginative proposals nor undermines the competitive nature of the game. Make sure that all teams are fully informed of any such decisions.

9.   Announce a timetable and make it clear to all that it will be strictly adhered to. The timetable must allow at least 30 minutes total for the presentation and discussion of all the proposals. For example, if the overall length of the session is 1 1/2 hours the following timetable might apply for 3 teams.

Introduction and negotiation	10 mins.
Teams work on proposals	45 mins.
Presentation and discussion	35 mins.

    For certain problems a longer work time (and hence total time) may be needed if proposals of sufficient quality are to be achieved.

10.   Act as referee to ensure that the instructions are clear and being followed. You may need to make interpretations and variations from time to time. These should be within the context

of the game and, unless there is good reason for not doing so, should be announced to <u>all</u> participants.

11. Should the Assessors' Panel ask whether they may communicate with the teams or vice versa, advise them to decide that for themselves in the context of the whole exercise, or just ignore the question.

12. You may also act as a neutral resource person in any way appropriate to the content of the exercise.

13. The teams will invariably be oblivious to the passage of time. They will therefore need reminding of approaching deadlines and of any other responsibilities.

14. Keep a check on any other decisions implied in the two Instruction Sheets.

15. Review (at least 30 mins). There are several ways in which the review session can be conducted. A lot will depend on whether the game was run primarily as an exercise in group and inter-group dynamics or as a way of producing a rich variety of ideas and plans on the problem under consideration; whether the emphasis was on process or product. The main thing is to give some recognition to things that will have gone on both within and between groups and the fact that the experience will have been both an intellectual and emotional one for most participants.

Before embarking on any discussion of process or product you may find there are a few feelings floating around which may need to be defused. You might do well to ask:

'How is everyone feeling - anyone want to get anything out of their system?'

or something similar, but then, as soon as the immediate response to the question has taken place to quickly pass on to the <u>process</u> discussion.

After this you might adopt the following pattern:

(a) Ask the teams separately to discuss and

report back in plenary, questions about:

Leadership and the distribution of tasks

How conflicts were resolved and decisions made

The effects of time pressure

The criteria by which Assessors were elected

How the Assessors felt during the presentation phase

How the Consultant teams felt about the Assessors

(b) In plenary, draw out the answers to the above questions and try to build up a more generalised picture of the events in the game and the implications with questions about:

How easy participants would find it to join one of the other teams to implement the winning, or any other, proposal and what that implies

What parallels there were with 'back home' experiences, structures, relationships

How they might use the format of the game in their own work

What they learned from the game generally/about themselves

What things they might wish to do or change as a result

(c) Then there are questions about the product:

What they thought of the quality of the proposals

How the proposals compared with equivalent ones 'back home'

What improvements they could make to the proposals

How they might use the ideas in their own work

Of course the opportunity to ask questions at pre-ordained times rarely arises. You will probably have to be fairly selective and pragmatic in the sequence of the above questions.

Training Methods and Activities

Instruction Sheet I

<u>Consultants' Team</u>: Your main task as a team is to prepare a proposal on the agreed topic. After 10 minutes you will be asked to choose a member of your team to leave and become part of an Assessor's Panel. You will then have an agreed period of time in which to formulate your proposal.

You will be expected to present your proposal to the panel at the agreed time. You will have 5 minutes (10 if time allows - check with tutor) to present your proposals. After your proposals have been heard there will be 2½ (or 5) minutes for a question and answer session with the Assessors' Panel which will then evaluate the separate proposals.

The Assessors' Panel has 3 tasks:

* to determine criteria for judging the merits of the proposals submitted.

* to take full responsibility for the conduct of the presentation session.

* to make an open adjudication on the various proposals presented to them.

You should also decide how you are going to present your proposal bearing in mind the strict time limit.

Training Methods and Activities

Instruction Sheet II

Asssessors' Panel: You are independent assessors and in no way represent the teams from which you were elected.

Your task while the teams are preparing their proposals is to establish criteria for their evaluation. In addition you should agree a procedure for the adjudication.

Each of the teams will decide for themselves how they are going to present their proposal. They will each give a five-minute presentation followed by five minutes of questions and answers with you (times may be extended by the organiser). All the presentations should be completed before the question and answer session starts.

You should set up the room for the presentation roughly in the pattern showed by the organiser at the start, and establish a reasonably formal atmosphere.

Once the presentations and questions are complete you will naturally wish to discuss your impressions and make the necessary decisions. This discussion should last no more than five minutes and be conducted openly so that all the teams can hear.

The adjudication may take two forms. One is to announce one of the teams as the winner. The other is to discuss openly the relative merits of the proposals. In either case you should make public the reasons for your assessment and reveal the process of arriving at it.

You are responsible for the conduct of the presentation session.

Building a Team - A Simulation Exercise

1. Aims

   To encourage students to discover something of
   the talent, skills and qualities they bring to
   a team to help them consider their adequacies
   and deficiencies as a team.

2. Time Required

   Thirty minutes to one hour, depending on size
   of teams.

3. Numbers

   It is better if several teams do the task
   simultaneously so as to provide a richer
   variety of understanding about group dynamics.

4. Procedure

   (a) The tutor distributes the task and asks
       each team to take regard of the time
       limit.

   (b) After 20 minutes (the timing is flexible -
       the main point is to ensure that the teams
       can reach agreement in the time allowed)
       invite the teams:

       (i)   to explain and justify their choice;
       (ii) to describe how they arrived at
             their choice;
       (iii) to talk about what the procedure
             described in (ii) told them about
             their team and the different people
             in it;
       (iv) to predict how they might best use
             their collective strengths and
             weaknesses as a team.

5. Variations

   (a) The details of both the task and the
       profiles may be changed to suit.

   (b) Teams can be invited to exchange members
       to enable each to achieve a better
       balance.

Task: You are working as a group of final year students in Community Studies on an educational project designed to examine the problems of teaching professional courses in the health-care field. The project is to be marked as a group task and you will also function as a tutorial group up to and including separate exams, each of which will include a question in interdisciplinary studies. Your team is short of one member. Various other students are interested in joining you and their profiles are given on the attached sheet. You have 20 minutes to choose by consensus the final member of your team from those described on the profiles. You will then be asked to explain your choice and how you went about making it.

Profiles

Philip: A 'mature' student, he has had a lot of experience in industrial management with a special interest in committee work. He actually likes writing reports and hopes to become an NHS administrator. Is married with a family of 4 children. In groups he tends to create a sort of safe and trusting atmosphere.

Yvonne: Is a very attractive blonde who matches her good looks with a fine sense of humour. She is also very intelligent, is full of ideas, but does need a lot of encouragement to succeed. Yvonne tends to invest energy in her work only as long as promising results are just round the corner.

Mary: An interesting and caring girl with an unhappy home life, she seems to cover up for her problems by working hard and successfully. However, she does return home every weekend, and is then not contactable. She is very critical of the way most systems are managed and her views on health and care tend to be very radical. In groups she has difficulties making her intentions understood.

Harry: Is a great raconteur who can make the most pedestrian incident sound fascinating. He writes well too, though his academic standing is low. He has however a lot of drive and is usually liked by all who work with him. Groups tend to depend on his presence, once he has established himself.

Gill: Is an excellent organiser. She achieves this

through a mixture of charm, flirtation and sheer persistence and she would be the first to admit that she consciously manipulates people when it suits her. She is good at directing the attention of the group to its own process and likes to talk openly about personal behaviour.

Geoffrey: Is very conscientious and particularly good at searching out and piecing together detailed information. He has, however, a stammer which makes him embarrassed to contribute to discussion and he would probably rather work on his own. His work is however always completed with great diligence.

Winnie: An acerbic partner for anyone, she has developed a fine critical intellect which frightens many people away. She gathers many admirers but has few if any close friends. She is much respected by the tutors and will probably stay on to do research. She is often valued for the intellectual discipline she exerts on a group.

Training Methods and Activities

NASA Exercise: Seeking Consensus

Aims: To compare the process of individual decision-making with group decision-making. To develop an awareness of teamwork skills.

Class Size: Any number - several groups may be directed simultaneously.

Time Required: Approximately one hour and a half.

Materials: (i) Pencils

(ii) Individual task and work sheets

(iii) Group instructions

(iv) Answer sheets containing rationale for scoring

Physical Setting: An open room where participants can sit in face-to-face groups, preferably in circles.

Procedure: (i) Give each participant a copy of the work sheet and tell them that they have fifteen minutes to complete Step 1 of the exercise.

(ii) Give each team a group instruction sheet and tell them:

(a) Individuals are <u>not</u> to change any answers on their individual sheets as a result of group discussion.

(b) The teams will have thirty minutes in which to complete Step 2 on the work sheet.

(iii) When the teams have completed their rankings, then either hand out or read out the NASA 'answer' sheet. Do not get drawn into arguments about the correctness of the answers. They have been made by a 'NASA expert': you are merely passing them on.

(iv) Ask them to complete steps 4 and 5 and invite each team to call out

(a) its group score.

(b) its average individual score.

(c) the highest and lowest individual scores in the team.

(v) Draw up a chart such as the following (I have added sample numbers to illustrate)

Score Group	Average Individual	Range	Consensus
A	55	27-71	20
B	36	20-53	57
C	41	36-45	40
D	50	30-67	26

and write explanations of the differences especially Team B: 'What went wrong?' and Team C 'Was there not enough difference of opinion?'

(vi) Draw comparisons between the NASA ratings (page 267) and those of the participants.

(vii) Invite open discussion on issues like:

(a) Whether teams had any agreed procedures for making decisions and if these worked.

(b) What sort of arguments seemed most convincing.

(c) What leadership roles emerged and what function they served.

(viii) If time permits, hand out the 'Teamwork' checklist and ask each individual to fill it in separately with their rating of their team. Then ask them to compare ratings and discuss any discrepancies.

(ix) Finally, invite comments on what everyone has learned about teamwork and what they, personally, might do about it in the future.

Task Sheet

Situation: You are a member of a space crew originally scheduled to rendezvous with a mother ship on the lighted surface of the moon. Because of mechanical difficulties, however, your ship was forced to land at a spot some 200 miles from the rendezvous point.

Problem: During landing, much of the equipment aboard was damaged and, since survival depends on reaching the mother ship, the most critical items available must be chosen for the 200 mile trip.

Task: On the task sheet are listed the 15 items left intact and undamaged after landing. Your task is to rank them in terms of their importance for your crew in allowing them to reach the rendezvous point. Place the number 1 by the most important item, and 2 by the second most important, and so on, through to number 15 the least important.

Step 1: You have 15 minutes to complete this phase of the exercise by yourself. Please do not confer with anyone while deciding on your rank order.

Step 2: Now rank the items as a team. Once discussion begins, do not change your individual ranking. Follow the group instructions on the separate sheet.

Step 3: Fill in the expert's ranking.

Step 4: Compute the difference between Stage 1 and Stage 3 (all differences positive).

Step 5: Compute the difference between Stage 2 and Stage 3 (all differences positive).

Total the differences in both the above steps. Compute the average, for your team, of the total individual differences in Step 4 and compare these with the team total (Step 5).

NASA WORK SHEET	Step 1 Your Individual Ranking	Step 2 The Team's Ranking	Step 3 Expert's Ranking	Step 4 Difference Steps 1 and 3	Step 5 Difference Steps 2 and 3
Items					
Box of matches					
Food concentrate					
50 feet of nylon rope					
Parachute silk					
Portable heating unit					
Two .45 calibre pistols					
One case dehydrated milk					
Two 100 1b. tanks of oxygen					
Stellar map (of the moon's constellation)					
Life raft					
Magnetic compass					
5 gallons of water					
Signal flares					
First aid kit containing injection needles					
Solar-powered FM receiver-transmitter					

NASA Exercise: Group Instructions

Instructions: This is an exercise in group decision-making. Your group is to employ the method of Group Consensus in reaching its decision. This means that the prediction for each of the 15 survival items must be agreed upon by each group member before it becomes a part of the group decision. Consensus is difficult to reach. Therefore, not every ranking will meet with everyone's approval. Try, as a group, to make each ranking one with which all group members can at least partially agree.

Here are some guides to use in reaching consensus:

1. Avoid arguing for your own individual judgements. Approach the task on the basis of logic.

2. Avoid changing your mind only in order to reach agreement or to avoid conflict. Support only solutions with which you are able to agree somewhat, at least.

3. Avoid 'conflict-reducing' techniques such as majority vote, averaging, or trading, in reaching your decision.

4. View differences of opinion as helpful rather than as a hindrance in decision-making.

NASA Exercise: NASA's Answers to Decision Task

15. Box of matches. Since there is little atmosphere on the moon, the matches wouldn't burn. So they would have little or no use.

4. Food concentrate. This would be very nutritious, and food would be one of your concerns.

6. Fifty feet of nylon rope. It has a number of uses - tying people together, climbing small mountains, tying all the equipment together and pulling it.

8. Parachute silk. This would be ideal protection from the sun's rays. One thing the task requires you to figure out is that you are on the lighted side of the moon.

13. Portable heating unit. This would be useful only if you landed on the dark side of the moon.

11. Two .45 calibre pistols. NASA says that self-propulsion devices could be made from these.

12. One case dehydrated milk. This could be useful as food mixed with water for drinking but less so if you already had food concentrate.

1. Two hundred-pound tanks of oxygen. Oxygen was seen as the most pressing need. Because the gravitational pull of the moon is only one-sixth of what it is here on earth, these tanks would weigh only about 30 pounds.

3. Stellar map. NASA saw this as the most important single means of navigation.

9. Life raft. This has a variety of uses. Inflated it gives protection from the sun, a means of carrying injured or equipment. NASA favoured using CO_2 bottles on the raft for propulsion across chasms, etc.

14. Magnetic compass. If there is a magnetic field on the moon, it doesn't seem to be polarised. The needle would probably spin and angle and be of little use.

2. Five gallons of water. You get into 200+ temp-
    eratures on the moon's lighted surface. There
    would be a pressing need for water to replenish
    fluid loss.

10. Signal flares. Possibly useful if you could
    get close enough to the ship for them to be
    seen.

7. First-aid kit containing pills and injection
    needles. The pills or injection medicine
    might be valuable.

5. Solar-powered radio. This could be used as a
    distress signal transmitter and for possible
    communication with the mother ship.

NASA Ratings

    0 - 20 Excellent

  20 - 30 Good

  30 - 40 Average

  40 - 50 Fair

  over 50 Poor

Training Methods and Activities

Teamwork Checklist

The following faults frequently impede the progress of discussion and decision making.

		A	B
1.	Failure to listen to what other members are saying	___	___
2.	Constantly re-iterating arguments	___	___
3.	Constantly interrupting	___	___
4.	Trying to put others down	___	___
5.	Failure to participate	___	___
6.	Silent members not drawn in	___	___
7.	Dominant members allowed to dominate	___	___
8.	Everyone pushing own views, not clarifying, developing, encouraging	___	___
9.	Unwillingness to make accommodations/compromises to others' views or needs	___	___
10.	Raising irrelevant or unhelpful points	___	___
11.	Not recognising how members are _feeling_ about the discussion	___	___
12.	Concentrating on making impressions rather than getting the task completed	___	___
13.	Failure to be aware of the effect of one's contributions on other members	___	___
14.	Disturbing the overall process with private conversations	___	___
15.	Failure to clarify the task or objective	___	___
16.	Failure to follow agreed directions and procedures	___	___
17.	Not checking on progress	___	___
18.	Failure to keep eye on time	___	___
19	Not being clear about what has been decided	___	___
20	Lack of agreement on _who_ is to take action on decisions	___	___

Please rate each item 5, 4, 3, 2, 1, or 0 on the following scale:

    5 = the error, weakness or failure is evident most of the time;

    1 = the error, weakness or failure hardly occurs at all;

    0 = the fault is irrelevant in this instance.

In column A give your rating of how typical, in your experience, each particular item is for teams/groups/committees.
In column B give your personal rating of according to how you saw the problems in your team/group.

Fig. 9.8

268

Training Methods and Activities

Styles of Teaching and Learning

Aim: To look at ways in which we approach a simple teaching task and the limits we set ourselves in defining the task.

Materials: Ten index cards per group with one word on each (see below) or a set of ten random objects (some unusual). Observer's instructions.

Time Required: 1 1/2 hours.

Class Size: Any number, divided into sub-groups of 6 to 10

Procedure:

1. Invite participants to form groups of six to ten members. Read the above aim and explain that they will shortly be given a teaching task. Invite two people in each group to agree to be teachers, three to six to be students; the remainder to observe.

   Hand the teachers the cards or objects with the following verbal instruction: 'Your task is to teach these.' (give them cards or objects), 'You have 10 minutes to plan your teaching and 20 minutes to do it! The task is clearly stated and there should be no discussion on its interpretation.

   Hand the observers their checklist.

2 While the teachers are planning their teaching, ask the students to consider their thoughts and feelings about their impending class.

3. After 30 minutes precisely has elapsed call a halt to the teaching and ask the observers to use the questions on their checklist as a basis for discussion with the 'teachers' and 'students'. This should take another 20 minutes.

4. At this stage the discussion may be opened across groups in order to share findings. Ten to 20 minutes should suffice.

5   Repeat the task with the roles in each group rotated. The same or different words/objects may be used.

Possible Words:

METAL
GROUPS
CRICKET
POETRY
EXPERIMENT
EGREGIOUS
MACHINE
MOLECULE
RELATIONSHIP
CAVITY

One of the best series of objects is the office stationary cupboard.

Adapted from: John E. Jones and J. William Pfeiffer, Eds., The 1973 Annual Handbook for Group Facilitators, San Diego, CA: University Associated, Inc., 1973.   Used with permission.

Observer's Checklist

Ask teachers:

1. What did you think the task was?
2. What teaching strategy did you use?
3. In what way did you involve the students?
4. What was your impression of the students?
5. How did your perception of the task and the students influence your behaviour?
6. What limits to the task did you assume and why?
7. How did you feel about the teaching?
8. How well did you operate as a team?

Ask students:

1. What did you think or talk about in anticipation of the teaching session?
2. How was the learning task presented to you?
3. How did you perceive the task: meaningful, useless, how?
4. What was your impression of the 'teachers'?
5. How did your perception of the 'teacher' and the task influence your behaviour?
6. What limits did you assume in your learning and why?
7. How did you feel as learner?

Peer Consulting: A Monitoring Technique
The value of a close and confidential discussion
about personal problems has been well known in the
health/care field for many years. Peer consulting
is merely an extension of this principle. The
structure is simple. Two (or three, but no more)
colleagues, preferably from different subject fields
agree to meet for a fixed time period, anything from
20 minutes to two hours, on a regular or an ad-hoc
basis. Their dialogue is organised according to the
following schedule:

1. A describes a plan she has:

   - an idea she wants to develop
   - a critical interaction

   or

   - just what she has done since the
     two last met.

2. B listens attentively and supportively,
   occasionally asking gently probing questions for clarification or to help A out
   of a circular or confused pattern of
   thinking.

3. This procedure lasts half the time (less
   five minutes) that the pair has allotted
   for the consulting.

4. At this point A tells B in what ways he
   was helpful to her in 1 and 2.

5. The above procedure is repeated with A in
   the listening role.

Training Methods and Activities

Planning a Course
Below are three cases which represent problems to do with the choice and organisation of teaching and learning methods. You are asked in your group to draw on your knowledge of different methods and their particular virtues in proposing a solution to each problem.

Damned Lies: A class of 20 first year students is studying Statistics. There are five other separate subjects to be studied concurrently. In past years the lectures have been poorly attended - only overseas students seemed interested. An essay and a sheet of examples are set, but they are rarely done except by overseas students. Again, in the examination in the subject, most people scrape through, revealing only a bare knowledge of the subject.
You have been asked to take this course for a study entitled 'Statistical Significance and the testing of Hypotheses'. You have a three-week period with 6 one-hour periods allocated to this topic. What teaching/learning methods might you use and how would you sequence them?

Jumblies: In the second year of the course, the students study six separately organised course units. During the second term they also undertake integrated projects. Partly the idea is that they should thus become better acquainted with each course unit in order to make a more informed choice of two of them as third year options and, partly that they should have a chance to integrate their understanding of the separate elements. The theme of the projects is to be 'For the Greater Benefit of Mankind'.
In previous years the number of students in the second year never exceeded 30 and projects were pursued individually with regular one-to-one supervision by teaching staff. This year there are 50 students and it is proposed to try out the idea of group projects, dividing the students into ten groups of five, each group undertaking a separate project. There are ten members of teaching staff potentially available and there is a period of three weeks during which the students are freed of all class commitments. This block of free time must occur simultaneously for all the students, but its timing has yet to be fixed. How would you suggest

the learning experiences within the project be organised?

'And What Seems to be the Problem?': There are troubles in the first year of clinical training. Among a string of complaints about the style of their education the students have cited the learning of interviewing skills. In the last few years they have been taught how to conduct interviews through three lectures by a research psychologist from the College of General Practitioners and by subsequently sitting in with consultants on diagnostic interviews with real patients. The students feel this procedure is not thorough enough for what they feel will be a pivotal activity in their future profession. How would you organise the learning activities of the students?

Card Exchange: A Starting Exercise

Aims: To help a large group of students get to know each other; to share values about given issues; to form teams.

Class size: 10-40

Time Required: One to one and a half hours

Materials: Five times as many index cards as the number of participants

Physical Setting: An open-plan room.

Procedure:
1. Before the class starts, prepare several index cards by writing on them comments on the subject of the course or the topic under discussion. Make some positive, some negative and some neutral, e.g.:

   I think ... is the deadest duck in the Academic pond.

   A knowledge of ... is essential to any well-run organisation.

Prepare about twice as many cards as there are students and hold these in reserve.

2. In class, hand out four blank cards to each student and ask them to write comments like those above - one on each card. Encourage them to be witty, cynical, encouraging, political, philosophical or whatever. (Allow five minutes.)

3. Collect the cards from the students and shuffle them well with your prepared cards. Then hand back to each student an arbitrary selection of five cards. Tell them that they will find they now have cards they would or would not wish to be associated with. Their task is to walk round the room exchanging cards until they have a set they are happy with. It is important to emphasise that exchanges should be done on a one-for-one basis with cards unseen and that the wish to give

or receive a card of a type should be justified, e.g.:

'I want to swap a card which cocks a snook at ... because I don't like .... Have you got anything more positive?'

or vice versa.

Scatter the spare cards on a table with the comment that these may be freely swapped with any cards. (Allow 15 minutes and encourage everyone to circulate.)

4. Having checked that everyone is reasonably happy with their hand of cards, ask them to form teams, each of whose task it is to select one of their pooled cards to represent their outlook or to devise a new statement with the same object.

There are two ways these teams may be formed and you as organiser should decide which to choose beforehand:

(a) participants freely team up with any number of colleagues according to shared values as represented by the cards

(b) they form pre-ordained groups of a fixed size (this is particularly useful when work is to continue in these teams thereafter).

Once they have chosen a team statement, ask each team quickly to choose a name by which it should be known.

Finally, invite the teams to announce publicly their choice of statement and title with a short justification for each.

This is adapted from 'Game Game' by Thiagarajan (1978).

Training Methods and Activities

A VARIETY OF GROUP TECHNIQUES

Please tick each of the Group Techniques listed below according to how frequently you use them now on your teaching scheme.

	TEACHING METHODS	Now	Future	Comments
1	Seminar			
2	Case discussion			
3	Group tutorial			
4	Individual tutorials			
5	Peer tutoring			
6	Buzz groups			
7	Snowball groups			
8	Cross-over groups			
9	Horseshoe groups			
10	Fish bowls			
11	Groups in laboratory classes			
12	Groups in field exercises			
13	Group projects			
14	Role playing			
15	Games and simulations			
16	Video playback of individual or group activity			
17	Syndicates·			
18	Brainstorming			
19	Synectics			
20	Associative discussion			

Having read about and/or discussed the various techniques listed above, mark up how often you intend to use them in the future. Explain your choices to a partner and discuss how you propose evaluating them.

Fig.9.9

Training Methods and Activities

Small Group Teaching Workshop
(Run by University Teaching Methods Unit, London in June 1980).

Programme

Introduction

The main aim of the workshop is a practical one of providing an opportunity for participants to improve their skills and sensitivity in group work through participating in a range of different types of group under different forms of leadership. There will be discussion about these experiences and about pre-recorded video tapes. Video recordings of some of the workshop activities will be made and some of these will concern problems which participants are asked to submit in advance.

There will be two or three sub-groups with about eight members in each. Most of the time will be spent in these groups although for some purposes groups of different sizes will be formed and at other times, of course, there will be plenary sessions.

First Day

0930 - 1000	Registration and Coffee
1000 - 1005	Welcome to the Workshop
1005 - 1045	Values in Small Group Teaching

We should like to begin with an exercise in which we write a large number of positive and negative statements about group work on cards. From these, individuals select the ones which come closest to their own values. We shall then move into groups to compare them and select those which represent the values of the group.

| 1045 - 1100 | Coffee |
| 1100 - 1230 | Paired Introductions |

The groups will have met in the opening

exercise but we should like to spend
this session getting to know each other
initially through paired introductions.
You will be asked to introduce not
yourself but your partner and explain
some of the reasons why he or she has
come to the workshop. We shall then go
on to explore participants' good and
bad experiences of group work and begin
to draw out the characteristics which
make for success and failure in groups.

1230 - 1345   Buffet lunch

1345 - 1400   <u>Triads</u>

We feel it could be useful for participants from different groups to have
the experience of a continuing group of
three to share ideas about the workshop
and what it means to them personally.
As there will not be too much ,to share
at this first meeting (of three) we
should like to consider the checklist
at the end of the chapter, which was
sent to you. Could it be useful in
watching the video tapes in the next
session?

1400 - 1530   <u>Step-by-step discussion of pre-recorded
video tapes of Small Group Discussion</u>

Although the workshop will be actively
involved in group work, the only opportunity we have of meeting real students
is through video recordings of actual
teaching sessions. In this session we
shall look at extracts, stopping
frequently to discuss the style of
leadership and other issues mentioned
in the background paper and the checklist for observation of small group
discussion.

1530 - 1545   Tea

1545 - 1630   <u>Why Teach in Small Groups?</u>

We feel it will be useful for you to
think for yourselves about your own
priorities for use of small groups and

to broaden your horizons by engaging actively in comparing your own ideas with those of others. We should like to use a system of progressive doubling (snowballing) starting with individual thoughts on the purposes of group work and going on to compare these with a neighbour and then moving to groups of four and eight, then finally coming back to a plenary session where two groups present their final agreed statement of the five to ten most important purposes for use of small groups. The suggested timing for this part of the session would be five minutes as individuals, ten minutes as pairs, ten minutes as fours and ten minutes as eights who should prepare a flipchart summary which might form a useful basis for a set of guidelines to be given to students.

1630 - 1730   Devising Group Discussion Guidlines

This activity consists of a role play in which students and staff draw up guidelines on leadership and particip-ation for a series of discussions on an interdisciplinary theme. Examples of learning contracts will be introduced.

1730 - 1800   The bar in the student refectory will be open.

1800 - 1930   Dinner

This will not be provided but there are restaurants and pubs nearby as well as refectories.

1930 - ?   Party and Games   -   Evening Option

The games will begin at least with some educational justification but where they end will depend on the dynamics of the group.

Second Day

0930 - 1300   Discussion and Video Recording of
   or 1530   Members' Teaching Problems

0930 - 0945   <u>Setting up of the Problems</u>

Through the whole of the morning we
shall be in the original mixed small
groups and each group will have copies
of all the problems submitted beforehand by members of that group. The
initial setting-up phase will be a task
for the group itself. They will have
to decide how many problems they want
to deal with, how many might be amal-
gamated into single problems and how
they will go about it - after considering the following suggestions.

0945 - 1130   <u>Problem Discussion</u>

Here we suggest that you take each
problem or cluster of problems in turn
and go through three phases, each
requiring a different approach and run
by different members of the group. The
three phases are:

1. <u>Problem Clarification</u>. This might
require a case discussion type of
approach where the essential feature
is that the person with the problem
presents it with the help of the group
'leader' whose job it is to make sure
that the problem is stated in a clear
and manageable way.

2. <u>Production of ideas and a wide
range of possible solutions</u>. This
phase might require a different sort of
leadership, perhaps of the brainstorming type, to make sure that the group
is active and productive without being
too critical.

3. <u>Deciding on a solution</u>. Here the
leadership may need to be more directive to make sure the discussion is
focused and time is used economically.
Problems of authority versus democracy
may well arise.

After each cycle there should be five
minutes' discussion of different styles
of leadership and general reflection

on the way the group has progressed. It will be up to the group to decide whether there are two or three cycles. During this time all the group activity will be video taped to be used later. During such a session or cycle a different member of the group may observe and evaluate the group process.

1130 - 1300   Replay of the video tape

The workshop tutor should keep record of the most useful phases for replay. Groups might use a number of these or concentrate on one whole cycle.

1300 - 1400   Lunch

1400 - 1415   Triad Groups

1415 - 1530   Continuation of the Morning's Activities or Options to be Decided

1530 - 1545   Tea

1545 - 1730   Syndicate Work

In this session and for the first two on the third morning we shall be combining the experience of syndicate work, discussion about it and studying within syndicates the problem of evaluation in group work.

The syndicate method is where a class is divided into groups of four to six who work outside a formal class situation on the same or related problems with intermittent teacher contact. They write a joint group report which is discussed by the tutor and the whole class and may continue over several weeks or months with guidance on resources from the tutor. In this case the reports will have to be written by 1100 am tomorrow when Gerald Collier from the University of East Anglia will be joining us to discuss the reports and the general question of teaching through syndicate work.

Resource materials will be provided at the first session to be divided between members of each syndicate.

1730 - 1800 Bar Open

1800 - 1930 Dinner (not provided)

1930 - 2100 Evening Option - A discussion based on a video tape about McMaster University's problem-orientated medical course.

Third Day

0930 - 1100 Syndicate Work Continues

1100 - 1115 Coffee

1115 - 1245 Syndicate Work Continued with Gerald Collier

1245 - 1400 Lunch

1400 - 1530 Consultants' and Assessors' Game

We should like to combine the evaluation of the workshop with experience of the Consultants' and Assessors' Game. Two or three teams will devise a scheme for evaluating the workshop and present it to a team of assessors whose task is to define criteria for evaluating the reports and to make and justify their judgement as to the 'best' scheme.

1530 - 1545 Tea

1545 - 1630 Evaluation of the Workshop

The 'best' scheme will be used to evaluate the workshop.

1630 - 1645 Triads

In this final meeting we should like the triads to look back over the workshop and consider what practical application it might have for the future.

1645 Say Goodbye

Learning Through Groups

The activities described in this chapter represent but a sample of the many that are available to interested readers. Miles (1981), Napier & Gershenfeld (1973) and Johnson & Johnson (1979) all include further samples of well-tested training activities. Yet whatever games, exercises or methods we may use, there are certain assumptions and principles which perhaps need to be underlined.

1. The accent is on 'whole person' learning: learning that involves both thinking, feeling and behaviour.

2. There must be practice of behaviour and skills; practice that is informed by guided experience and constructive feedback (see page 54).

3. There should be a strong focus on the 'here and now'; the 'there and then' is of great use with a video playback (see Kagan, 1982) but while it makes discussion of behaviour safer, it may also make it less immediate. The 'here and now' approach helps in the learning of monitoring skills.

4. There should be general acceptance that everyone has unique styles of personal behaviour, different needs and their own way of seeing the world.

5. The emphasis should be on the 'social self' rather than on the 'inner world' of participants.

6. That personal change is best achieved where there is a judicious blend of support and challenge (Smith, 1981).

7. The primary orientation should be towards the development of skills, but these should be seen within a wider framework of attitudes and values (Miles 1981).

The whole of this chapter, and indeed the book, is based on the supposition that participants, whether they be college students or practising teachers, are willing not just to learn, but to learn how to learn and to integrate this into their future development. Learning is a cyclical process and includes the taking of risks, willingness to share, acceptance of feelings and the ability to monitor one's own experience and progress. 'Experience', as someone once said, 'is not what happens to you, it's what you do with what happens to you'.

Discussion Points

° What principles of learning seem to be incorporated in the various activities included in this chapter? What sequences are evident?

° Draw up a contract for the work of your group.

° You have been asked to design and run a 1-day workshop on group teaching. What are you going to include? How will you approach it?

BIBLIOGRAPHY

ABERCROMBIE, M.L.J. (1969)
The Anatomy of Judgement,
Penguin, Harmondsworth, Middx.

ABERCROMBIE, M.L.J. (1979)
Aims and Techniques of Group Teaching
(4th Edition)
Society for Research into Higher Education,
Guildford, Surrey.

ABERCROMBIE, M.L.J. & TERRY, P. (1978)
Talking to Learn,
Society for Research into Higher Education,
Guildford, Surrey.

ALLEN, E.A. (1965)
'Group Methods of Teaching in Higher Education'
Educational Review, 18, November.

ALLPORT, F.H. (1924)
Social Psychology,
Houghton Miffin, Boston.

AMARIA, R., BIRAN, L. & LEITH, G. (1969)
'Individual versus Cooperative Learning
1: Influence of Intelligence and Sex'
Educational Research, 11.2.

ARGYRIS, C. (1968)
'Some Unintended Consequences of Rigorous
Research'
Psychological Bulletin, 70.

BIBLIOGRAPHY

ASEE (American Society for Engineering Education)
(1976)
Experiential Learning in Engineering Education,
(ASEE, Washington).

BAKER, F. (1974)
Personal Communication to ABERCROMBIE, M.L.J. (1979)

BALES, R. (1970)
Personality and Interpersonal Behaviour,
Holt, Rinehart & Winston, New York.

BANET, A.G. Jnr. & HAYDEN, C. (1977)
'A Tavistock Primer'
in Pfeiffer, W. & Jones, J. (Eds.)
Annual Handbook for Group Facilitators,
University Associates Inc., San Diego.

BARKER, R. (1968)
'Ecological Psychology: Concepts and Methods
of Studying the Environment of Human Behaviour',
Stanford University Press

BEARD, R., & HARTLEY, J., (1984)
Teaching and Learning in Higher Education
(4th Edition) Harper & Row, London.

BEARD, R., BLIGH, D. & HARDING, A. (1978)
Research into Teaching Methods in Higher Education
(4th Edition)
Society for Research into Higher Education,
Guildford, Surrey.

BENNIS, W., BENNE, K. & CHIN, R. (1970)
The Planning of Change,
Holt, Rinehart & Winston, New York.

BENNIS, W. & SHEPARD, H. (1956)
A Theory of Group Development, Human Relations
IX

BIBLIOGRAPHY

BERNE, E. (1968)
Games People Play:
The Psychology of Human Relationships,
Penguin, Harmondsworth, Middx.

BIGNELL, V., PETERS, G. & PYM, C. (1977)
Catastrophic Failures,
Open University Press.

BION, W. (1961)
Experience in Groups,
Tavistock, London.

BLIGH, D. (1972)
What's the Use of Lectures?,
Penguin, Harmondsworth, Middx.

BLIGH, D., EBRAHIM, Z., JAQUES, D. &
WARREN PIPER, D. (1976)
Teaching Students,
University of Exeter Press.

BLIGH, D., JAQUES, D. & PIPER D.W. (1980)
Methods & Techniques in Post-Secondary Education,
UNESCO.

BLOOM, B.S. et al (1956)
Taxonomy of Educational Objectives   Vol. 1,
Longman, London.

BLOOM, B.S. et al (1964)
Taxonomy of Educational Objectives   Vol. 2,
Longman, London.

BLUNT, M.R. & BLIZZARD, P. (1973)
'Development and initial Assessment of a
Teaching-Learning Programme in Anatomy',
British Journal of Medical Education, 7.

de BOARD, R. (1978)
The Psychoanalysis of Organisations;
a Psychoanalytic Approach to Behaviour
in Groups and Organisations,
Tavistock, London.

BIBLIOGRAPHY

BOUD, D. (1981)
Developing Student Autonomy in Learning,
Kogan Page, London.

BOUD, D. & PROSSER, M. (1980)
'Sharing Responsibility: Staff-student
Cooperation in Learning'
British Journal of Educational Technology,
1.11. January.

BOUD, D., KEOGH, R. & WALKER, D. (1985)
Reflection: Turning Experience into Learning,
Kogan Page, London

BRADFORD, L., GIBB, J. & BENNE, K. (1964)
T-Group Theory and Laboratory Method,
Wiley, New York.

BRADFORD, L. (1976)
Making Meetings Work,
University Associates Inc., Mansfield, U.K.

BRAMLEY, W. (1979)
Group Tutoring,
Kogan Page, London.

BURNS, T., & STALKER, G. (1966)
The Management of Innovation
Tavistock, London.

BRONFENBRENNER, U. (1977)
'Toward an Experimental Ecology of
Human Development'
American Psychologist, July.

CARRIER, M.H. (1981)
Take Five,
Harrap, London.

CARTWRIGHT, D. & ZANDER, A. (1968)
Group Dynamics (Third Edition),
Harper & Row, New York.

BIBLIOGRAPHY

CHESLER, M. & FOX, R. (1966)
Role Playing Methods in the Classroom
Science Research Associates Inc., Chicago.

COLLIER, K.G. (1968)
New Dimensions in Higher Education,
Longman, London.

COLLIER, K.G. (1969)
'Syndicate Methods: Further Evidence
and Comment',
Universities Quarterly, 23.4.

COLLIER, K.G. (1980)
'Peer Group Learning in Higher Education',
Studies in Higher Education, 5.1.

COLLIER, K.G. (1983)
The Management of Peer-Group Learning:
Syndicate Methods in Higher Education,
Society for Research into Higher Education,
Guildford, Surrey.

COOPER, C. (Ed) (1976)
Theories of Group Processes,
Wiley, London.

CORNWALL, M.G. (1979)
Students as Teachers: Peer Teaching
in Higher Education,
C.O.W.O., University of Amsterdam, Holland.

COWAN, J. & MORTON, J. (1973)
'MOCO - A structural Game for Undergraduates',
Programmed Learning and Educational Technology,
10.4.

COX, R.(Ed) (1975)
Evaluating Teaching in Higher Education,
University Teaching Methods Unit,* London.

BIBLIOGRAPHY

CRYER, P. (Ed) (1982)
Training Activities for Teachers in Higher
Education,
Society for Research into Higher Education,
Guildford, Surrey.

DAVEY, A.G. (1969)
'Leadership in Relation to Group Achievement'
Educational Research, 11.3.

DAVIS, J. (1969)
Group Performance,
Addison Wesley, Cambridge, Mass.

DAVISON, A. & GORDON, P. (1977)
Games & Simulations in Action,
Woburn Books, London.

DEUTSCH, M. (1949)
'Experimental Study of Effects of Cooperation
and Competition on Group Process',
Human Relations, 2.3.
also in CARTWRIGHT & ZANDER (1968)

DEWEY, J. (1916 and 1944)
Democracy and Education,
Free Press, New York.

DUNPHY, D. (1968)
'Phases, Roles and Myths in Self-Analytical Groups',
Journal of Applied Behavioural Science IV

EASTON, G. (1982)
Learning from Case Studies,
Prentice Hall, New York.

EDWARDS, J. (1980)
'The Engineering Syndicate Study',
Proceedings of Institution of
Electrical Engineers, No.8. November.

BIBLIOGRAPHY

ENTWISTLE, N. (Ed) (1976)
Strategies for Research and Development
in Higher Education,
Swets & Zeitlinger, Amsterdam.

ENTWISTLE, N. (1977)
'Strategies of Learning and Studying:
Recent Research Findings'
British Journal of Educational Studies,
XXV.3. October.

ENTWISTLE, N. (1981)
Styles of Teaching & Learning,
Wiley, London.

ERIKSON, E. (1971)
Identity: Youth & Crisis,
Faber, London.

FESTINGER, L., SCHACHTER, S. & BACK, K. (1950)
Social Pressures in Informal Groups: a Study
of Human Factors in Housing,
Harper & Row, New York.

FRAZER, M.K. (1977)
Problem Solving in Chemistry,
Mimeograph, University of East Anglia.

FRANSSON, A. (1976)
'Group Centred Instruction: Intentions and
outcomes' in Entwistle, N. (Ed)
Strategies for Research and Development
in Higher Education,
Swets & Zeitlinger, Amsterdam.

FREUD, S. (1972)
Group Psychology and the Analysis of the Ego,
Edited and translated by Strachey, J. (1975)
Norton, New York.

GAFF, J. & WILSON, W. (1971)
'Faculty Cultures and Interdisciplinary Studies'
Journal of Higher Education, 42.3.

BIBLIOGRAPHY

GIBB, J. (1961)
'Defensive Communication'
Journal of Communication, 11. September.

GIBBS, G. (1984)
Using Role Play in Interpersonal Skills Training:
a Peer Learning Approach, in Jaques D & Tipper E
Learning for the Future, SAGSET
University of Loughborough

GIBBS, G., HABESHAW, S. & HABESHAW, T. (1984)
53 Interesting Things to do in your Lectures
TES Publications, 37 Ravenswood Rd., Bristol, U.K.

GOLDSCHMID, B. & GOLDSCHMID, M. (1976)
'Peer Teaching in Higher Education - A Review'
Higher Education, 5.

GOLEMBIEWSKI, R. (1962)
The Small Group,
University of Chicago Press.

GOODLAD, S. (1978)
'Projects'
in UTMU
Improving Teaching Higher Education,
University Teaching Methods Unit,* London.

GORDON, W., (1961)
Synectics
Harper & Row

HABESHAW, S., HABESHAW, T. & GIBBS, G. (1984)
53 Interesting Things to do in your Seminars
and Tutorials
TES Publications, 37 Ravenswood Rd., Bristol, U.K.

HARRIS, T.A. (1973)
I'm OK - You're OK,
Pan Books, London.

BIBLIOGRAPHY

HAVELOCK, R.G. (1973)
The Change Agent's Guide to Innovation in
Education,
Educational Technology Pubs.,
Englewood, Cliffs, New Jersey.

HEARN, G. (1979)
'Small Group Behaviour and Development: A
Selective Bibliography'
in PFEIFFER, W. & JONES, J. (Eds.)
Annual Handbook for Group Facilitators,
University Associates Inc., San Diego.

HEDLEY, R. & WOOD, C. (1978)
Group Discussion for Seminar Leaders,
Mimeograph, Faculty of Education,
University of Manitoba.

H.M.S.O. (1963)
Committee on Higher Education
(Robbins Report),
Her Majesty's Stationery Office, London.

H.M.S.O. (1964)
Report of the Committee on University Teaching
Methods (Hale Report),
Her Majesty's Stationery Office, London.

HERON, J. (1974)
The Concept of a Peer Learning Community,
Human Potential Research Project,
University of Surrey.

HERON, J. (1976)
Six-Category Intervention Analysis,
Human Potential Research Project,
University of Surrey.

HERON, J. (1981)
'Assessment Revisited' in BOUD, D. (Ed)
Developing Student Autonomy in Learning,
Kogan Page, London.

HILL, W.F. (1977)
Learning Thru Discussion
Sage, London.

BIBLIOGRAPHY

HOYLE, E. (1972)
The Role of the Teacher,
Routledge & Kegan Paul, London.

HUBERMAN, A.M. (1973)
Understanding Change in Education,
UNESCO

HUDSON, L. (1966)
Contrary Imaginations,
Penguin, Harmondsworth, Middx.

JAQUES, D. (1980)
'Students' and Tutors' Experience of
Project Work' in OXTOBY, R. (Ed.)
Higher Education at the Cross-Roads,
Society for Research into Higher Education,
Guildford, Surrey.

JAQUES, D. (1981)
Behind the Scenes,
Report to Nuffield Foundation.

JOHNSON, D. & JOHNSON, F. (1975)·
Joining Together: Group Theory and Group Skills,
Prentice Hall, New Jersey.

JONES, R.M. (1972)
Fantasy and Feeling in Education,
Penguin, Harmondsworth.

JORDAN, W.J. (1961)
Synectics,
Harper & Row, London.

KAGAN, N. (1982)
Interpersonal Process Recall: Basic Methods
and Recent Research,
Mimeograph, Department of Counselling Psychology,
University of Michigan, E.Lansing.

BIBLIOGRAPHY

KLEIN, J. (1965)
Working with Groups,
Hutchinson, London.

KNOWLES, H.C., KNOWLES, M. (1972)
An Introduction to Group Dynamics,
Association Press, Folletts, Chicago.

KNOWLES, M. (1975)
Self-Directed Learning: a Guide for
Learners & Teachers,
Association Press, Folletts, Chicago.

KNOWLES, M. (1979)
The Adult Learner: a Neglected Species?,
Gulf, Houston.

KOLB, D., RUBIN, I., & McINTYRE, J. (1979)
Organisational Psychology: an Experiential
Approach,
(Third Edition)
Prentice Hall, New Jersey.

KRUPAR, K. (1973)
Communication Games,
Free Press, New York.

KUHN, T. (1973)
The Structure of Scientific Revolutions,
University of Chicago Press.

KUIPER, R. (1977)
'Group Project Work: a Self-Managed "Learn and Work"
Process'
in CORNWALL, M. SCHMITHALS, F. & JAQUES, D. (Eds.)
Project Orientation in Higher Education,
Brighton Polytechnic/University Teaching Methods
Unit,* London.

LEWIN, K. (1951)
Field Theory in Social Science,
Harper & Row, New York.

BIBLIOGRAPHY

LEWIS, H. (1979)
'The Anatomy of Small Group'
Studies in Higher Education, 4.2.

LEWIS, R. & MEE, J. (1981)
Using Role Play: an Introductory Guide,
National Extension College, Cambridge, U.K.

LUFT, J. (1970)
Group Processes: an Introduction to Group Dynamics,
Mayfield, Pal Alto, Ca.

McKEACHIE, W. (1969)
Teaching Tips,
(6th Edition)
D.C. Heath & Co., Lexington, Mass.

McLEISH, J., MATHESON, W. & PARK, J. (1973)
The Psychology of the Learning Group,
Hutchinson, London.

MAGIN, D.J. (1982)
'Collaborative Peer Learning in the Laboratory'
Studies in Higher Education, 7.2.

MANN, R. et al (1967)
Interpersonal Styles and Group Development,
Wiley, New York.

MARRIS, P. (1965)
The Experience of Higher Education,
Routledge and Kegan Paul, London.

MARTON, F., HOUNSELL, D., & ENTWISTLE, N. (Eds.)
(1984)
The Experience of Learning,
Scottish Academic Press, Edinburgh.

MARTON, F. & SALJO, R. (1976)
On Qualitative Differences in Learning I & II,
British Journal of Educational Psychology, 46,
1 & 2.

297

BIBLIOGRAPHY

van MENTS, M. (1983)
Effective Use of Role Play,
Kogan Page, London.

MILES, M. (1955)
'Human Relations Training: How a Group Grows'
Teachers College Record LV

MILES, M. (1981)
Learning to Work in Groups: a Program
Guide for Educational Leaders,
(2nd Edition)
Teachers College Press, Columbia, New York.

MILLER, C. (1975)
'Evaluation of Teaching and the Institutional
Context' in COX, R. (Ed),
Evaluating Teaching in Higher Education,
University Teaching Methods Unit,* London.

MILLER, C. & PARLETT, M. (1974)
Up to the Mark - a Study of the Examination Game,
Society for Research into Higher Education,
Guildford, Surrey.

MILLS, T. (1967)
The Sociology of Small Groups,
Prentice Hall, N.J.

NAPIER, R.W. & GERSHENFELD, M.K. (1981)
Groups: Theory and Experience, (2nd Edition)
Houghton Mifflin, Boston.

NEUFELD, V.R. & BARROWS, H.S. (1974)
'The McMaster Philosophy: an Approach to
Medical Education'
Journal of Medical Education, 49.

NEWCOMB, T.M. (1967)
'Student Peer Group Influences'
in SANFORD, N.
The American College,
Wiley, New York.

298

BIBLIOGRAPHY

NISBET, S. (1966)
'A Method for Advanced Seminars'
Universities Quarterly, 20, Summer.

NUFFIELD GROUP (FOR RESEARCH AND INNOVATION
IN HIGHER EDUCATION) (1973-76)
Newsletters 1-7,
Nuffield Foundation, London.

NUFFIELD GROUP (FOR RESEARCH AND INNOVATION IN
HIGHER EDUCATION) (1977)
The Container Revolution,
Nuffield Foundation, London.

N.U.S., (National Union of Students) (1969)
Report of Commission on Teaching in Higher Education,
N.U.S., London.

NYLEN, D., MITCHELL, R. & STOUT, A. (1967)
Handbook of Staff Development in Human
Relations Training,
National Training Laboratories, Arlington, Va.

OSBORN, A. (1963)
Applied Imagination: Principles & Procedures
of Creative Problem Solving,
Scribners, New York.

O.U. (Open University) (1975)
P.I.G. - Problem Identification Game,
designed by JACQUES, R. & TALBOT, R. for the
Man-made Futures Course.

PARKER, J.C. & RUBIN, L.J. (1966)
Process as Content: Curriculum Design and the
Application of Knowledge,
Rand McNally, Chicago.

PARLETT, M. (1977)
'The Department as a Learning Milieu'
Studies in Higher Education, 2.2.

PARLETT, M. & KING, R. (1971)
Concentrated Study - a Pedagogic Innovation
Observed,
Society for Research into Higher Education,
Guildford, Surrey.

PARLETT, M. & SIMONS, H. (1976)
Learning from Learners: a Study of the Student's
Experience of Academic Life,
Nuffield Foundation, London.

PARLETT, M., SIMONS, H. & JASPAN, A. (1976)
Up to Expectation: a Study of the Students' first
few weeks of Higher Education,
Nuffield Foundation, London.

PASK, G. (1976)
'Styles & Strategies of Learning'
British Journal of Educational Psychology, 46.2.

PERRY, W.G. (1970)
Forms of Intellectual and Ethical Development
in the College Years,
Holt, Rinehart & Winston, New York.

PFEIFFER, W. & JONES, J. (1973)
Annual Handbook for Group Facilitators,
University Associates Inc., San Diego, and
Mansfield U.K.

PFEIFFER, W. & JONES, J. (1973, 74, 75, 76, 77,
78,79, 80, 81, 82, 83, 84)
Structured Experiences in Human Relations Training,
University Associates Inc., San Diego, and
Mansfield, U.K.

PIPER, D.W. & GLATTER, R. (1977)
The Changing University,
University Teaching Methods Unit,* London.

PIRSIG, R.M. (1976)
Zen and the Art of Motorcycle Maintenance,
Corgi Books, London.

BIBLIOGRAPHY

POLYA, G. (1957)
How to Solve it,
Doubleday Anchor, New York.

PRINCE, G.M. (1970)
The Practice of Creativity,
Harper Row, New York.

PRING, R. (1973)
'Objectives and Innovation: the Irrelevance
of Theory'
London Educational Review, 3. Autumn.

PRING, R. (1970)
'Teacher as a Researcher' in LAWTON, D. (Ed)
Theory and Practice of the Curriculum,
Routledge and Kegan Paul, London.

RAINER, T. (1980)
The New Diary: How to use a Journal,
Angus and Robertson, London

REDL, F. (1942)
'Group Emotion and Leadership'
Psychiatry, 5.

RICE, A.K. (1971)
Learning for Leadership Interpersonal
& Intergroup Relations,
Tavistock Publications, London.

RICHARDSON, E. (1967)
Group Study for Teachers,
Routledge and Kegan Paul, London.

ROSS, M. & HENDRY, C. (1957)
New Understandings of Leadership,
Association Press/Follets, Chicago.

ROWAN, J. (1976)
The Power of the Group,
Davis - Poynter, London.

BIBLIOGRAPHY

ROWAN, J. & REASON, P. (1981)
Human Inquiry: a Sourcebook of New
Paradigm Research,
Wiley, London.

ROWNTREE, D. (1978)
Educational Technology in Curriculum
Development,
Harper & Row, London.

RUBIN, L.J. (Ed) (1867)
Facts and Feelings in the Classroom,
Ward Lock, London.

RUDDUCK, J. (1978)
Learning Through Small Group Discussion,
Society for Research into Higher Education,
Guildford, Surrey.

SANFORD, N. (1967)
'Student Performance in Relation to Educational
Objectives' in SANFORD, N. (Ed.)
The American College,
Wiley, New York.

SCHMUCK, R. & SCHMUCK, P. (1979)
Group Processes in the Classroom,
Wm.C. Brown, Dubuque, Iowa.

SCHUTZ, W. (1958)
FIRO: A Three Dimensional Theory of Interpersonal
Behaviour,
Holt Rinehart & Winston, N.Y.

SHAFFER, J. & GALINSKY, M. (1974)
Models of Group Therapy and Activity Training,
Prentice Hall

SHAW, M.E. (1977)
Group Dynamics
The Psychology of Small Group Behaviour,
Tata - McGraw-Hill, New Delhi.

BIBLIOGRAPHY

SHORT, A.H. & TOMLINSON D.R. (1979)
'The Design of Laboratory Classwork',
Studies in Higher Education, 4.2. October.

SMITH, P. (1973)
Groups within Organisations,
Harper & Row, London.

SMITH, P. (1980)
Small Groups and Personal Change,
Methuen, London.

SNYDER, B. (1971)
The Hidden Curriculum,
M.I.T. Press, Cambridge, Mass.

SOMMER, R. (1969)
Personal Space: the Behavioural Basis of Design,
Prentice Hall, Englewood Cliffs, New Jersey.

SRHE (Society for Research into Higher Education)
Working Party on Teaching Methods (1975)
Project Methods in Higher Education,
SRHE, Guildford.

STADSKLEV, R. (1974)
Handbook of Simulation Gaming in Social Education,
University of Alabama.

STANFORD, G. & ROARK, A. (1974)
Human Interaction in Education,
Allyn & Bacon, Boston.

STARTUP, R. (1977)
'Staff Experience of Lectures and Tutorials'
Studies in Higher Education, 2.2.

STEIN, M. (1975)
Stimulating Creativity, Vol.2:
Group Procedures,
Academic Press, New York.

BIBLIOGRAPHY

STENHOUSE, L. (1972)
'Teaching Through Small Group Discussion:
Formality, Rules and Authority'
Cambridge Journal of Education, 2.

STENHOUSE, L. (1975)
Introduction to Curriculum Development,
Heineman, London.

STERN, G. (1967)
'Environments for Learning'   in SANFORD, N. (Ed.)
The American College,
Wiley, New York.

TABA, H. (1962)
Curriculum Development: Theory and Practice,
Harcourt, Brace and World, New York.

TAYLOR, W. & WALFORD, R. (1972)
Simulation in the Classroom,
Penguin Books, Harmondsworth, Middx.

THELEN, H. & DICKERMAN, W. (1949)
'Stereotypes and the Growth of Groups'
Educational Leadership VI

THELEN, H. (1963)
Dynamics of Groups at Work,
University of Chicago Press, Phoenix Books.

THIAGARAJAN, S. (1978)
'Thiagi's Game - game VI described as a fast
paced Introduction to Gaming'
Simulation/Gaming, May/June.

TREADAWAY, J. (1975)
'Do Seminars Work?'
University of London, Institute of Education Reporter.

TUCKMAN, B. (1965)
'Developmental Sequence in Small Groups'
Psychological Bulletin LXIII(6)

TUCKMAN, B.W. & JENSEN, M.A.C., (1977)
Stages of Small-Group Development,
Group and Organisational Studies 2,4.

BIBLIOGRAPHY

TUCKMAN, J. & LORGE, I. (1962)
'Individual Ability as a Determinant of Group
Superiority'
Human Relations, 15.1.

U.T.M.U. (1972)
Varieties of Group Discussion in University
Teaching,
University Teaching Methods Unit,* London.

U.T.M.U. (1978)
Improving Teaching in Higher Education,
University Teaching Methods Unit,* London.

WHEELER, D.K. (1967)
Curriculum Process,
Unibooks, London.

WICKELGREN, W. (1974)
How to Solve Problems,
Freeman, San Francisco.

WILSON, A. (1980)
'Structuring Seminars: a Technique to allow
Students to participate in the Structuring
of Small Group Discussion'
Studies in Higher Education, 5.1. March.

WOODS, D.R. CROWE, C., HOFFMAN, T., & WRIGHT, J.,
(1977)
'How can one teach Problem Solving?'
Ontario Universities Program for Instructional
Development Newsletter, No. 16. May.

WORSLEY, P. (1970)
Introducing Sociology,
Penguin, Harmondsworth, Middx.

ZUBER-SKERRITT, O., (1983)
Video in Higher Education
Kogan Page, London

* Now 'Centre for Staff Development in Higher
Education', 55 Gordon Square, London WC1H 0NU.

CENTRE FOR STAFF DEVELOPMENT IN HIGHER EDUCATION,
55 Gordon Square, London WC1 0NU.
Courses, Training Materials and Consultancy on
Teaching Methods and Course Development.

GROUP RELATIONS TRAINING ASSOCIATION, 15, Nursery
Close, Acle, Norwich, NR13 3EH.
Annual Conference, T-Group Laboratory and numerous
local events. Quarterly Newsletter.

SAGSET (SOCIETY FOR THE ADVANCEMENT OF GAMES &
SIMULATIONS IN EDUCATION & TRAINING), Centre for
Extension Studies University of Technology Lough-
borough, Leics. LE11 3TU, U.K.
Quarterly Journal: Simulations/Games for Learning,
Resource Lists, Annual Conference.

SMALL GROUP TEACHING PROJECT, Centre for Applied
Research in Education, University of East Anglia,
Norwich, UK.
Various documents and edited video tapes available
from Jean Rudduck.

TAVISTOCK INSTITUTE OF HUMAN RELATIONS, 120 Belsize
Lane, London NW3 5BA.
Conferences and Study Groups on Group Relations.

(ULAVC) UNIVERSITY OF LONDON AUDIO-VISUAL CENTRE,
North Wing, Senate House, London WC1.
Video Tapes: 'Learning in Groups' and on Perception
by M.L.J. Abercrombie & P.M. Terry.

NAME INDEX

(T.A.) 55-61;
applied to teaching
and learning 57-60
transactions: com-
plementary, crossed
and ulterior 58-9;
in teaching and
learning 150
transference 3-4, 6
tutorial technique
xiv, 90, 96, 103-5,
148, 169, 216, 234,
239, 243, 277
tutor's role (see
role of tutor)
tutorless groups 36,
100, 103, 105

unconscious processes
4, 13, 36, 51, 133,
146, 153; and
tutor's fears 147

values 24, 85, 284;
faculty differ-
ences in 12; in
aims 63, 65, 71,
73, 78
variety in group
teaching xi, 133-4,
277
video-recording/tapes
38, 149, 188; as
distancing mechanism
236; as prelude to
discussion 192-3,
210, as substitute
for lecture 208,
210; as task 82;
for monitoring/evalu-
ation 145, 149, 224;
for training 210,
242-4, 278-9, 282,
284; in role play
122; in step-by-
step discussion 91;
of simulation 120,
122, 186; on experi-
mentation 195;
playback 277, 284
Veterinary Science

teaching 209
vocational needs
12-13; through
Chemistry teaching
194

warm-up exercises
241-2, 275
workshop(s) 10, 131,
199, 221, 234, 240;
format of 10, 137,
140, 239-41; on
small group teaching
278-83; tutor's role
in 148-9